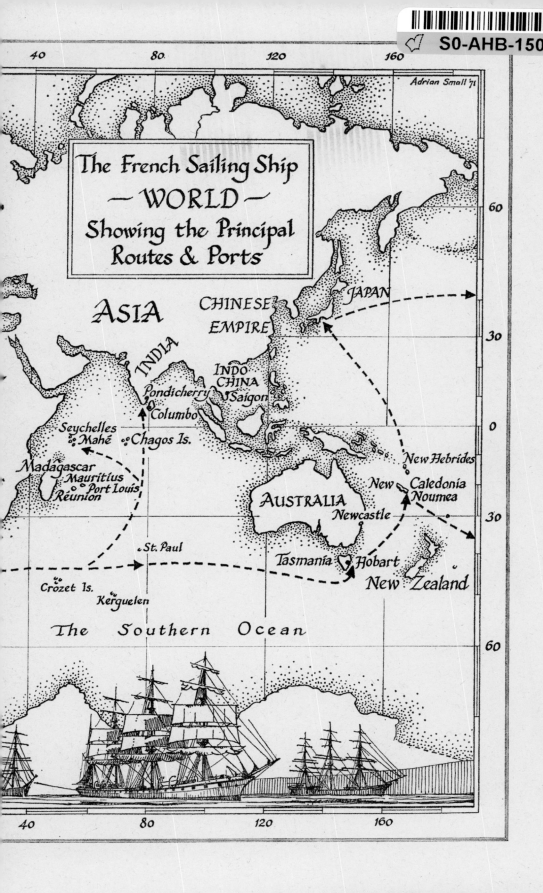

Adrian Small '71

The French Sailing Ship
— WORLD —
Showing the Principal Routes & Ports

ASIA

CHINESE EMPIRE

JAPAN

INDIA

INDO CHINA

Saigon

Pondicherry

Columbo

Seychelles
Mahé

Chagos Is.

Madagascar
Mauritius
Port Louis
Réunion

New Hebrides

New Caledonia
Noumea

AUSTRALIA
Newcastle

St. Paul

Crozet Is.

Kerguelen

Tasmania Hobart

New Zealand

The Southern Ocean

The Bounty
Ships of
France

The Bounty Ships of France

The Story of the French Cape Horn Sailing Ships

Alan Villiers & Henri Picard

CHARLES SCRIBNER'S SONS
NEW YORK

A - 11.72 (I)

Printed in Great Britain.
Library of Congress Catalog Card Number 72-6842
SBN 684-13184-6 (cloth)

Illustrations

Maps and line drawings by Captain Adrian Small
Jacket painting by Mark Myers
Jacket designed by Martin Treadway

Introduction

AMONG SEAMEN and all who have known the sea, French ships have been famous as long as any in Europe—ships-of-war, of discovery, merchantmen, East and West Indiamen, Grand Bankers, Greenland and Iceland fishermen. Early English warships designers learned a deal from the French. Perhaps France did not develop a special sort of "clipper", the allegedly—and sometimes real—superfast vessel, for she had no special need for them. She had few sluggards either, no cumbersome wall-sided blocks of more-or-less shapely wood drifting along as well as they might manage. She had a great empire, a great sea trade. But she had no Californian or Australian "Gold Rush" to give ephemeral spurt to a few pampered ocean greyhounds, to rush briefly round the earth in the last days of Sail and wear themselves swiftly out while the powered leviathans slowly panted to sea supremacy. *All* her ships were built to sail reasonably well, and her seamen knew how to handle them. She built really fast vessels when she needed them, even in the 1850s.

France had a great sailing merchant fleet of barques, ships, and four-masted barques well into the second decade of the 20th century, and later. In the far-off Australia of that era, I knew them well, for where the sea winds blew they sailed. They were distinctive, shapely, unmistakable, somehow always *French*. France had large fleets of sturdy, sea-kindly fishermen too, the Grand Banks and Greenland barquentines and topsail schooners out of Fécamp, St. Malo, and other ports of Brittany and Normandy: I saw the last fishing off Greenland in 1950. The first was there before Jacques Cartier sailed west from St. Malo in 1536 to look for a North-West Passage, and find the St. Lawrence route into Canada.

I saw the great French square-rigged merchantmen, racing visions of pale grey loveliness beneath towering, perfect suits of gale-filled sails heading towards Hobart in Tasmania (for I was raised round those parts), towards Noumea in New Caledonia, or perhaps Chile or California. Seamen called them "bounty ships", for their government had the sense to take real interest in them and look after them and their seamen. The ships were distinctive for their hull-shape, their abundance of dry accommodation, their almost continuous upper-decks which kept the Cape Horn seas from breaking with full and murderous strength on board. Their crews were unique for their curious homogenous quality in that otherwise most international of worlds. The French crews were French; and their rate of desertion in distant ports was the lowest of all seamen—not a sixth, for example, of the British. Even in our small Australian barques the crews were always international: the only thing they often had in common was that they were all seamen.

I remember once, early in my time at sea, serving in a Tasman Sea and South Pacific barque, plugging along to the westwards in the South Tasman —that ugliest, foulest, stormiest of stretches of miserable water—wide open to the Antarctic in the south and all the hell of the Roaring Forties to the westwards. It had its own array of vicious sudden storms called "southerly busters" that flung themselves out of a clear sky at you without a moment's warning, and continuity of nothing except an appalling desire, apparently, to blow all ships that ventured there from the face of the earth for ever. We were staggering from some southern timber port in New Zealand bound for Melbourne, and the going was hard. We had a gutful of sawn timber, and the fact that the main deck was also full of the stuff did not make the ship easier to work. The watch of us, I remember, were trying to get the main topgallantsail in—trying means succeeding, in that life, and that can take time. We felt as if we had been aloft all day. The cold wind screamed and the hail squalls lashed and the old barque gyrated and jumped and leapt and plunged as if she were heartily sick of the whole enterprise, or desperately seeking at least one square hundred yards or so in that squall-tormented sea where she could be still, if only for a moment. The wind was ahead, of course; right in our faces. This makes the going hard for square-rigged ships at any time, but especially in the Tasman Sea. It can continue that way for weeks, months—forever, apparently. And it brings up such a sea as can penetrate everywhere through the ship and through your bones, too, and oilskins, and sea boots, and sou'-westers, and keep the galley swamped and the fo'c'sle dripping, the deck there often knee-deep in cold sea. The main topgallantsail was, through some error, made of American cotton canvas— tough, steely stuff that rips out your fingernails (if any are left) by the roots. It was rough up there on the topgallant yard, not to say thoroughly nasty.

Suddenly there was old Bill Barrett staring to wind'ard.

"Look!" he shouted. "There in the clearing. Lord almighty!"

There within a couple of ships' lengths of us (so it looked: probably it was further) a sudden clearing showed a great sailing-ship running magnificently towards the east, the westerly gale a fair wind for her, and the long, lithe, lean form of her gloriously beautiful hull revelling in it. A ray of sunshine broke out of the storm wrack, just for her, lighting her like some stage beauty, shining upon the fantastic symmetry of her gale-distended suit of straining sails as they hurled that lovely hull along through and yet always above the sea, at a rate that looked to us like 18 knots and was certainly over 16. Sea after sea rushed snarling at her only to part and let her drive buoyant on her way: she rolled heavily but never rail under (as we did). No weight of water fell upon her though sea after sea lapped her to the top of her railing: it found no place to assault her, no spot to roar on board, for her poop reached for'ard almost to her mizzen-mast and her fore-castle-head stretched aft towards her main, and what might have been open deck between was occupied by a large donkey-boiler-house and other con-structions. She had a high freeboard though she was well laden, and she ran with a delicate grace as if the beautiful woman at her prow—her magnifi-cent figurehead—was picking a way for her, avoiding the worst of the seas, bewitching them. All these things one saw in a flash, and the perfection of her perfect sails: then she was gone like a great gazelle that had leapt into view suddenly among sunbeams in a forest glade, and fled.

"One of A. D. Bordes' ships," Bill broke the silence. "She'll be from Hobart now, bound south of New Zealand belike, towards Chile or Aca-pulco, or Santa Rosalia—some place like that. Running her easting down. She'll have a gutful of coal . . . "

It seemed crude to think of a "gutful" of coal being carried in so much loveliness: but it was proper. She was a working ship. I never forgot that sight. I knew the firm of A. D. Bordes, then of Dunkirk, had long been one of the great French sailing-ship lines particularly in the Chilean nitrate trade—possibly the only line that rivalled the Hamburg House of Laeisz of the Flying "P" Horn-defiers, whose thoroughbreds included the five-masted barque *Potosi* and the big ship *Preussen* of 5,000 tons. The French built their ships strong and well, and when they bought former British ships their policy was to acquire none but the best.

I never forgot that Bordes ship, but for 50 years after that I learned little if anything more about her or her many sisters. Somehow the "windjammer" books left them out. Their own masters wrote no books*, though it was the French Cape Horn shipmasters who established the only international brotherhood of their kind—the famous St. Malo-based A.I.C.H., *Amicale Internationale des Capitaines au Long-Cours Cap Horniers,* in which the rank of Albatross (Cape Horn shipmaster, experienced as such in command of engineless square-rigged ships doubling the Horn) still stands pre-eminent in the merchant-ships' sea world. Today there are few such Albatrosses—not a hundred left on earth—almost all are in France, Finland and Germany.

No Albatross of France wrote any book as far as I knew, or Mollyhawk (ex-Mate) either. It seemed odd, for I knew that it had been France, too, which introduced the first great square-rigged five-master—the *France*, built for Bordes in 1890. I knew that during the heyday of the big steel ship, that illustrious country had built over 200 fine ships between 2,500 and 4,000 deadweight tons within five years from 1897—212 of them, to be precise, a magnificent fleet, right at the end of the sailing-ship era. Indeed, after

---

* Although one remembers the many fine books of Captain Lacroix.

another five years, no real plain working Cape Horn square-rigged ship dependent only on God's wind was ever built, except a handful—*Pola, Priwall, Padua*—in Germany. When the first World War began in 1914, there were 140 Cape Horners built in France under the bounty system still flying the Tricolour, and these found plenty of useful work to do and suffered casualties at no greater rate than powered vessels did. Her policies gave France not only this big fleet, but a host of good seamen both for her fighting and her merchant ships. I read in an English book, written by the indefatigable Mr Basil Lubbock, that the Bordes and other French ships had made as splendid passages as anyone, especially in the Chilean nitrate trade—little more than a couple of months, for example, between the Channel and Chanaral or Iquique, or Valparaiso outward-bound deep-loaded past the savage ship-wrecking Horn, thrusting deep from Andes rim towards the Antarctic Ocean where a Tasman Seas Southerly Buster was like a summer air, and the sea turned to ice as it touched steel. Think of it! This was sailing, consistent, and quietly done, without fanfare or other interference by publicist or promoter, loudmouth or fabricator, and the crudest microphone then still by God's grace a quarter of a century away or more.

I searched for something of the real story of these French ships in vain. Mr Lubbock's was a lone voice, perhaps overly concerned with records real and alleged, seeing all ships as "clippers" which they were not. His book about what he called the "nitrate clippers" was better than nothing by far, but brief indeed, written almost with a sense of patriotic shock that any nation other than Britain and U.S.A. should have sailed such ships so consistently and successfully at all. Then one day out of the blue I heard of Henri Picard, through my friend Commandant Marc Paillé, of Nantes: Henri Picard had made a real study of the French ships over years, going back to sources. He had been a sailor in a French barque, the big steel *Bretagne* of 2,197 register tons, a "bounty" ship built at Nantes in 1901 and sailing out of there, until an accident forced him to abandon his sea career early. He never gave up his interest. Beginning before the 1939-45 war when records were still readily at hand, he traced the stories and the passages of almost 300 iron or steel French ships from the 1890s to the early 1930s—an enormous task, aided by many, but inevitably—he says—still with some errors lurking here and there. For these, apologies.

Monsieur Picard thanks all who have helped him in his long quest. For my part, I am delighted that he undertook such a task and successfully completed it, and I thank him. His work, and my own researches into the records available at Lloyd's (who covered all ships, not at all just British) and in the older shipping journals filed at the National Maritime Museum at Greenwich, and in Sydney and Newcastle, N.S.W., Hobart, Tasmania and elsewhere form the basis of this book.

Oxford, October 6 1971.

                                                            ALAN VILLIERS

PART ONE

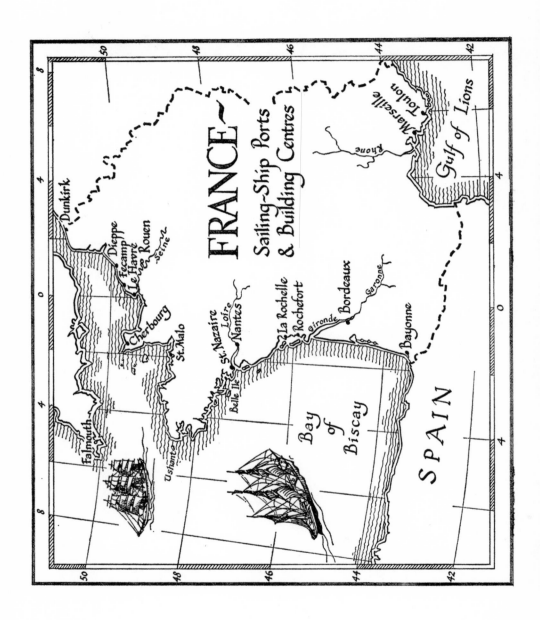

FRANCE

Sailing-Ship Ports & Building Centres

Dunkirk

Dieppe
Fécamp
Le Havre
Rouen

Seine

Cherbourg

St. Malo

St. Nazaire
Nantes
Loire

Belle Ile

La Rochelle
Rochefort

Gironde

Bordeaux
Garonne

Bayonne

Rhône

Marseille
Toulon

Gulf of Lions

Bay
of
Biscay

SPAIN

Falmouth

Ushant

Chapter One _____

The French were Different

JOSEPH CONRAD spent his first two years at sea in the French merchant service. Between 1874 and early 1877 he sailed out of the port of Marseilles in a couple of those beautiful little square-riggers—graceful wooden barques and shapely barquentines—which the French sent to the West Indies and Central America, mainly in the logwood and sugar trades with, perhaps, a bit of gun-running on the side. The strange young Pole never forgot his sea beginnings in the 400-tonners *Mont-Blanc* and *Saint-Antoine*. Had he really been interested in professional seafaring as a career, he might have been well-advised to remain with the French rather than change suddenly to the British, with their difficult new language, odd insularity, far less security for seamen and—especially for the foreigner—much poorer prospects both of continuity of employment and hope of advancement. For France has looked after her merchant seamen for centuries, and has long regarded all her shipping as a national asset.

Conrad had his reasons, which could have had nothing to do with a preference for the tough Limejuicers. After all, though no-one was more Polish than he, in fact he was a Russian citizen by birth (in a part of Poland then —and now—compulsorily Russian) and, as such, should have had Russian permission to sail in foreign ships, for he was subject to Russian conscription. To be that much further from Czarist Russia for the patriot Pole was a very good idea, as his 21st birthday approached. If the Russians ever got hold of him in conscript service, in those Czarist days it would be for life: his father was well remembered as a Polish patriot, transported to Siberia. As a child, Conrad had existed there briefly himself. So he made his way to England and joined the British merchant service in mid-1878. It was tough. Looking into the official records, one notes that his first British sailing-ship was the 254-ton collier *Skimmer of the Seas*, a barquentine on the coal-heavers' "run" between Lowestoft and Tyneside, and he stood that only for about ten weeks. In those ten weeks, Conrad (J. C. Korzeniowski then) made six round trips between Lowestoft and Newcastle, in ballast northwards, back with coal. It was a backbreaking job shovelling it out at Lowestoft and trimming it in at Newcastle, for his wage of one shilling a month as ordinary seaman. It could have been curious English the young Pole picked up among those Norfolk lads, his ship-mates. The Master's idea of the "Scale of Provisions to be allowed and served out to the Crew during the Voyage" is spelled out on the Articles (still existing) as: "SURFISHANT NO WASTE".

No, the *Skimmer of the Seas* must have been something of a shock, after the little French square-riggers. That "wage" was derisory, too. The Norfolk ordinary seamen aboard had £2.5s. a month.

It took some influence to get Conrad his next ship—a berth in the Australian trader *Duke of Sutherland* where he made one round voyage, still as ordinary seaman at one shilling a month. When he qualified as officer, he had to accept a third mate's job, as a sort of glorified boatswain not in charge of a watch and so not reckoning as officer's service towards advancement. His first real second mate's berth (in the 400-odd tons old-timer *Palestine* which took nearly a year to get started on a voyage at all and then burned out before reaching her destination) could scarcely have been much sought after. His only command was of an unimportant little barque, the 400-odd tonner *Otago,* and he left her after a year-and-a-half of the Australian coast and the Mauritius trade, to step back as mate. He was almost as much ashore looking for a ship as at sea in one, and that was no fault of his. One thinks that he would indeed have done better among the sympathetic French.

Of course, Joseph Conrad was exceptional. His French experience led to the great novel "Nostromo", the fiery *Palestine* to "Youth", the *Otago* to "The Secret Sharer" and much else. But it was France that first welcomed him, and gave him his indoctrination to the sea, pleasantly: in the very beginning with the Marseilles pilots, then in the small barks *Mont-Blanc* and *Saint-Antoine,* with intervals ashore. His road to command in such ships was clear-cut and open, and the owners were family friends. His French was excellent, his English then non-existent.

France then had an immense merchant service. The sea world had long known the excellence, the sea grace of the French frigates and majestic strength of her ships-of-the-line. The whole world knew, too, of the long line of France's probing, gallant seamen questing in the Pacific, the South Indian Ocean, the waters of Antarctica where only that quiet Yorkshireman James Cook forestalled them. Brought up in part in that farthest British island of Tasmania, perhaps I was more conscious of the French Pacific seamen than those who learn their sea history only in English schools, for the names of great Frenchmen were thick upon our shores—Bruni d'Entre-casteaux, Huon de Kermadec, the mysteriously lost La Perouse, Yves de Kerguelen-Tremarec had all sailed these seas. Almost as much of the South Pacific (disregarding Australia and New Zealand) was French as was British —New Caledonia, the New Hebrides, the Society Islands, the Tuamotus.

In the Indian Ocean, Mauritians still spoke French though the island had been British for more than a century. What qualities had these extraordinary French that their roots struck so deep, and seemed always to remain?

Unlike many living nearer France, I knew as a lad, too, of their magnificent modern merchant service, for their great ships, barques and four-masted barques called often at Hobart, capital of Tasmania, and at Melbourne. There were always some large French square-rigged ships in Melbourne during the first two decades of the 20th century. They were there, usually, to load wheat for Europe, or sometimes for Peru: some brought cargoes of benzine or kerosene, then transported in 5-gallon tins two to the wooden case, from Philadelphia or Hoboken; or nitrates from Chile. I could identify them at one quick glance because they were unmistakable—well-kept, their steel hulls looking well in a light-grey shade so distinctive it was called French-grey, sometimes touched off by a line of the painted-ports (false gun-ports), a hangover from pirate days when big sailers in the Eastern trade found it expedient to look like ships-of-war.

The French ships had hulls quite different from the usual. The ordinary British, American, or Scandinavian ship was strictly utilitarian. She had a cargo-carrying hull with the minimum accommodation built on top of it— a bit of a raised fo'c'sle-head right forward and a poop aft, both as short as possible, the first an anchor-working place and the second a steering position and control station so-to-speak with, just below, accommodation for a minimum group of officers, a store-room or two and the master's saloon. On the main deck was a steel house, very square and utilitarian, for the accommodation of her crew: this was known as the forecastle. Some ships had the galley incorporated in this, others a "donkey"-room (for a small boiler used in ports) as well: larger ships might have a hutch of a house further aft in the wettest part of the waist where the apprentices lived. The key-note was utility with minimum cost.

Not so with the French. They had roomy long forecastles extending often to well abaft the foremast, large houses on deck, big donkey-rooms, long poops with large charthouses above, almost invariably. They looked as if they were designed to provide maximum accommodation, not minimum. I was to discover that indeed they were, and one reason was that, needing them and having some national appreciation of those who sailed them, the French Government subsidised their building in French shipyards: the larger the gross tonnage the larger the subsidy, naturally. They could afford to be generous. This also meant that they were safer ships, as I learned when I went to sea. There was less free space for the great seas to wash and drown and destroy when they broke aboard. They had to reach higher to get aboard in the first place: when they got aboard, there was far less volume to them, less weight to pin the ship down and so cause more seas to follow.

B

Looking at ships in a quiet basin in Melbourne or at anchor in the Derwent at Tasmania did not indicate such points. I learned of them later. Some of those great four-masted barques like the *Parma* or full-riggers like the *Grace Harwar* would let the gale-whipped seas storm over them, filling them from rail to rail dangerously, putting the mariners at grave risk: for as the ship rolled they could be washed out of her, as the murdering hand of the violent sea reached inboard to pluck them away on the next rail-down roll. Once knocked off his feet, there was little but luck to keep the seaman aboard, and in bad weather his quarters were also invariably wet, his bunk a wooden shelf with nothing provided by the ship at all—no bedding, not even the plainest eating utensils, never enough to eat on too many British ships, and often barely sufficient to drink. Such quarters, called the forecastle because they had gravitated from an even bleaker, wetter space beneath the forecastle-head, had usually one skylight not waterproof, a few small ports kept screwed fast (if possible), and two doors one each side, so that it was often possible to keep the weather door shut and some sea out. The same steel house usually housed the galley—one stove, one fire (often out, always doused at night), one coal-bunker, one water-tank, a few pots, one cook—and that was very vulnerable, too. Such quarters were hangovers from the old-type wooden ships, which sailed drier and more buoyant than the big, deep-loaded, steel sea bruisers.

I saw at first only that the French were different and quite distinctive. I heard too at Hobart, where I wondered what brought so many of them there though few if any unloaded or loaded anything in Tasmania, that the French sailing-ships were paid a mileage subsidy. Hobart was a safe port placed ideally in the so-called Roaring Forties belt of the Southern Hemisphere, where the predominantly westerly winds could drive a strong square-rigged ship swiftly and reliably round the world—at least give her the longitude she needed, no matter where she might be bound. If she were making a passage from North Europe, say, towards San Francisco or Puget Sound, or Chilean or Peruvian ports, or Acapulco or Hawaii—all then places importing much bunker-coal from Europe and other heavy cargoes such as cement and railway-iron—the simplest though also longest way to sail there was to run out round Good Hope and hare along eastwards in the Forties, north of the drift-ice line, south of the baffling winds.

Roughly half-way between the turning-point towards the Cape, about long. 20° or 25° W. in the South Atlantic Ocean and the turning-point towards the north again 8, 9, or 10,000 miles further on in the South Pacific, Tasmania stood conveniently athwart the gales. On its lee side, just round its southern corner, was the wide estuary of the Derwent River which led to Hobart—easy to make, safe to enter without pilot or tug, a secure and commodious anchorage that was also easy to leave. A rich food-producing island, Tasmania was a good place also to replenish sea stores, to buy plump chickens and fat hogs, and good fruits and fish and all those things appreciated by men come in from sea.

Many of the big French ships had no real occasion to touch at Hobart. Few had cargo for Tasmania, though some did lift a token tonnage, in case of questions on their mileage bounties—perhaps five or ten tons. Hobart was a most convenient and cheap port to touch at inexpensively for further orders, and this could be useful in times of difficult freight markets. This was before the days when ships could be communicated with by wireless telegraphy at sea. When this questionable boon came, for that matter, few big sailing-ships bothered with it, for they had no facilities for re-charging batteries, and their people liked things the way they were.

The French ships, to remain internationally competitive, were for some years aided by building and sailing subsidies. The building subsidies allowed owners to acquire them for a reasonable investment. The sailing subsidies were paid at so much a thousand miles on all their voyaging. Such payments were known as bounties and the ships were called "bounty ships". It was a concrete expression of the French people's appreciation of their worth to the nation, a payment in cash to help them through hard times, for they were a magnificent fleet of cargo-movers independent of foreign fuels or power-plants of any sort, a noble expression of the French genius in naval architecture, and a splendid reservoir of hardy, able and courageous seamen. More than that, through their sailing, they were constantly replenishing and adding to the national "stock" of seamen. These French ships were French and they were French manned, down to the deck-boys and the scullions (if any). The seamen were reservists, and pensionable. They had national rights and they had national duties, clearly defined. They knew where they stood, and so did their countrymen. Indoctrination in a long-voyage square-rigged ship might at times be thought harsh but it was effective, swift, and permanent. It weeded out the misfits, too, likewise quickly and for ever.

Of course, I did not know these things as a boy in Melbourne. For one thing, it was rather difficult to get to know the French. One could board a Scots ship or a Norwegian or a Dane or German, and the language was like as not English of a sort for they were thoroughly international. But the French ships were wholly French, and the seamen spoke a language which bore no resemblance to the French taught in Melbourne schools, especially seamen in the beautiful ships of St. Nazaire and Nantes. These were manned by Bretons who spoke a language of their own, older than French, a sort of Welsh. All I realised then was that it was quite incomprehensible to me. I soon had friends in other ships, but this barrier with the French ships was then insurmountable. Later, in the few years I was in deepsea sailing-ships myself while French ships still also sailed, I saw that French crews did not mix much internationally, either. Even in the extraordinary human mix-

tures common before the mast in British ships, no Frenchman sailed. Few
if any Britishers sailed in French ships. A French master, it seemed, had
to comply strictly with French maritime law and fill vacancies with consular
approval: only in the absence of French nationals might he engage a foreign
replacement at all. The British, Scandinavians and American masters looked
after themselves and had much more freedom in shipping crews or replace-
ments, and so had the Germans. But no one had any pension rights aboard
them—certainly never as a seaman—nor any claim during the sailing-ship
era on public health services if provided, or workmen's compensation. In
some British ships especially, the seamen must have been the most thoroughly oppressed working-men on earth, even in the first decade of the
20th century, and their officers were little better off than the foremast crowd
was.

It was not a simple matter for the Australian or any seaman other than
the French to learn much of French ships. They figured in the occasional
yarn, of course—the wonderful rescue by France's big ship *Bérangère* of the
crew of the dismasted, bashed-up Britisher *Garsdale* in one violent winter
storm off the Horn in the dreadful year 1905*, the splendid record of the
Dunkirk ships of A. D. Bordes, the feats of their pioneering five-masted
barque *France*. Plenty of them were bashed up off the Horn, too, forced
to run back for the Falklands or Montevideo in distress, or wrecked, or just
gone missing—that endless silent fate of mystery forever associated with the
fight to survive at sea.

We all knew the French ships. There were hundreds of them, all somehow managing to look unmistakably French even if some were built
originally in Britain. What we did not know then were the French seamen,
except as worthy members of the great brotherhood, going quietly and
effectively about their work in their own ships. The French had nitrates
interests in Chile, as the Germans had, and these gave them many cargoes.
They had special interests in New Caledonia with its rich deposits of nickel
ore, which they moved by hundreds of thousands of tons (in the aggregate)
in ships driven by the wind alone. They had their own interests in the
Eastern trade as other nations had, particularly in India and Indo-China.
They had particular interests in Madagascar and in the West Indies,
especially in the sugar and log-wood trades: the economy of the great port
of Nantes was largely founded on this. And they joined competitively in the
sailing carrying trades of the world while these survived.

There were those who criticised, of course: foreign owners alleged that
the French were too greatly subsidised through those building and sailing
bounties, which gave them an "unfair advantage" over other ships. Even in
France, this legislation was criticised at times, for it is not everyone who

---

* See *The War With Cape Horn* by Alan Villiers (Hodder and Stoughton, 1971), (Charles
Scribner's Sons, N.Y., 1971).

can appreciate the true value of seamen and ships. France is quite a substantial piece of Europe, much of it remote from the sea: most French, like any other landsmen, were content enough to live in forgetfulness of their seamen. In Britain, it could be a different matter. At a meeting of the International Sailing Ship Union held at Glasgow on June 8 1906, attended by representatives from Liverpool, Aberdeen and other British ports as well as from Nantes, Paris, Bremen and Hamburg, there were many complaints about the alleged bad effects of the French bounty system and its possibilities for "unfair competition". The international group was set up to try to maintain minimum freight rates, below which owners would agree not to accept charters.

"Let us stand together, shoulder to shoulder, loyal to our union," declared the Chairman, Scots sailing-ship owner William Law, to acclamation, "and good times may come for the sailing-ship again."

But international freight markets were not to be controlled by any union of hopeful owners. When too many ships sought cargoes on a shrunken market—down because of plain economic or natural causes such as a poor grain harvest in California or Australia, or a slump in the demand for nitrates in Europe—the attempt to set up minimum acceptable freights broke down. "Lloyd's Weekly" had pointed out in December 1905*, how the French system paid. The Bounty Law of 1881 had seen an increase in the French deepsea sailing fleet from 735 ships of 325,000 tons in that year to 1,157 of 520,000 tons ten years later. This was the building subsidy, introduced because it was "necessary for the support of French ship-building and necessary for the defence of the country and the national prosperity". A great and healthy merchant fleet "should exist as an adjunct to the state arsenals, to produce a Navy, for the training of seamen, formation of a reserve, and the defence of the colonies".

Another news item in the London shipping press (on June 15 1906) referred to the fact that the French ship *René Kerviler*, 2,200 tons, which had recently cleared in ballast from Dunkirk bound for Hobart for orders, was more than reimbursed for the lack of outward freight by the sailing bounties accruing to her for the 14,000-mile outward passage and, when she reached Hobart, she would be "well placed for the Newcastle (N.S.W.) coal trade to Chile, to go to San Francisco for grain or even direct to Chile for nitrates homewards, and she would have additional bounty payment for the distances sailed to any of these."

There were loud complaints, and they continued. But the French policy showed its effectiveness in many ways other than as a useful commercial subsidy. For example, during a discussion of the Merchant Shipping Bill in the House of Commons in June 1906, Mr. Lloyd George, then the responsible minister, told the House of Commons that there were "probably 27,000

---

* Issue dated December 7.

cases of desertion from British ships in a year"—an appalling and expensive
rate of loss. The remarkably low proportion of British seamen in British
ships was constantly being bewailed in the same House, and elsewhere. In
the same issue of "Lloyd's Weekly Summary" which drew attention to the
appalling desertion rate, another item spoke of the fact that "statistics have
shown that for some time past the number of British seamen is steadily
decreasing," laying the blame at least in part on the seamen's "poor pay,
poor food, and poor housing" and suggested that the merchant service should
"be a pensionable calling, instead of one of maximum insecurity". There
was also an appalling casualty rate, particularly under sail.

It is a plain matter of recorded fact that the French did better. For
example, the British Consul at Portland (Oregon)—a notorious port for
"crimps" and other exploiters of seamen—reported in May 1906 a "welcome
decrease in the numbers of deserters from British ships calling there . . .
from 40 per cent (of all crews) in 1903 to 21.26 per cent in 1905," but, he
added, the French rate throughout was steady at less than 7 per cent.
Reasons he gave for this were that the French "were more diligent in pursu-
ing deserters, and fighting off crimps" (whose charge for supplying a man
to ships from whom they had previously stolen the crews was then £6 each).
He wished, added the consul, that the British were as resolute as the French.

But the consul seems to have missed the crux of the problem. The French
seamen had a real stake in their calling. As for the British, they had little
or none, and there was evidence that in several Puget Sound and Californian
ports, some British crews were deliberately driven out of their ships with
the connivance of their own captain, who then received a "consideration"
out of the blood-money, as well as filching the men's hard-earned wages by
means of concocted accounts for "advances," and tobacco and clothing sold
at "sea prices" from the only store on board—his own. Once a man deserted
or could be so entered in the Official Log, his earnings were fair game as
he was not entitled to them until the voyage ended. There were honest
masters: there were also others. None was overpaid, and with the seamen
gone, the men's wages were forfeit anyway. The temptation was there. At
£3 a month less one month's advance, even an average passage to San Francisco or Puget Sound (of five months or so) should give an A.B. a £12 credit
with the ship, and this was real money in the early 1900s. If the ship had
made a longer passage—big sailers signed Articles for three years—the men
could have far larger credits, for advances of pay in ports were purely "at
master's option", i.e. they might be allowed to draw £1 or so perhaps once,
or nothing at all. Alone among workers, the British seaman had to complete
the whole voyage to have legal claim on his hard-earned pay, and very few
left allotments. Some masters had concluded that, as the crimps in some
ports were bound to take the men anyway, they themselves might as well
also make something out of the evil. For the masters and officers were very

poorly paid and badly treated in British sailing-ships then, with no pensions, no leave, and no "job security".

There were other ways to subsidise shipping than by the straightforward payments made by France. Most of those same shipowners who roundly condemned the French bounties secured from a fourth to a third of their crews—some as much as half—by a system of callous exploitation of teen-age boys and young men. This was the so-called apprenticeship system, by which lads of good background, strong physique and reasonable education were recruited as company apprentices, indentured to serve four years for no pay at all or (in some cases) a pittance, to work loyally in whatever ship they might be appointed to, in return for a poor allowance of poor food and a shelf to sleep upon as the watch system might permit.

The fiction was that the lads would be "taught the business of a seaman" —and they were, by the ship and the sea and their own friendly shipmates, rarely indeed by the master responsible (under the owner) for them. They lived in a small steel hutch usually in the wettest part of the ships. Far from being accorded any privileges, the lads had to keep time—strike the bells— during night watches at sea, and "loblolly" as master's boatboys in port, in addition to the performance of more than their fair share of the ship's work including manhandling heavy cargoes.

There were good British companies and there were excellent masters who really looked after the lads, but for the most part, the system worked as a crew-saving "subsidy" in flesh and blood. Each of those lads saved his owner an able seaman's wages, after he had been a voyage at sea, and an ordinary seaman's from the start. There were six, eight, or even ten or twelve in a ship, saving anything up to £40 or so a month on the wages bill even when able seamen were paid £3 or £3.10s. the month. Many became unpaid acting third or second mates, before their indentures expired, for British sailing-ships were then required to carry only two certificated officers, the master and the chief or first mate (always known as *the* mate). In tramps, second mates required no certificates, and third mates were luxuries.

The apprentices' casualty rate was very high, and there was yet another bad feature in such a system. It was not necessary for anyone to be an inden-tured apprentice to qualify to sit the simple deck officers' examinations of the time. A true apprenticeship system was necessary for the tradesmen's qualifications of sailmaker or ship's carpenter, but the requirement for deck officers was four years on deck in deepwater vessels in any capacity from deck-boy (the first year) through ordinary to able seaman. One chief result of the British system was to staunch the flow of good youth into the forecastle, and to help promote the enlistment of foreigners. Worse than that, a side-result was, very largely, to introduce the best youth into an exacting service with a tradition *against the men,* and this was foolish. A ship's company is a unit or nothing: it is remarkable how well they usually did.

One speaks in the matter from a background of some experience. In Australia and New Zealand, there was no such system as this premium-paying indentured apprenticeship, though one could (and I for one did) begin in a small group of teen-age lads together in a half-deck. We were there as cadets signed on the ship's voyage articles, like the men, *not* as indentured apprentices bound to the owner. One began that way, perhaps, but soon graduated to the forecastle among the other young fellows there—one's countrymen, and with them some of those 27,000 deserters from the British ships (by no means all British by nationality) whom I recall as the salt of the earth.

There were other forms of "subsidy", owner-promoted or fostered: such could be and were at times carried to ridiculous lengths, such as requiring masters (at £12 a month, without paid leave, pension, or security, and most with few if any legitimate sources of commission or other genuine earnings) to provide their own sextants, charts, and even the chronometer. Minimum charts could cause wrecked ships, and so could indifferent chronometers. The French in their hey-day carried no half-decks of "apprentices", and furnished their ships' full equipment. Those bounties helped not only owners but masters, officers and crews, and morale. The French merchant service was a reliable national asset in peace and war. Without its hordes of foreign seamen both in Sail and steam and its thousands of Asiatic firemen, trimmers, and greasers down below in its steamships, the British merchant service then could not have existed. (Though it was a marvellous national asset here too, when needed, thank God.)

In a remarkable small book called "England's Duty to Her Merchant Seamen"* written by a former British able seamen named A. E. Gay, never widely distributed and now rare—it is one of the few documents by an educated working seaman before the mast in British sailing-ships of those days—the writer has something to say about the far better treatment of the French seaman.

"It is not generally known among the British public," he writes, "that French seamen have many advantages over the British. A French merchant seaman on attaining the age of 50 years, providing he can prove twenty-five years' service in merchant ships, is entitled to receive 600 francs annually as pension for life (400 before January 1907) and on his decease his widow receives half this sum annually for life. Apart from that (unlike the British) he can demand part wages abroad. French ships are more fully manned than ours, and on visiting seven French sailing-ships in succession I found in each case the crew's quarters were furnished with a mess-room specially built for the purpose, separate from the sleeping quarters. The British sailor generally has his dinner on the floor of his sleeping quarters." (Seated on his sea-chest, if any, mug, knife and tin plate in his hands: no table provided.)

---

* Published (printed) at Adelaide, South Australia, by Sands and McDougall, Printers, King William Street, 1907. My copy by courtesy of the Australian Federal Librarian, Canberra, A.C.T.

"In all these French ships the crew's quarters had nearly twice as much space allotted to them as would our men have in British ships. They received daily at least two hot meat (or fish) meals. They are not so bullied and otherwise harshly treated as our British sailors usually are. I consider Frenchmen have far more inducement to follow the sea in their own ships than our men in theirs."

The French certainly formed far more stable crews. As reservists, they had duties too but, in war or peace, their principal place of duty was in their merchant ships so long as these could keep the sea. French consuls and shipping authorities were required to exercise a proper supervision over the treatment and behaviour abroad of French crews, and masters, who were held responsible for their acts. Unlike men serving in British ships, French seamen were required to be properly identified and medically fit—two important qualifications. There was no medical check of men seeking to sign aboard British ships in the sailing ship era (which lasted both under the British and French flags into the 1920s): even a man's name might be fictitious, or that upon whatever flimsy discharge-paper he presented to the powerless clerk at the signing on table. His state of health and competence showed up quickly aboard, but that was too late, for crews were signed on just before sailing.

Able Seaman Gay writes of the treatment of other able seamen as he knew it, in British ships. In truth, most British masters and mates were not much better off. When France still offered reasonable employment prospects and conditions (not only in the wind-driven ships), and masters were the trusted, contracted employees of owners who appreciated them, many British masters and almost all officers outside a few large lines had no proper contract with their owners at all. Masters might own a few shares in later days, particularly in the one-ship companies when they had somehow acquired sufficient capital—a matter of near impossibility out of their wages. Even in the 1890s, most were elderly men (often Welsh, Irish, Scots or Canadians mainly from the Maritimes) who had left it too late to change into the steamships they despised, many of them hanging grimly on to command of some great, gaunt Cape Horner making what they could and, as the years passed, becoming the more embittered. The watch-keeping officers consisted often of elderly mates past hope of command or, in some cases, former masters stuck with the sailing-ship life but unable to command through failing vision or health —splendid old boys who toiled on in that most rigorous of lives until they fell dead in their sea-boots and oilskins, aged 75 or more, for they had no beds to die in ashore.

With these were juvenile second mates aged between 18 and 22, some of them senior apprentices, others with their first certificates fresh from the crammers, anxious to serve the necessary sea-time towards their next certificates (chief mate's) in Sail. The time needed for this was 12 months only—

less than half many Cape Horning voyages—and this had to be served as officer in charge of a watch. Hence the preference for Sail, where the custom was to employ two watch officers only so that each had one watch. The same young fellows sometimes stayed on for a year or so as mates, to qualify to sit for a master's licence—again more readily gained from Sail and (since they were paid slightly better than A.B.s, the crimps and other criminals let them be, and with few ports visited, temptations were few and so were chances to spend money) it was easier to save the essential sum to pay for crammers and shore lodgings that way. (French schooling was free.)

For none of these people (except the good master with his own shares) did the British long-voyage sailing-ship offer real career prospects after the year 1895, though many failed to realise this for at least another ten years. In the French merchant service things were different, and stayed so until the end of the First World War.

Conrad came to England from France in 1878. He had a spread of 15 years in the British merchant service. Paid the derisory wage of one shilling a month in his first two sailing-ships, qualifying as second mate only after rigorous examination and then forced to ship in the elderly and decrepit barque *Palestine,* with later long spells ashore seeking employment between ships, his advancement was by no means assured nor his career straight-forward. Britain was then short of merchant service officers. Conrad was competent, sober, highly intelligent. His spoken English though imperfect was adequate for his duties in Sail or steam, and certainly no worse than thousands of other continentals who then helped to keep British ships at sea. Yet he served for more than one round voyage in only two of his British sailing-ships, the barque *Otago* in command, and (later) the ship *Torrens* as mate. In most of his British ships he remained only for half a voyage. Burned out of the *Palestine,* badly injured in the *Highland Forest,* dismissed summarily by the alcoholic master of the *Riversdale* (a few weeks before that incompetent stranded the ship), one homewards passage only (from India) in the *Narcissus,* with intervals for passing his three Board of Trade examinations, Conrad was almost as much ashore or in port as at sea between 1878 and 1892, when he left the *Torrens* and the sea. He was never more than weeks in the few steamships he joined.

The strange forces which may influence the career of genius have no effect on the lives of more ordinary humans, ashore or afloat. Conrad is exceptional. But a 350-ton colonial barque was an indifferent command for so gifted a seaman: professionally he should certainly have done better had it been possible for him to remain sailing in French ships, from France. His British ships were to give the world many books of enduring magnificence and power, as well as such word-pictures of the sea as had never been produced in English or in any other language before, or since. But his two little French barks gave us "Nostromo".

Chapter Two

More about those Subsidies

THE SUBSIDY LAWS of French merchant shipping were much publicised and criticised but little understood outside France—indeed, they were not always appreciated by landsmen ashore in France either. France introduced free trade in 1866, removing the penalties formerly existing against cargoes not carried by ships flying either the flag of France or of the country providing the cargo. There was an outcry against the effects of this liberalism on French shipping, of course: but it was not until 1881, 15 years later, that the first measures to assist both French ship-building and ship-operation were passed. These were in the form of a building subsidy (60 francs a ton gross for iron or steel) and an operating allowance of one and a half francs for each net register ton over each 1,000 miles sailed, based on the direct sailing route between ports necessarily made. (This included calls for orders, of course, as sailing-ships handling bulk commodities traditionally touched at cheap and convenient outports for instructions where to discharge, or to load.) The franc-and-a-half was for new ships only: after the first year this was reduced by 5 centimes annually for metal ships, by 7.5 centimes for wooden. New ships built elsewhere for French owners received half-subsidies.

According to the researches by Monsieur Henri Picard into the subject, these 1881 subsidies did not work perfectly. Perhaps some slump in world trade with accompanying low freights helped to deter owners, and in the 1880s the competition of steam tramps built in Britain was seriously affecting many long-voyage freight markets formerly profitable for Sail. So was the successful operation of the Suez Canal. Only eight large metal square-rigged ships were built in French yards during the decade following the introduction of these first "bounties": French merchant shipping fleets declined to ninth place in world figures.

In January 1893, a new Act therefore came into force to last for the following ten years, increasing payments considerably, not only for sailing-ships. Building payments, offered for the first ten years of a vessel's life (for sailers of 80 tons or more and for powered vessels over 100 tons), were increased to 65 francs the ton (the first year) for iron or steel vessels, and 40 francs for wooden construction. The sailing bounty, again operating on each 1,000 miles necessarily sailed, became 1 franc 70 centimes for each *gross* ton, which was very different from net. This sum decreased by 6 centimes annually on a steel ship. Steamships were similarly subsidised but at slightly lower rates, and all subsidies were for ships on long voyages as officially defined—i.e., beyond 15° W. or 44° E. longitude, reckoned from Paris. Two-thirds bounties were paid for shorter passages. Main or auxiliary machinery drew its own bounty, and so did useful innovations in sailing-ships such as donkey-boilers to provide steam for working the windlass, and winches for cargo-handling. It was no part of the Government's intention to foster the older type of ships at the expense of progress. One irate member of Parliament, representing a constituency well inland, shouted in the debate about the larger subsidies for sailing-ships, "You are subsidising the stage-coach at the expense of the railway-train!"

The bounties had nothing to do with Sail as Sail, but as an important, large, efficient and valuable section of the French Merchant Marine. When the Bounty Acts were passed, not only France still operated big fleets of sailing-ships large and small. Britain was developing more and more efficient steam tramps, cargo-liners, and passenger vessels, but still operated an enormous (though declining) fleet of sailing-ships. The idea that such ships would ever be wholly abandoned was not entertained, certainly not by those operating and sailing them.

The French Act of 1893, which operated for ten years like its predecessor, did not cause an immediate great increase in new building or voyaging but a rising freight market about 1897 really got things going. A shipbuilding boom brought 212 large new sailing-ships, almost all between 2,500 and 4,000 dead-weight tons, into the French merchant service within the following five years. The payment on gross tons, which included non-earning superstructure, encouraged owners to increase this—hence in large part the excellent accommodation, the large deckhouses, long poops and fo'c'sle-heads which then became such a feature in French ships. It did not pay to give the ships continuous upper decks, as this also increased dues charged by other authorities. A few British owners increased the safety factor and accommodation in big four-masted barques and a few full-rigged ships by building them with so-called three-island hulls—that is, with a substantial midships section of generous length carried out to the ships' sides, in which were the seamen's accommodation, galley (usually, not essentially), sail-locker and loft, carpenter's shop, and so forth. Germans soon went better with much larger midships sections where all hands were accommodated, and the tonnage of assaulting sea able to smash round the well-decks was much reduced. Such ships were intended mainly for the Chilean nitrate trade, which involved a wild beat past Cape Horn to windward every voyage, summer or winter. France built some of these big three-islanders, too, notably the second of her two five-masted barques, which benefited by the same subsidy arrangements as other French ships.

British barque

French barque

The bounty system caused some international clamour, of course, but mainly in bad times when poor freights (or none) offered. There were owners who exploited it, drawing all the money they could for the ten-year period each subsidy was intended to last, both for building and sailing. When their ships were ten years old (and still good for another 20 or 30) they sold them. A few sent ships on voyages (in poor times) which were obviously planned as maximum bounty earners and little else—right round the world in ballast, seeking a cargo. This could happen genuinely, and often did: it was ruinous for owners of other nations. Many of these complained that the French ships could undercut them on the freight markets, as they sometimes did. It was galling to a British owner to see big French sailers load, for example, all the grain cargoes offering in a bad Californian season at rates which would cause the Britisher loss.

By the first decade of the 20th century (the last French bounties Act was passed in 1902, operative in 1903 and for ten years afterwards) British owners had in fact considerably less capital tied up in their ageing ships than the French invested in new vessels, despite the subsidy. Quite soon, as big British Line after Line decided to get out of Sail and develop steamships in their tramping trades, even their big four-masted barques and full-rigged ships could be bought for a few thousand pounds, and were sold by the dozen. Nor were they all sold to Scandinavian countries and Italy. Many continued under the skinflint management of British one-ship companies of a sort, some of them notorious exploiters of their masters and officers, and the nefarious "apprenticeship" system. This was a parsimony the French never practised.

One reason for the absence of the indentured apprentice in their ships was that, traditionally, merchant ship officers had graduated from small ships to large, from for'ard (as sailors) to aft (as officers). They did not *begin* as embryo officers by status real or imagined, purchased or granted, but as seamen pure and simple. French advancement, just as British formerly had been, was by developed, noticed, and proven merit. The system bred practical and able seamen, but as steamships increasingly took over liner trades and most—soon, all—passenger carrying, there grew a requirement for social polish and so forth which the seaman in Sail had neither cultivated, nor needed. So there was some recruitment to "crack" French liners from among naval officers. Great British lines got around difficulties of this kind by early recruitment of the best sail-trained men (they could be licensed deepsea masters at 23) and training them to liner ways; and the sailing-ship indentures system did succeed in attracting many better educated boys. Its rigours also weeded out the unfit and the unsuitable. France kept her preference for the practical man, properly indoctrinated in small ships first.

Each subsidy lasted for ten years from the time of enactment. In 1903, a new law provided that, to earn full sailing bounties, a ship had to carry a minimum cargo of two-thirds her gross tonnage for at least two-fifths of the sailing distance claimed for. This meant that if she began by sailing outwards to Hobart for orders, she would draw full subsidies if she were to load grain, say, at Geelong back to Europe (which would give her cargo for half the voyage), or coal from Newcastle, N.S.W., to a Chilean port, back thence across the Pacific in ballast to N.S.W. for more coal, and finally homewards from Chile round the Horn with nitrates, or perhaps with heavy lumber or grain from Puget Sound, having sailed northwards again in ballast. These were all common rounds in the sailing-ship days. She was still able to sail three-fifths of her whole voyage without cargo, seeking. Tramp sailing-ships had often to make one leg of a long voyage in ballast in order to get any cargo at all, simply because—for example—there were just no bulk cargoes to lift outwards to San Francisco or Puget Sound at a time when prospects of a good grain harvest promised paying homewards freights from either place. The desirable thing was to have ships located where at least some paying cargo could be expected to offer, and to earn what they could, where they could. With or without bounties, too much voyaging in ballast or waiting idly in ports could be ruinous. So could the acceptance of too low rates of freight, and the bounty payments were a cushion against these. Above all, they helped the maintenance of reasonably good conditions for crews of French ships, and so of good morale. They did not merely favour the owners, nor were they intended to.

Undoubtedly the bounty system greatly aided France and her Merchant Service. When the First World War broke out, there were still 140 fine French sailers, built under that system, none old, all in good order, between them able to lift 600,000 to 700,000 tons of cargo on long voyages without consuming anything beyond the wherewithal to sustain their crews and maintain their sails and rigging. It is probable that none of these ships would have existed then had there been no bounty system. Moreover, they were manned by French seamen, almost exclusively. Even after the essential naval reservists had been called to the colours, there still existed a great and sufficient reservoir of competent French masters, mates and seamen to man this large and exacting fleet which, though it suffered heavy casualties, did excellent work throughout the war.

Long before that war, most of the other maritime nations—the Scandinavians, Italy and Russia among them—were operating their sailing-ships on capital values which were far from their real worth, having bought cheaply good ships discarded by a Britain concentrating increasingly on steam. The United States had effective forms of subsidy of its own, though its governors included few who were sea-minded. The great bulk of the American population cared little about sea matters.

There was never real difficulty about manning the French ships. The policy of accepting and fostering deepwater seafaring as a profession had been encouraged in France since the time of the great Minister Jean-Baptiste Colbert, who controlled Louis XIV's navy from 1661 to 1683. Colbert laid down rules covering all branches of the maritime profession. Every man and boy working in deepwater, coastal, short-voyage, and even river sailing, or sea fishing in all its forms, was required under these rules to register as a naval reservist, subject to call-up when required. For this obligation they were granted privileges. While the notorious press-gang was slugging British seamen and landlubbers, desperately grabbing anything like an animated male body to serve the King's ships when needed, Minister Colbert set up widely-based pensions schemes both for the invalided and the elderly, established the principle of responsibility for shipwrecked, ill, or stranded French seamen, insisted that French ships be French-manned for'ard and aft, and that crews be properly maintained and paid while their ships lay in ports abroad. There was no inducement to desert: indeed, privileges could be lost by doing so.

Of course this sort of direction could put French shipping at a commercial disadvantage, internationally, and this was a real basis for the subsidies called bounties. But the *Inscription Maritime* (as it was known) worked well: French merchant-men helped greatly to man their navy over the centuries. Compulsory naval service, when required, lasted for France's merchant seamen well into the 1960s and was modified in 1967 only to the degree that the young seafarers were allowed then to choose to serve in the Army or Air Force, if they wished. I am told that 90 per cent of them still choose the Navy.

Some three-quarters of the men manning France's fleet of deepsea sailing-ships were from Brittany—men with a long tradition of seafaring. One of Brittany's greatest assets has always been men—hardy, competent, resolute, well prepared to be independent but equally competent in those demanding joint enterprises which compel full co-operation for success not to say survival, such as off-shore fishing. Whoever sets out to sea from Brittany's ports to wrest a living from the sea must face at once the stormy treachery of the Bay of Biscay, that forever lee shore wide open to the storms of the Atlantic beyond 40° North latitude, lined with savage rocks merciless to ships and men. Fishing, deepwater seafaring, or the endless struggle of wresting a hard living from over-small areas of hard land—these were the choices. Younger sons had little if any future on the land. So the Breton was the seaman *par excellence* of France, particularly in those great and beautiful ships of the long-voyage sailing trades hailing out of Biscayan and Channel ports. He served ships, and France, well.

Many masters were also Bretons. Almost all the sailing-ship masters began at sea as their men did, as deck-boys or perhaps when very young as cabin boys in small ships. There was a rating known as *pilotin,* and this was

An unidentified big French barque alongside in San Francisco. The wireless indicates that this is probably about 1920. (*Tod Powell Collection, San Francisco Maritime Museum.*)

Alaska Packers' ships in Uminak Pass, en route for the Behring Sea, including the old French barque *Bougainville*. (*San Francisco Maritime Museum.*)

Typical French "bounty" four-master, in the Derwent River, Tasmania, about
1912. (*Beattie, Hobart.*)

A fine example of a big four-masted barque of the Bordes Line.
(*Henri Picard Collection.*)

roughly the equivalent of the apprentice in British ships as far as duties aboard ship went. A ship might have one *pilotin,* or none. There was no obligation on officers to serve as *pilotins* at all. The general custom was that masters came up the hard way. It was against the Breton character to pay a premium to work at sea or anywhere else. To them a *pilotin* was a *fils à papa*—son of a Somebody—at sea by influence; certainly not one of them. Owners do not seem to have been in favour of the idea either, for they required the *pilotin* (if any) to pay 200 to 300 francs a month for his berth in advance, as well as to put up a substantial deposit against his possible illness, accident, desertion, or repatriation costs. Aboard, the *pilotin* easily became a dog's-body. One of his principal jobs was to act as "captain of the chicken-coops"—"*officier de cages à poules*"—but a useful lad could make a good job of that. Seeing that the eggs the fowls lay found their lawful way aft could be almost a full-time business in most ships, and so could the equally important matter of making certain that a succulent bird was always available for the captain's Thursday chicken dinner, for no scraggy broken-down fowl would do. Living aft, the *pilotin*-cum-chicken-man was well placed to learn a great deal about the business of being a practical ship's officer.

Conrad appears to have signed aboard as *pilotin* in one of the small West Indies traders, probably for his second voyage in the 394-ton barque *Mont-Blanc* to the West Indies in 1875 when he was nearly 18 years old—much older then than French youth usually began in the sea profession. He was probably still a *pilotin* in his next ship, the 432-ton *Saint-Antoine,* whatever he was nominally called—purser, steward, even by some writers passenger (which he was not). Conrad's uncle had influence with the owners, Delestang et Fils of Marseilles. There was obviously a certain looseness in this matter of designations, especially when family influence came into it.

Monsieur Picard told me that when he joined the barque *Bretagne* to begin his sea career in July 1920, he was at first a *pilotin,* but his job was really store-keeper. "I also did four hours or so at the helm every day," he said, "and of course helped with all the necessary jobs on deck and aloft. I didn't feel much like an officer."

The Master of the *Bretagne* was Captain Abel Chevalier, a typical Breton. Beginning at sea in the mid-1890s at the age of 14, he found his sea-legs in the little brigantines and barquentines of St. Malo in the Newfoundland trade. After a year or two of this, he shipped as ordinary seaman in the long-voyage barque *Jules Verne.* Average voyages were a year or more then. When considered big and strong enough as well as competent, he was advanced to able seaman—the sea craftsman's rating——and continued in long-voyage square-rigged ships. At 20, four years of service in the navy began: he was a mature and experienced 25 before passing for his first certificate which was as deepsea mate. (France, like Germany and many other maritime nations,

C

wasted no time on alleged second mates' certificates, requiring her future master mariners to qualify first as mates only.) Three years later, after long voyages abaft the mast in big ships including the barque *Amiral de Cornulier*, Monsieur Chevalier qualified as master at the age of 28. He had then been a working seaman for half his life—14 years. Command came in 1912 when he was just over 30, with the full-rigged ship *Desaix*. The *Desaix* was a steel ship of 2,255 tons, then only ten years old, built in St. Nazaire in 1902 for Nantes owners. Captain Chevalier had been mate of the *Général Faidherbe* (2,188 tons) for the same owners for several voyages, immediately before promotion to command. His last command was the steel barque *Bretagne*, another big vessel of over 2,000 tons.

When after seven years he left the *Bretagne* at Bordeaux in the post-war shipping slump of 1921, he was still only 40 years of age and had been 16 times round Cape Horn, westwards and eastwards. He had reason to feel satisfied with his sea career. The *Général Faidherbe* was a smart ship credited with several good runs: all those 2,000-tonners were roomy, strong, well-manned and comfortable sailing-ships. He had been well paid, had enjoyed reasonable leave (when this was possible: it was difficult during the war) and had earned the percentages paid to good masters for the contributions they made to the earning power of their ships.* All this enabled him to build up sizeable savings. He had reason to feel that he was a member of a worth-while and respected profession.

Captain Louis Lacroix, who has as much right as anyone to be called, perhaps, the historian of the French sailing-ship days, had a similar career. Beginning as deck-boy, he became successively ordinary then able seaman, was promoted second mate at 22, mate at 24, master at 26 of the big barque *Maréchal de Gontaut* (a 2,240-tonner, Nantes built and owned) and commanded two other large square-rigged ships before retiring from the sea in 1910. Such masters became well-known men in the maritime profession and, being naval reservists as well, usually had no great difficulty in finding some suitable and rewarding berth when the time came to move ashore.

French merchant-ship masters had been required by law to qualify by some sort of examination since A.D. 1584: in 1825, the strictly regulated certificates for deep-sea (*capitaine au long-cours*) and coasting master (*maître au cabotage*) were introduced. This was long before British cargo-ships were required to carry certificated masters: indeed, the general regulation of seamen employed as masters and mates in British ships was somewhat haphazard and unsatisfactory throughout at least the first half of the 19th century, both deepsea and coastal. Big companies took their own steps, which was sensible: the appalling loss-rate of most others is sufficient commentary

---

*See typical ship-master's contract of 1904, at the end of this chapter.

on the quality of their commanders.* Well into the second half of the 19th century, the space on the first page of the Official Log Book wherein the British master was required to enter the number of his certificate was still headed "No. of his Certificate (*if any*)". The French certificated rank of *Capitaine au long-cours* was modified by a new law in 1967, bearing in mind the changing position with the possibility (and the fact) of engine-handling by controls from the bridge, especially in smaller vessels. This law set up masters first class (deep-sea) and second class (coastal), but there will be plenty of surviving *Capitaines au long-cours* until the end of the 20th century, at any rate.

There was often a real attempt to use the French sea-officers' merchant-ship experience when he did his naval service, too, rather than try to mould all in the general duties branch. For instance, the well-known Captain L. F. Bourgain who began his career in fishermen at the age of 13, was mate ten years later and qualified master at 25, was in command of half-a-dozen of the big Cape Horners of the famous Maison Bordes Line of Dunkirk, mainly in the Chilean trade, and rounded the Horn 56 times, chose to do his necessary naval service early in his career, and spent the whole in four sailing-ship naval transports. Their employment was largely the movement of convicts, for whom France maintained one or two rigorous overseas establishments. So the naval service being all in non-auxiliaries helped the young man's merchant service career, too, though it can be understood that he did not really learn much about the passenger side. No matter: Maison Bordes did not operate passenger ships.

Captain Bourgain was mate (executive officer) of the five-masted barque *France* in the early 1890s, and later commanded several of the splendid Bordes "bounty" four-masters, among them the handsome *Atlantique* and *Antonin* which has a passage of 72 days between La Pallice and Antofagasta to her credit, made not long before that cheerful "pirate", the Count Felix von Luckner, sank her from his full-rigged ship *Seeadler*. Captain Bourgain also commanded the *Rancagua* and *Dunkerque*. The *Dunkerque* was another noted sailer, credited by the English sailing-ship historian Basil Lubbock* with at least four passages between Chilean ports and the Channel of 70 days or less, most of them made with full cargo. The best was 67 days from Port Talbot to Iquique with coal in 1905.

The Maison Bordes often bought fine old British ships and did well with them, but these big four-masters were French designed and built. Bordes were for a long time the only company in the Chilean trade at all comparable with the German Flying "P" Line of the House of Laeisz. Both built up the long-haul trade in Chilean nitrates to their respective countries, for

*See *The War With Cape Horn*, Alan Villiers (Charles Scribner's Sons Ltd., 1971: Hodder and Stoughton, London).

*In his book *The Nitrate Clippers*, Brown Son and Ferguson, Glasgow, 1932.

nitrates were then invaluable for two of Europe's great needs, fertilisers and munitions. Both bought British ships (doing very well with them) and also built their own. Both built great square-rigged five-masters—the French Bordes pioneering in 1890 with the first *France,* a five-masted barque of 3,326 net tons which was lost, following her with another larger vessel of 5,630 tons with the same name and (with slight variations) rig: Laeisz building the successful *Potosi* (4,026 tons) in 1895 and the world's only five-masted full-rigged ship *Preussen* (4,790 tons) in 1902.

The first *France* was a slim, good-looking vessel of little greater tonnage than some large four-masted barques. But her gross tonnage was 3,800, being a bounty ship: though she was British built (to Bordes order) she was a special case and qualified for half-bounties. She was the world's first big metal five-masted square-rigged ship (there were many five-masted American schooners before her day, but their simple masts were much closer together and their handling infinitely easier). The *Potosi* did not follow until 1895. The square-rigged masts of the first *France* were 160 feet above the deck and she set some 50,000 square feet of canvas. A double bottom could carry 2,000 tons of water ballast, and a powerful donkey-boiler in a steel house on deck gave steam to drive four winches at each hatch, so that she could load and unload with steamship speed. She had no auxiliary main engine and no need of such a thing, as she quickly showed by sailing from Barry Dock to Rio de Janeiro in 32 days on her first voyage, with over 5,000 tons of best Welsh coal in her one enormous hold. She had only the one collision bulkhead right for'ard, like most sailing-ships: though many steamships of much greater tonnage were being built, for years the *France* had the largest hold in a deep-sea ship anywhere, for the steamships were much more bulk-headed of necessity.

This first *France* did not last long. She showed that she could sail consistently and well—71 days from the Channel past the Horn to Valparaiso full of coal in 1892, 73 days for the same passage the following year (when she had to fight her way into the North Atlantic from the North Sea and later past the Horn, both in mid-winter), 76 days again outwards and 78 homewards in 1900, this time to and from Iquique. She carried a full crew of 46—enough but no more. (All these big five-masters carried a few over two-score men, except the auxiliaries *R. C. Rickmers* and *Kjøbenhavn* which required an engine-room complement as well.)

The first *France* was lost in 1901. She sailed from the Tyne with 5,100 tons of coal in March of that year bound round the Horn towards Valparaiso but never arrived. She was missing for a while, but another outward-bounder came in from sea to report having seen her somewhere off the Plate, deserted, over on her beam-ends, her lee yardarms dipping in the sea as she lurched with that awful gait of the dead ship, and the South Atlantic rollers breaking along the length of her. What had caused this—a pampero? She

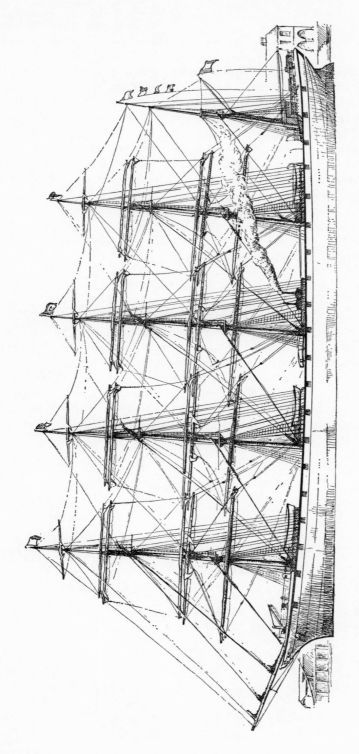

The FRANCE, built at Port Patrick in 1890, was the first 5-masted barque

was in the area where these sudden violent storms could be expected. Some
seamen said she was "crank"—too tender. Her under-water lines, some said,
were too fine to give the hull grip enough of the sea to keep her stable if
struck by a heavy squall on the beam, with four tall masts of square sail set
up there. This was quite an acreage of canvas: in sudden squalls it is not
very tractable. But a hold full of coal should have held her up in anything:
perhaps that had shifted, if it did not fill the hold. The crew were rescued
by the gallant efforts of the German four-masted barque *Hebe* and landed
at Valparaiso on June 9 1901.

The next *France* was stiff enough from the stocks and provided with
auxiliary power in the form of twin-screws driven by diesel engines, when
she was built at Bordeaux in 1912 by the Ch. and Atel. de la Gironde.
Registering 5,633 tons gross and 4,554 net with these engines, she was just
on 4,700 tons under-deck—some thousand tons larger than the first *France,*
and she looked it. With a terrific sheer (I thought her forecastle-head would
have made a splendid toboggan-run so pronounced was its slope from knight-
heads to after-railing, when I saw her in Melbourne about 1918) and a somewhat squat "jubilee" rig (that is, with nothing set above double topgallants), she was something removed from the more graceful French four-
masters, ships and barques of my earlier acquaintance.

The diesels were out of her then, and two of Melbourne's best tugs had
their hands full to keep her properly in the channel going up the Yarra. She
was 419 feet long by 56 feet beam, within an inch or two, and 25 feet deep
—larger than the *Potosi* or *Preussen.* Her stump-topgallant rig (as sailors
then called the square-rigger without royals) looked square and squat. When
I read of her loss on a New Caledonian reef a year or two later (in 1922), I
reflected that an interesting ship had gone, but perhaps the world had lost
no beauty. I never saw her under sail, but that gaunt great version of square-
rig lacked much of the older grace and symmetry. She looked massive, over-
sized, astonishing—extraordinary indeed, but somehow wrong, almost something of a freak.

I wish I had seen the first *France.* She must have been the best-looking
of the few such giant five-masted barques ever built, though the *Potosi* was
a fine ship, too.

Master's Contract in the Barque Molière

As for treatment of their ship-masters, a typical form of contract signed
in 1904 between the owners MM. René Guillon and René Fleury of Nantes,
and Captain Henri Lozet of their steel barque *Molière,* 2,198 tons, is of
interest. Among other points, it makes clear the master's responsibilities
regarding the establishment of proper claims to bounty payments: it gives
him good salary, commissions, and leave and it emphasises economic and
proper maintenance of ship and sails, compliance with conditions laid down
by government regulations, and proper treatment of the crew.

The *Molière* was built by the Ateliers et Chantiers de la Loire at Nantes in 1899, and was a typical Bounty-type barque.

Here is the contract. It meant just what it said.

Conditions for command of Captain Henri Lozet on board the three-master "Molière".

Owners: René Guillon and René Fleury at Nantes.

1. The fixed wages will be 250 francs per month, payable likewise during a three-month stay ashore, but only if the Captain takes up command of the same ship or of another of the company indicated by the owners.

2. A commission of 2½% shall be granted to the Captain on the profits of every voyage; the repayment and the interest on the capital not to be taken into account in the expenses.

3. The owners, before each voyage, will fix a bonus for speed. Should the wages added to the commission on the gross profits not give an average of 5,000 francs per annum, this fixed sum of 5,000 francs per annum is guaranteed to the Captain during his time at sea. Time spent at sea includes time spent in ports other than European ports, except such time when the ship is immobilized by calling at a port to lay-up.

4. The Captain will be responsible for the quantities recognised by him on the Bills of Lading.

   He will supervise the stowage and see to it that the ship is properly laden according to her trim, so that the ship may lie in her best position in the water to sail most effectively.

   The Captain will likewise ensure, if his cargo is in sacks, that no sacks will be cut, to take a note of the number embarked, any sacks short being always claimed as full by the consignee. (The *Jules Verne*, after its first voyage, has had to pay at Rouen 813 francs for missing or light-weight sacks, although that ship had delivered the weight as per Bill of Lading, less 2% waste.)*

5. The Captain shall at all times make arrangements for the departure of his ship, before the end of its loading, so that, weather permitting, the ship may sail within 24 hours after the completion of loading.

6. In no case is the Captain to charter the ship without seeking our authorisation by telegram.

7. If the Captain finds himself detained in port, either by a strike or by any circumstances beyond his control preventing him from loading, he will send a telegram at least once a week, stating the position as exactly

---

*It was important that all cargoes had to be carefully tallied inboard and out again. A 2% wastage might be allowed for (evaporation, shrinkage, lost in the bilges, etc.) but the total weight must be landed and the sacks it was shipped in though this last was not always enforced.—AUTHOR.

as possible and mentioning any proposals of cargoes which might be made to him.

Sailing Bounty. Accounts.

8. Immediately on arrival in every port, the Captain shall send regularly to his owners, by registered mail, the passage certificate for the sailing bounty, and take good care to verify personally that the name of the port, the date and the seal are duly imposed thereon by the Consul, and to ensure that the spelling of the owner's name is correct on the certificates.

He will likewise, on his departure, get his new passage certificate signed by the Consul.

When the Captain arrives in a port under orders in Europe, he will carry out the normal formalities at the Consulate in order to draw the bounty; but when he leaves, when he has his new passage certificate certified by the Consulate, he must make it quite clear that he has not carried out any kind of business in that port, and that the bounty due from the port of orders to the end of the voyage, must be the deep-sea and not the coastal one. The Captain must, in every port, have his orders-port noted by the consul. This document is indispensable for the regulation of the fifth parts of the bounty.

9. When the ship is in a foreign country and the Captain is obliged to replace some men, he is obliged to take only men of French nationality; if he is unable to find any Frenchmen and is compelled to make up his crew with sailors of foreign nationality, he must obtain a certificate from the French Consulate, in the port where he has embarked these men, stating that it has not been possible to find French sailors to replace the deserters or the sick.

The Captain will likewise obtain a similar certificate in the ports where he touches, bearing in mind that he is under an obligation to replace the foreign sailors in the first port where he is able to find French sailors.

Should the Captain be unable to find any further French crew in the second port of call, he will obtain a certificate from the Consulate stating that he is keeping the foreign sailors signed on and embarked at the former port, since it has proved impossible for him to find French sailors to replace them.

10. Before leaving each port, the Captain will send to his owners his accounts of outgoings and expenses with the receipts in support. He will mention the rate of exchange, so as to enable the owners to draw up their accounts in francs.

11. Advances to the crew during the voyage will be certified by the Consul or the maritime authorities, so that when the crew is paid off, the owners do not have to keep accounts of these advances.

12. The Captain will telegraph, using the company's code, his arrival and departure from ports, the beginning and end of unloading and likewise of loading.

In the telegram announcing his departure, he will mention the quantity he has unloaded. In addition, he will give a regular account, by letter, of the progress of his operations.

13. When he considers that circumstances permit it, the Captain is authorised to throw into the sea a part of his ballast, when he is about to arrive in port. For that to take place, he must ensure that he has a charter to load in that port and that his ballast cannot be sold; the discharge of ballast being then an expense for the ship, the captain can thus save money for the owners.

14. When the Captain puts into port for orders, especially in Melbourne, he will, as much as possible, remain out in the roads so as to avoid the expense of towage, etc., if possible.

The crew are to be strictly confined to the ship, only the Captain going ashore, with all the papers necessary to have the voyage bounty certified. Having done this, he will put in the post, by registered mail, the certificate which is to enable his owners to draw the bounty with a letter giving an account of his passage: a letter which will have to be written at sea while the voyage is in progress.

Without any delay, after collecting the orders awaiting him at the French Consulate, the Captain will have his departure for the destination indicated certified and will set sail, avoiding expenses and delay.

It is clearly understood that a telegram will always be sent to inform the owners of the arrival at the port for orders as well as the departure from that port.

15. The Captains are authorised, in order to save time on lay days, to pay a sum to the shippers, if they think that they will obtain nothing without that.

Bearing in mind the sum (531 francs) which each day saved can gain, they will exercise their intelligence as to whether the sacrifice is worth it. But if the sum demanded is of a certain importance, they will first cable their owners, mentioning the sum.

16. In the event of the ship putting into port because of damage, the Captain will telegraph his owners, who, in agreement with the insurers, will give him authority, if there are grounds for it, to act as if he were not insured.

When the ship is in ballast and when, therefore, no settlement of ordinary damages can be considered, the Captain will avoid all judicial and consular expenses, etc.: and depart from the port of call as quickly as possible, making only the repairs vitally necessary to continue towards his destination. Only there will he do what is necessary.

When the ship has a cargo on board, the Captain will be obliged to put in order any ordinary damage. Because of the expenses of putting into a port of call, essential expenses common to the hull and the cargo only should be incurred. As for the damage to the ship accepted by agreement with the insurers, he will avoid all expenses, and carry out indispensable repairs with the same economy as if he had not been insured.

Food

(1) On each departure from Europe, a year's stores will be put on board.

(2) The Captain will be responsible for quantities consumed in excess, the voyage being of one year's duration.

(3) In the event of his being given food in bad condition, the Captain will draw up a report which he will have signed by the officers and leading members of the crew stating the quantity of defective food.

(4) The Captain is forbidden to re-victual without our authority, unless the voyage lasts more than one year.

Maintenance of the ship

17. The exterior of the ship, its masts and spars, the interior of its bulwarks, superstructure, etc., are to be painted at least three times per annum.

   During a passage in ballast, part of the inner lining—that part which is detachable—is to be taken up so that it can be scraped and cleaned, and then treated with red lead. The hold must be painted with red lead at least once a year and so must the coal bunkers and other bunkers.

   All carpentering and caulking repairs are to be carried out by the carpenter on board during the voyage; likewise repairs and maintenance of the rigging by the crew.

   The sails are to be carefully maintained and repaired during all voyages: a third stitching is to be carried out on all sails after eight months in service. The sails are to be dried aloft and unbent from the yards in every port, then bent again three days before the anticipated departure, by the ship's people.

   In short, the ship arriving from sea is to be in good order, whatever the season.

18. The Captain will conform exactly with all these instructions; otherwise his owners will see themselves compelled to dismiss him.

Drawn up and signed by both parties, after reading, at Nantes on January 9 1904.

The Captain   The Owners
Henri Lozet.   Guillon, René.

_____

Chapter Three

The Seaman's Life

THERE WERE ALWAYS many aliens in British ships during the sailing-ship era. With some, one of the reasons for this was a desire to avoid their own conscription or national service, especially Russian. At that time, so many seamen who regarded themselves as of other nationalities (such as the Finns) were compulsory but reluctant Russians. Another reason was the desire or need to learn at least to speak sufficient seafaring English: a facility was the comparative ease in finding a berth aboard British ships, no questions asked, for in the sailing-ship era these were in some odd ways the least regulated of ships—indeed, of all international ways of life. In Britishers, not even elementary proof of identity was required. A single certificate of discharge from any ship, made out to anyone, was enough. So the reluctant conscript could avoid his call-up and desert: once signed on the Articles of the outward-bounder in any name, he was gone, a distant sea-tossed fragment lost in a lonely ship keeping the seas for years. Most went boldly in their own names, or whatever approximation of these the shipping clerk scribbled on the Articles of Agreement. They were never French nationals.

When the outward-bound Limejuicer was signing on, whoever could stagger to the shipping office and produce some sort of evidence of prior seafaring—even if only one discharge, and that not his own—might sign on. Some who signed melted away soon afterwords, and did not sail. These were noted on the Articles as "Failed to join", and their places were taken by whoever could be found as the ship undocked, usually "pierhead jumps" —derelicts and no-goods who haunted the locking-out basins looking for such a chance, for they were aware that they were unlikely to be signed on otherwise. The British ships' half-deck of six or eight "apprentices" was some insurance against the chance of a poor forecastle crowd even if half the apprentices sailed as little boys aged 14. Most of them soon grew big, or at least wiry.

In the French ships this was not so. It is unusual to find foreign seamen who have spent much or indeed any sea time in them. I know of two only, both Germans—old Bos'n "Charlie" Müller, and Captain Fred Krage. Bos'n Karl Müller, in 1972 95 years old, must be the last man on earth who, with some half-century at sea, never served in a steamship. Beginning at sea in 1890, he began in Sail and found in that a way of life which satisfied him. So he stayed with it. When there was no more Sail, there was no more sea for Charlie: power and Sail were different professions under any flag.

His first voyage was in a homely little German barque called *Luna* on a voyage to the South Seas under a master aged 70 with a bewhiskered crew whose average age was at least 50—"old-style men", Charlie called them, with Stockholm tar for blood so they didn't bleed easily and fish-hooks for fingers to get a better grip of frozen sails. Tough! They were the real thing: and a first-voyage boy among them was circumspect, good-mannered, industrious, and infinitely hard-working. They kept the same discipline and state of cleanliness in the small fo'c'sle that their officers maintained on deck and aloft. Charlie was called at 04.00 to scrub out the fo'c'sle, taking out the men's sea-chests (on which they sat to eat) noiselessly and having them back again by 05.30 ready for the men's coffee before regular turn-to at 06.00 for a 12-hour day (for daymen, and for all in port) or the regular watches at sea. A boy was kept in his "place", which did him no harm: among seamen he first earned the right to speak following upon his acceptance in that (then) skilled profession with its exacting standards of seamanship and helmsmanship and fearless indefatigability aloft, added to that indefinable but, if absent, instantly missed quality known as being a good shipmate.

The good shipmate (German, French, British, Scandinavian, American, anyone), was the standard—the stalwart reliable upon the swaying footropes aloft with the wild canvas blowing back threatening to murder all, if the weak let go their grip: the rugged helmsman reliable at the wheel hour after hour, nursing the ship with that inborn touch which keeps the worst of the giant seas from breaking aboard to murder his shipmates, the ship safe in his bare hands as she runs staggering through the endless morass of the gale-mad sea: the good shipmate ashore, too, ready to share his last quid, his last pint . . . ready to desert the bad ship, too, and take on the hostile world ashore for a while, where he will never meet the standards of the society of sailing-ship seamen nor hear of their existence.

Such standards are not for easy acquisition, and the way to their attainment was hard. But the two-year voyage of the little barque *Luna* set Charlie on the right path: he returned to Hamburg an utterly different person, and he never went again to the Black Forest whence he came. Perhaps one reason for this was that Charlie was a bit of an outcast, too. His family were prosperous local people, well respected. They and their neighbours regarded the wandering seaman—any such—as unstable by their standards: not the young men they wished their daughters to marry. For what possible reason should the young countryman want to turn his back on family and land and take up a career on the thoroughly insecure sea? It was different round the ports, different in crowded coastal towns, or in places where good land or local industry offered poor chance of an assured place for the industrious in their community. (Of course, it was different in Celtic Brittany, where the sea offered the principal, sometimes the only opportunity of a useful career to many.)

Another two-year voyage, and Charlie was graduated as A.B., soon shipping out in giant ships—the swift warriors of the great nitrate fleet of Hamburg which took the battle with Cape Horn in their stride four times a year. He was A.B. in the *Potosi* under Hilgendorf, the "devil of Hamburg"—not so called for evil reason but for what seamen noted as his extraordinary ability to outguess the wind, to defeat and to use the gale, to force and drive his great ship (the *Potosi* was a five-mast barque carrying 6,000 tons) to wind'ard past Cape Horn despite the scream of the hurricane and the onslaught of the sea. This could be done by greatly determined skill and endless tirelessness, by the magnificent leadership of the great shipmaster with the near-perfect ship and a splendid crew of dyed-in-the-wool shipmates, graduates of the small square-riggers of North Sea and Western Ocean, reared since later childhood with the roar of the gale in their ears —by autumn and winter, of course, for there are also summer seas when the seaman may lick his wounds, and his ship sail for a while upright and graceful like a Balinese girl walking, bathed in purest sunlight day after day, wafted pleasantly on her long way by the gentle trade winds.

In such ships Charlie sailed as a boy, youth, young man. He became a wanderer, as such men learned to be, for less and less could they find their own respected standards ashore, and a man may not survive for ever helping wind-ships to achieve the best use of God's system to make ocean voyages. There were never enough such seamen, especially in the last decade of the 19th century and first of the 20th. Charlie was in many ships: he found himself at times ashore. All masters were not Hilgendorfs (nor Learmonts nor Miethes nor de Cloux): sour old mates could be poor task-masters, fo'c'sle crowds could include an unnecessary proportion of bums when better men had cleared out.

So one day early in the 1900s Charlie shipped as A.B. in the French ship *Léon Blum* at Valparaiso—the only German among an otherwise all-Breton crew.

"I had lost a Norwegian barque in the South Atlantic outward-bound through fire in the coal cargo", he explained. "We were bound from Cardiff for Callao but had to leave the barque at sea when she was burning. We couldn't beat that fire. It was deep and it burst out, exploding the hatches, and then the wind fanned it. After being in the lifeboat 11 days, the lot of us were picked up by a big Limejuice four-mast barque called the *Somali*. She was bound for Valparaiso, so we helped to work her there: they were glad to have us aboard and we were glad to be there. She was hungry, of course, like all the Limeys (except some of those Scots like the little *Inver* barques: they fed well) but we got our 'whack', like her regular crew. She hadn't any jobs going or I'd have been glad enough to sign in her. At Valparaiso the next ship in the tier was this *Léon Blum*. The first thing I found out was that she needed a couple of A.B.s. She couldn't find any French nationals—not any seamen, anyway—in Valpo just then, and so the Captain got his Consul's permission to sign me on. They were very particular about looking for a Frenchman first, but there were none on the beach.

"This was my first French ship, and she was a big one—a full-rigger of nearly 3,000 tons gross. That is big for a three-masted full-rigged ship, but she had a good crew and she was nearly new at that time. Everything was in good order aboard and I'd noticed that the crew had a good and cheerful spirit, or I'd never have asked for the job. The accommodation for everybody was really astonishing, it was so roomy (and dry, too, when we got outside) and she had plenty of sheltered space, and big sills to keep the sea out of the quarters. She was very well fitted up aloft and on deck, with the Scots brace-winches* that we had in good German ships, and a big steam donkey for working the anchor in port, and some steam winches to help get the cargo in and out. She was big, yes, but she was no workhouse. Some of our big German ships had those Scots brace-winches, so I knew how handy they were. Two or three men work on a hand-operated series of six geared drums—three each side, one for each of the principal braces—secure in the middle of the deck out of the reach of the worst seas. They can grind the braces in in a few moments, instead of having to go to the ship's side to haul them in by hand, in the waist of the ship where she often rolls her side right under.

"I liked the look of the *Léon Blum* and I liked the look of her crew too. The *Somali* was a bit of a work-house, both for work and food—you remember, what we used to call pound and pint.

'You'll get your whack,
According to the Act'

and very lucky to get that—the strict survival allowance spelt out in the British Merchant Shipping Act, maybe to make sure the poor Limey sailors got something. Every Limey I was ever in made that allowance its maximum, with miserable substitutes whenever the master felt like it. And they worked their cargoes in and out by hand, out there on the West Coast.

"I liked the *Léon Blum*, but I couldn't understand the crew. They didn't speak any English or German of course, but they didn't speak French either.

---

* Many big French sailing-ships were fitted with the Scots Jarvis brace-winches, built under licence in France by Lesauvage and Patras of Le Havre. This company produced a very special ten-drum winch for the *France II*. The standard Jarvis brace-winch had six drums, one for course, lower topsail and upper topsail braces on each side: the ten drums were to handle the lower and upper topgallants as well, which were very square and heavy in that ship. She had no royals.

I'd learned that a bit at school. They were Breton fishermen, speaking their own language. We'd gotten along all right in the *Somali* and the Norwegian barque with seamen's English. Some of the *Blum's* officers spoke English enough. I noticed that when any of the men for'ard had a letter from home written in French, he had to take it aft to be translated into Breton. I was nine months in the ship and I picked up enough French—from aft, of course —before I paid off in Dunkirk, but I never learned the names of all the lines and gear in whatever language it was that the crew used on deck—a mixture, I think, of their Breton and French, or maybe some other sort of local French with a heavy Breton accent. I knew the orders all right. And you know, you don't have to be ten years at sea to learn what's going on, what's got to be done instantly and what should come next. That's all international. An A.B. doesn't need someone yelling in his ear.

"The food was plain but good and there was plenty of it—two good meals a day, the main meal at 11 a.m. on a regular routine between salt pork and salt cod or canned tunny or sardines, with canned beef and potatoes on Sundays and potatoes on other days too as long as they lasted. The evening meal was always soup and beans, right through the voyage. For breakfast there was good coffee and good bread with butter. The diet was not varied but it was sufficient and there was no sign of scurvy. The cook did well and there were no complaints. Of course as the voyage went on we had a few substitutes when things ran out. But the staples did not run out." (Monsieur Picard said he did better as a *pilotin* living aft, with fresh chicken on Thursdays and Sundays with a glass of bitters of Havre as appetiser, and now and again excellent canned foods from Nantes, and the same wine ration as the men.)

"I never liked the wine much—I missed the Bavarian beer—but I appreciated it", said Charlie. "It kept the scurvy away and the crew loved it. There was a good 'whack', dished out daily. The crew was big and beefy enough to do the work—she wasn't shorthanded like the *Somali* was before we came aboard. The French had no boy-'prentices at all. I always thought they were an odd part of Limejuicer's crews, where they worked like A.B.s and ran the captain's liberty boat in port for no pay at all and no privileges. I wondered where the owners had got all the optimists from. The girls liked them, though, in their brass-buttoned uniforms. The French wouldn't stand for the idea of binding their sons to serve a shipowner four years for nothing. We didn't miss apprentices. I hadn't been used to them in German ships either, or Scandinavian. There were always youngsters aboard and they did their share of the dirty work, of course, on their way to manhood. Same in the *Léon Blum*.

"The *Blum* ran on the two-watch system, like any other big sailing-ship— you know how it is. A watch is sufficient to work the ship under all reasonable conditions: so two equal watches alternate most of the voyage, being

strengthened in times of continuous bad weather by including the tradesmen—carpenter, sailmaker, donkeyman if any, who work as daymen in
settled weather—and by calling out all hands in a real jam. What keeps
things going more than anything else is a good spirit aboard, with a crowd
of competent men who respect and rely on one another's capabilities, without thinking about it, and respect the officers who give them the orders. My
French shipmates were all right.

"After the *Léon Blum,* I'd have gone in other French ships quick enough,
but I never got the chance."

Captain Fred Krage's French experience was a different matter. He was
another German sailing-ship wanderer except that, unlike Charlie Müller
who never wished to be anything higher than a big-ship bos'n, Fred Krage
intended to be a master. Neither was in a hurry. The road to boatswain, as
the senior petty officer—working foreman—among 20 or so able seamen in
a Cape Horn ship was long, arduous and searching. Theoretical qualifications had nothing to do with it. The boatswain had to be a rigger, an expert
in wire, hemp, and manilla line, an anchor man literally and figuratively,
a fearless and indefatigable leader aloft. In time the good seaman could
become all these things. He had to have natural leadership too, and he had
to come to the notice of hard-bitten mates and masters, who, in time, might
be willing to give him a chance—as bos'n's mate usually first, the starboard
watch bos'n. The boss bos'n was the mate's man: for the mate was prime
minister of the deck under the Sovereign, who was the Master under any
flag. The road to watch-keeping officer was ascended by paper qualifications
in the form of certificates gained in special schools or crammers ashore—in
both France and Germany, two for deepsea ships, as mate first and then,
after more sea time, as master. A certain stipulated amount of sea service in
long-voyage ships, a reasonably retentive brain and good maths, above all
a clear and reliable memory, could in due course gain the young man his
"tickets", as they were called. Then his progress was up to him.

Fred Krage had gone to sea in the approved manner for the intelligent
German lad before the First World War. About the time that the strong-
minded (not to say pig-headed) Lord Fisher was throwing the finest little
fleet of sail-training ships neck-and-crop out of the British navy, Germany
introduced a fleet of square-rigged ships for *ab initio* training of her seafaring recruits, some for the merchant service, others directly for the navy.
(The fit merchant service men would become naval reservists, anyway.) One
of these German ships was a full-rigger named the *Grossherzogin Elisabeth*
especially designed and manned to provide tough courses for embryo merchant seamen. She registered 1,260 tons and, when Fred Krage joined her
in 1907, was six years old. He had already graduated from high-school, for

French sailing-ships laid up in the Canal de la Martinière. (*F. Chapeau, Nantes.*)

Port of Nantes, 1919-20. (*F. Chapeau.*)

French Cape Horn seaman, A. B. Pierre Berthoud, in the ship *Grace Harwar* in 1929. (*Alan Villiers.*)

which his parents had made sacrifices hoping he would become some sort of civil servant, or teacher—those well-loved callings of the stable German citizen.

Such dull stuff was not for Fred: his home-town of Lübeck had an ancient seafaring tradition, and the idea of a career in sailing-ships appealed to him. He would have gone straight in some smaller merchant-ship, but his parents were told that the classic beginning should be in a school-ship. (The French managed very well without such things, with their vast fleets of smaller sailers and the great reservoir of the stout, sea-minded Bretons. Not for them the formalised sail-handling drill, the manufactured emergency coped with by numbers! They knew they could rely on the sea to provide what was needed to turn a fisher-lad or farmer's boy into a Cape Horn seaman.) The German merchant officer then had to serve a minimum of 45 months in sailing-ships, at least 24 of them as A.B. in a deepwater square-rigger.

The *G. Elisabeth* was an ocean-going full-rigged ship; time spent with her counted. She was based at Elsfleth near Bremen, where each year 120 boys mustered aboard for rapid indoctrination for a few weeks alongside before sailing to Baltic waters on a summer cruise. During this, the rudiments of the sailing-ship sailor's calling were rammed home—aloft all the morning working at practical sail-handling, the afternoons at sailorising—knots, splices, serving, marling, sail-sewing, cringle-making, all that endless work of the sailor's art. Hammer and tongs, spike and fid, sail-twine and hemp, block and tackle, foot-rope and jackstay the 120 lads were kept at it, their beautiful white ship always on show in port, and at sea, their master (one Dressler) a fearless and superb ship-handler setting standards of skill, cool judgment and nerve which gave the lads something to remember and try to emulate all their lives. Summer over, the graceful full-rigger sped to the West Indies and carried on in those blue waters with an even greater intensity. She had no power, of course—no one concerned with her would consider such a contamination. Captain Dressler sailed in and out of harbours no matter how difficult.

"He handled her as if she were a beautiful thoroughbred race-horse, responsive to the slightest touch on the reins, the smallest pressure from her rider's knees," said Fred at the Woermannhaus in Hamburg-Altona many years afterwards. He'd learned a little about horse-riding in Australia. "Of course, she was an old-style school-ship and she was good—beautifully balanced with fine lines, a wonderful hull and highly efficient rigging—and the greater part of his job was to sail her. He had a big crew and splendid officers who knew her perfectly, but I noticed that though he handed her over outside to the senior of these many times, none had anything like his skill. One of the exercises he did was to handle her with stern-way over several miles, picking up a flagged buoy that represented a man overboard. A full-rigged ship can be the bitchiest of all ships with stern-way. None of

D

the other officers could do this at all. We all felt mighty safe with Captain Dressler in charge, even if we did fall overboard."

It was a grand indoctrination, but 120 well-trained boys was a crowd to put on the employment market at the same time, even in the sailing-ship era at the end of 1907. Crack passenger-liners snapped up the lads, but sea-time in such ships was not on Fred Krage's programme. In time, he found an old former Down-Easter named the *Union* with a Methuselah of a master, sailing in the ice-trade to north Norway and along the Arctic coast beyond North Cape, hacking herself a cargo of ice-blocks from the pack and bringing that back to Germany for the fish trade. The *Union* was as different from the *Grossherzogin Elisabeth* as it was possible to be, but Methuselah was a superb seaman and ship-handler with more than a touch of the Dressler genius, and for the midsummer voyage each year he brought along his four beautiful blonde daughters. He was a stately, almost biblical character, bewhiskered and benign, who always dressed in the full frock-coat rig complete with tall hat when he went ashore, dutifully followed by the four daughters.

Fred was two summers in the *Union*: the trouble was to find another ship in the winters. As soon as he had served the time and acquired the skill to be rated A.B., this was easier: off he sailed to the ends of the earth in big deepwatermen—in the *Obotrita* to Chile, the *Urania* to Mexico, California and the Far East, the *Terpsichore* to Australia. Here he cleared out, to begin the wandering life of the adventurous sailing-ship seaman footloose ashore— to the back of beyond and further, the Broken Hill mines, the cattleman's life on and off the Birdwood track, the Territory and Western Queensland —roustabout, boundary-rider, miner, shearer's off-sider, on the coast in schooners. Australia then was a satisfying and adventurous place for the sturdy young seamen to roam: but such activities did not count towards those 45 months of sea-time he must serve in deepsea sail. So a ship out of Newcastle towards Chile with coal—the steel barque *Ravenscourt* of Grim-stad—got him across the Pacific to Valparaiso. Unlike most Norwegian ships, the *Ravenscourt* was in a rundown state, parish-rigged as seamen said, a bit of a menace with bad gear aloft and not enough to eat below.

At Valparaiso in September 1914, Fred found the European war on. What to do? The *Ravenscourt* was bound for Falmouth for orders next, with nitrates from Chile loaded at Antofagasta. Fred was on her articles as a German citizen. Arrival at Falmouth meant internment for him, if the war was still on then. The only thing to do was to desert at once, to melt away. There were many German ships in Chilean ports, but none was loading for the homewards run (nor was to do so for at least the following five years). With three Norwegian seamen from the *Ravenscourt*, Fred moved ashore the night before the barque was to sail, and—as had been arranged—hid for the time being in a hard-case sailors' boarding-house run by an opportunist named Brady. Here he became at once a Dane. Brady was a man who made his living by supplying crews to outward-bound ships, using his "house" as a convenient base for storing these until needed.

The line of demarcation between such a man and the full-time crimps who openly flourished in such places as San Francisco, Portland, Oregon, and Newcastle, N.S.W., was not finely drawn, except that the crimps were wholly callous, making an evil living from blood-money "earned" by any blood other than their own. Brady dealt with real seamen, respectable and sober (as they might personally wish at the time). In short, Brady was prepared to provide a real service. Fred Krage still had money from Australia as he was homeward-bound for Germany with his savings to go to mates' navigation school and to do his conscript service, finished with aimless adventuring.

Matters of nationality were of no concern to Mr. Brady. Seamen were international then, anyway. Fred kept all his German papers with him, as he would need them to prove his "time" and to enter navigation school. (He had already been over seven years getting those 45 months in.) His Norwegian shipmates accepted the flag-change of Able Seaman Krage: they spoke in Norwegian (the seamen's style is little different from seamen's Danish) or English. Fred's real papers were sewn in the bottom of his sea-bag.

"Brady found me a Finnish four-mast barque," Fred told me years afterwards, yarning at the Woermannhaus in Hamburg, "but she was manned mostly by real Finns—strange men. Somehow I didn't feel at home among them, and I didn't know a word of their language. Some of them didn't even understand Scandinavian, or pretended not to. One morning the crew knifed the mate, just suddenly after a short, fierce quarrel in their incomprehensible language. That settled it. I hadn't actually signed her articles. So I went back to Brady's place.

"'Well,' he said, 'if you're so fussy, there's a Frenchman at Mexillones loading for France direct. How about her? She's short-handed and I've no Frenchmen.'

"This shook me. The idea of a German going in a French ship to France, in time of war, hoping to get from there back to the Fatherland, *was* a bit of a shaker. My Danish-Norwegian would be no help there. Neither would my certificate of discharge from the *Ravenscourt* which clearly said 'Born in Germany' as my nationality. I suppose a real Dane could be born in Germany if his mother was there at the time, but it seemed too much. Papers didn't matter signing on, of course, but it was the simplest common-sense to expect my papers to get a thorough going-over when I reached France. It seemed to be taking a big chance to ship in that Frenchman: but one of the Norwegians suggested having that fatal word Germany altered. To what? It would at least have to be some place with the same

number of letters, starting with G. He suggested a town not far from Copenhagen called Gentofte. So Gentofte became my birth-place, at least on that
certificate.

"I made the alteration myself and it wasn't bad, and learned what I could
about Gentofte, which wasn't much. I was young and a born optimist. I
thought that if I landed in France paying off a French ship with a group of
Scandinavians, I ought to be able to pick up a coaster or something and get
to a port in Holland. Then I could get back to Germany. I knew that my
Scandinavian shipmates would never let me down, and the French of course
must never find out. You see, I had a duty to get back.

"So I shipped in that four-mast barque. Her name was *Chanaral* and she
was bound direct for La Pallice, on the Biscayan coast near the Ile de Ré.
The name on her bell was *Achnashie*, so I knew she was an old Britisher.
I knew at a glance that she wasn't French-built. She belonged then to the
big nitrates firm of Ant. Dom. Bordes, and she was well-kept and looked
handy enough—a four-master of some 2,400 tons, which is a handy size.
The Bordes line had a good name. The Master was a nice old man named
Hamoniaux. Of course, he'd signed us ashore, checking with the Consul
that there were no French seamen available in the area. He seemed to accept
me as a Dane without question, perhaps especially as I joined his ship with
three Norwegians. He was glad enough to have a full crew in those difficult
days, no questions asked.

"But I had a nasty shock when the four of us joined. A fierce young
fellow, eyeing us closely, suddenly came across the deck to me. He had some
sort of rusty old harpoon in his hands. Pointing this at me, he said, 'If you
was a German, I put diss tru you!' and he looked as if he meant it. Good
Lord, I thought, what can he know? But I grinned, and he grinned back.
He turned out to be the *pilotin*, the *Chanaral's* only apprentice and the
only one of the seamen who spoke some English. His name was l'Hotelier,
and we became good friends on the voyage. One of his jobs was looking
after a big coop of chickens, and another was dishing out the wine. He was
an important man, a sort of chief steward-purser and third mate combined.
I'd learned French for nine years at school, but I learned more from him
in the following months. I helped him with English and we got along fine.

"The voyage went all right. The *Chanaral* was in good order and well-
found, and we were bound round the Horn the downhill way in the southern summer—cruising stuff, with a bit of a change now and again in the
way of a gale or two. The crew were mostly from Brittany, a simple lot of
competent seamen who got on with the job. The style aboard was efficient
but easy, compared with some ships. The master never once raised his voice,
passing his orders through the mates. He was a whiskered, worthy old man
rather like the old captain of the ice-carrying *Union* without his daughters.
We seldom saw him: he stayed in or on the poop, a benign and competent

father-figure murmuring something to the mates from time to time as the
ship sailed on, or getting an observation with an elderly sextant religiously
at 08.00 and ship's noon. The mate was a splendid figure of a man, I think
from Royan: a grand seaman and a fine man. I got along very well with
him because I spoke reasonable French. The real Scandinavians were in the
mate's watch too—she was a two-watch ship, on much the same sea style
as a Limey—and I interpreted for them. The mate liked to practise his
English from time to time, too.

"The second mate was another fatherly type, a good seaman and always
friendly. The ship's routine ran very easily. The *pilotin* or purser or whatever he was seemed important. The cook was a huge ruffian not much
pleased with life, but the young purser kept him up to it. The sailors all
hailed from Brittany, though they also spoke fluent French. They were
good seamen and comrades. Discipline was excellent. Once I had my wine
stopped for two weeks (I deserved it) and that's all that happened. I didn't
miss the wine, except to wash the beans down. We had beans once at least
every day, and they needed washing down. But we always had enough of
them, and good baked bread too. About the only obvious difference between
the French seamen and other crews I'd been with was that they were tough
on albatrosses. When they caught them in calms, they made little ship
models in bottles from their bones. The carpenter was very good at this. He
made beautiful little models though he had hands like great hams.

"The most trying thing for me was the constant talk of the seamen about
their intentions of getting into the war as soon as they got home, and killing
Germans. They believed all the so-called 'atrocity' stories that had been
circulating, about German soldiers butchering women and children in
Belgium, and all that nonsense. They'd been told these things, of course,
and they believed them. One day one of the Norwegians said he didn't:
Germans were human too, he said. They did not bayonet babies. There was
a riot. The mate and the bos'n saved him from the very angry crowd.

"As we sailed along in the North Atlantic, everyone was concerned about
the submarines. We saw none. I don't think I'd ever known a more placid
passage, if it hadn't been for that sham I was trying, and the savage talk
about 'atrocities'. I sometimes thought it was rather mad to try, a German,
to land in France as a Dane and get back to Germany. Of course I had all
my German papers still with me, sewn in the bottom of my sea-bag along
with my little hoard of hard-earned Australian gold. Sailors don't spy on one
another: the matter of nationality doesn't come up—or it didn't, normally.
No one had any reason to believe me to be other than a Dane, except my
Norwegian ship-mates. They knew, but they were neutral. They regarded
the matter as none of their business."

So Able Seaman Friedrich Krage, alleged Dane (that is not the way Danes
spell Fredrik) stuck it out, reached La Pallice, passed rigorous French cross-

examination though he produced only the one flimsy *Ravenscourt* discharge, on which he'd converted Germany to Gentofte. The real Norwegians had real Norwegian seamen's books. There was a thorough examination of the four aliens at local police headquarters. The Norwegians went to the examination table first, Fred Krage anxiously watching the drill. Hardly a word was said to them and they were soon free. So Fred slapped his *Ravenscourt* flimsy down on the table, bold as brass.

" 'Is this all you have?' asked the officer, looking Fred straight in the eyes. 'Where are your pass, your registration certificate? All these essential documents?'

"That's all I sailed with and it's all I have, said Fred.

" 'There's something out of order here,' said the inspector, eyeing a large magnifying glass on the table beside him.

"I'd never been able to look at my handiwork through a magnifying glass, but I very much feared that, once he did so, the fraud was up. Suddenly my boldness returned and with it a desperate idea. Now or never!

"So I explained that my other papers had been stolen from me by a German at Brady's place in Antofagasta. (Might as well be thorough.) I suggested it would be a good idea to warn both British and French authorities to look out for this miscreant who'd turn up sooner or later in my name, with my Danish papers. I told him where this scoundrel really hailed from —Lübeck, of course.

"The inspector took a long look at me. Then without another word, he shrugged his shoulders and wrote my landing permit. I was free! For the time being, anyway. You know, regular sailing-ship seamen of many nations were a remarkably undocumented lot, none less than the British. But I couldn't pretend to be an Australian—they'd have passed me on to the British authorities at once. It was unusual to find four foreigners landing from any French ship, anyway: the fact that the other three were real Norwegians helped me."

Once allowed in, Fred Krage got out of France though it took several weeks. He shipped for Holland via Setubal in Portugal as A.B. in a small Norwegian steamer named *Borgur*. Examination of her crew later, in the Downs, was his undoing. Many German ships had taken refuge in the neutral Portuguese ports, and there was a traffic in seamen from them trying to do just what Fred was doing. Some had been found. This made the British examining officers suspicious. Fred knew he was finished when the inspector told him that he must check his nationality with his father in Gentofte. What was the address, please?

Fred didn't know the name of a single street in the place. He took a chance on Havnegade No. 21, on the assumption that every place in Denmark had at least a Harbour Street. It seemed that Gentofte had none. It was an inland town. The officials became not suspicious but convinced:

perhaps Fred did not really look like a Dane.

"Wait," said the inspector, speaking now in German. "I must check the matter more thoroughly."

Examination turned up his German papers. In due course, Able Seaman Krage found himself in an internment camp in the Isle of Man, and there he spent the rest of the war keeping fit by gardening work and studying mathematics and languages in preparation for mates' school in Germany some day.

"I was not in a French ship again," said Fred, "but I have pleasant memories of the old *Chanaral* and my shipmates. It was a pity there had to be a war."

There was to be another war later. By that time an experienced master-mariner, Captain Krage became a successful blockade-runner in the motor-ship *Ermland,* operating between Germany and Japan. In this he rounded the Horn at least once more—a very different kind of rounding from that of the *Chanaral.* Under the former able seaman allegedly from Gentofte in Denmark, the *Ermland* made the first successful break-through between Japan and Germany—at the time, to German-occupied France. For this tough voyage, her captain received the Iron Cross, Second Class, and the ship was presented with a portrait of Hitler five feet high, signed by the Führer himself.

But the *Ermland,* renamed *Weserland,* was intercepted on a later voyage. Once again the adaptable Captain Krage became a P.O.W., this time at Phoenix, Arizona, by way of a fatal brush with the U.S.S. *Somers* in the South Atlantic early in 1944.

The German school-ship *Grossherzogin Elisabeth* in which Captain Krage began his sea career was turned over to France as part of reparations in 1945, then in good condition. Renamed *Duchesse Anne,* she lay idle at Lorient for some time. Rigged down and used as a floating barracks for naval ratings at Brest in 1951, it would appear that no attempt was made to use her as a seagoing, square-rigged ship. At the end of 1971 she was still at Brest, doing useful work as a hulk.

Chapter Four

Shipmates

I HAVE HAD only one French shipmate before the mast, an able seaman from Fécamp, I believe, in the Finnish full-rigged ship *Grace Harwar* in 1929. She was an unusual ship—then the last full-rigged ship left in the Cape Horn trade, a tough old Limejuicer built in Scotland, at that time flying the Finnish flag: she was bound from Spencer Gulf in South Australia towards Falmouth, Plymouth or Queenstown (Ireland) for orders with 3,000 tons of South Australian grain, and she would have to pass the Horn in mid-winter. She was an old dog with a bad name, said to be a "killer". She had come in short of food to Spencer Gulf, and her crew had mostly "run". That is, they had deserted. No crimp speeded them. They'd had enough, for she was already out some 24 months on a long globe-wandering voyage that had begun with coal from the Bristol Channel to Luderitz Bay in former German South West Africa, thence to some wretched Peruvian island to fill herself with guano—that hateful cargo, the deposits of millions of sea-birds overfed on fish from the Humboldt current—for Wilmington, North Carolina. Thence—all this had taken time: a long time—to Spencer Gulf for orders in ballast, hoping to pick up grain. She'd been stopping steamships on the way down to ask for food for her crew, a bad sign.

She was two years out of dry-dock and the sea-growth sprouted like Neptune's beard (untrimmed for 10,000 years) from all her underside. She'd killed a man or two, and flung her master across his quarter deck in the Roaring Forties and broken his leg. Her crew came in with some incipient scurvy. So half of them had melted away: and every real seaman round the Gulf and Port Adelaide knew it. Who would ship out in this lame old dog with a bad name? She'd had that name for years. She'd killed her master's wife once, it was said (and truly): and the bereft man had buried her in the ballast to bring her body in for burial, on the long run from Tocopilla towards Sydney Heads for orders, that he might not leave her in a canvas shroud weighted in the sea. She had asked for this. The crew was against the idea, holding that any woman aboard was "bad luck", and a dead woman probably fatal. The poor wife still haunted the full-rigger's poop, they said. Perhaps her tormented wraith was asking pitifully not to be buried in the sea.

The *Grace Harwar* was a sombre ship. But she *was* a ship, a classic full-rigged ship, and her hull had grace, her rigging an appealing symmetry, with that perfection of design that sometimes man evolved for those machines or vehicles that he had developed down the thousand years to use Nature's forces to help him do his work. Of these the most perfect was the Cape Horn ship.

And so the Frenchman also joined, for he was a man used to such ships and he loved them, in his own way. In 1929 France had no more: the last remnants had been clutched even from the Canal de la Martinière and sold as scrap for what they would bring. The Frenchman had reached the Gulf in the last Limejuicer, a gaunt four-poster of bald-headed rig and little grace. Beside the full-rigged ship this four-masted barque sat like a large heavy-sterned goose in company with a swan. So the Frenchman left the bald-headed Limejuicer and joined the sinister but lovely Finn. He did not desert. He did things properly as he had been trained to do, signing off in the approved manner from the stiff Limejuice Articles, and on the Finn's, all documents in order.

I was A.B. in that Finn. She had only six. I was there because she was then the world's last working Cape Horn full-rigged ship. Perhaps our French comrade did not know her story, for there was already then a shortage of the old shell-backs to pass such things on. The Finns were young men —very young. They were aware that the *Grace Harwar* was a hard ship for they had found out that much for themselves: but they had no memories reaching back to her Limejuice days.

We sailed, our crew a handful—13 before the mast, 19 all told. We were bashed up in the Tasman Sea, that grim, cold nastiness between South East Australia and New Zealand. We had to turn away from the passage round the south of New Zealand, to sail through Cook Straits and reach the Roaring Forties, to run then—we hoped—before the westerlies east-south-east towards the Horn. But the wind howled with mad laughter in our faces: when it shifted it was to the south'ard, bringing with it the whipping sting of that white hell down there. The ship, like most such ships, had no warmth, no heat. She was old—40 hard years old. She had too many of those wretched defects of the old ship—forecastle doors, ports and skylights not closing properly, capstan gears near worn out, the windlass primeval like Drake's in the *Pelican* but heavier—that sort of thing. She had an open wheel, and no charthouse: no shelter anywhere for the helmsman, watch-keeping mate, lookout—anyone. That guano cargo sent up fumes which had rotted some of the rope running rigging. There were no spares for she was parish-rigged, homeward-bound. She had no money (or not enough) to spend on spares.

She was two months between New Zealand and the Horn. She began to leak a little, for she was worn and weary with the strain of the great seas forever smashing at her hull, picking her up and flinging her now high upon their crests, now deep in their deepest troughs, as if to keep her there. One month out, an ordinary seaman was killed aloft. She killed him: she gave him no chance. He was doing his work aloft and she dropped the steel fore upper-topgallant yard across his back and killed him instantly, with a scream of the wind and a roaring of the sea. "Old ship," that wind screamed, "you are too old. Be gone! Be gone, lest we blow you for ever from the face of the ocean. And your rigging is worn out—rotten!"

When the daylight came we saw the white canvas high aloft stained heavily with blood—the ordinary seaman's young bright-red blood burst from his heart as the steel yard fell on him. We buried him from the quarter-deck in the morning in Finnish, Swedish and English, and we wondered, in the backs of our minds, who might be next: what next of that rigging might part fatally, rotted by foul guano fumes and hot Peruvian sun. It was all vital. We looked to it and did all we could, turning this halliard end-for-end so that the worst chafe and strain might come upon different parts and the whole survive at its work a little longer; long-splicing that brace, doubling this or that sheet with wire preventers. But we could achieve little without many coils of new rope, and these were not on board.

In the South Atlantic the second mate broke down. He could no longer send his sailors aloft where they must go: and he could not do the going for them. A Horn-doubling sailing-ship mate or master is a lonely man: mate and second mate alternate at their rigorous, soul-twisting watches, 24 hours each day. Each takes the half, day and night. In that undermanned ship, only the helmsman was on the poop with them, at the open wheel, groping to see the compass course by the feeble binnacle light, feeling the direction of the lashing wind upon his neck, his bare hands alert to all shifts and vagaries, all attempted twistings of the driven ship from her appointed course, all assaults of the sea and shifts of the forever screaming wind— howling tormented in the rigging as if maddened by the failure of more of it to carry away: and the squalls rising to a mad crescendo, and the great black seas roaring above the ship with a snarl of breaking crest whipped away by the screaming wind to drive bodily on board.

Four hours and five were the night watches: and the second mate broke down. He slipped overboard: We saw him go, flung a buoy, backed the mainyards to stop her way, to brake her in her killing stride; got out a boat with miraculous speed though no falls were rove. (They had been taken to meet greater need aloft.) We rove off line, working furiously. The ship lurched and rolled heavily, making foothold precarious. As it lifted, the heavy boat lurched at us murderously with the ship's motion, as if now it was free it turned into a killer boat, whelp of that killer ship. Over-side and into her! Fend off! Out oars! Get her away before the ship's side smashes her!

No one spoke, for orders were quite unnecessary. The mate had charge. The master was on the poop. Five went in the boat, led by the mate. We found him, though it seemed hopeless. We found him because in the cold dawn we saw the albatrosses circling over him, waiting, when the boat was thrown up on the crests.

We found him. We saved him. But then he was quite broken down. The crew was then an effective 11, still 10,000 miles from port. The ship's underside was foul as she had been unable to get into any dry-dock on her long voyage. Normally she was a good sailer: now she was sluggish and hard to steer. We were nearly four months to the Line. The food began to run out. The master, mate and carpenter were managing with the watch-keeping. We were used to hunger. It keeps you fit, and clear-minded. In the better weather, the master gave the second mate back his watch for which he had begged, to save his sanity. It was worrying for us. The state of the rigging became no better, and always there was that blood upon the sail. No gale or lashing rain washed that away. Even in the moonlight it scarred heavily across the canvas, especially on the sail below the yard that had fallen.

It was a dreadful voyage—searching, scarring, unforgettable. We were five in the second mate's watch—two Finns, an Englishman and an Australian, one Frenchman. All were real seamen, Cape Horn seamen. On such a voyage one sees men tested to extremes and the testing goes on—never with sleep enough, rarely food enough (though we got some once from a Scots steamer we spoke to at the edge of the north-east trades) and always the knowledge that more of the cordage could go. And the strained face of the young second mate in charge of us, sometimes seeming horribly close to final breakdown.

In such a ship on such a voyage one *knows* one's shipmates—through and through, tested as in savage active service in some horrible civil war: yet relieved, too, for our war was wholly clean, under God, with grand shipmates, good officers, men without guns fighting clean under conditions they accepted and well understood. The greatest victory was to save the sanity of the fine young second mate.

We did just that: and we brought that ship in from sea by God's grace, 137 days out from Australia. I knew my French and Finnish shipmates as I had known no other men. French, Finn (Ålander or mainlander), English, Australian—what were these labels amongst us? In the hard world of the Cape Horn ship, nothing at all. When the gale blew and the canvas thrashed, when the combination of terrible circumstances which can rise against any man suddenly snatched a shipmate from among us, then were the survivors moulded the more surely together, with stronger bonds, ready to go on.

That was more than 40 years ago, but good shipmates in that brotherhood are not to be forgotten. In this list I count high Pierre Berthoud, of Fécamp, in France.

Chapter Five

Some Accounts of Ships

THE BOUNTY ships of France indeed were different from all others. The fleet was a national asset, the crews a national reserve. The State helped them, the State demanded duties from their crews when necessary, the State recognised ships and men as worthy of financial support. The State also regulated them but only to see that the nationally enacted laws were properly observed aboard them, and there was real authority vested in consular officers who were trained in shipping matters—a field in which some other great maritime countries could have been more efficient. The ships were privately owned and operated by competent owners who took a close and informed interest in them. Officers and seamen alike were treated fairly.

Some French ships went missing, as other sailing-ships did. In the course of time, many were wrecked—embayed and stranded, caught in bad icefields in the vicinity of the Horn and the Falkland Islands, lost at times by bad landfalls, run down by steamers, as the barque *Eugene Schneider* was in the English Channel—that dangerous place for sailing-ships at any time but especially after the powered vessels had taken over, increasingly officered by men who had no sailing-ship experience. Any survey of the deepsea sailing-ships of the late 19th and earlier 20th centuries shows many losses, but it must be remembered that sailing-ships lasted through long lives during which they necessarily made a good many difficult voyages of some unavoidable hazard, at times of extreme danger, in the ordinary course of their careers. Their sailing routes lay through the stormy zones of the world, for they needed wind and plenty of it. The fact that the passage of Cape Horn was difficult and at times hazardous—many were lost in the area—kept the long-voyage trades for Chilean nitrates, Peruvian guano, Californian grain and Puget Sound lumber in their hands in the days before the Panama Canal was cut. Steamships could more easily use the Straits of Magellan, but while the sailing-ship could effectively move most nitrate or guano, or great baulks of lumber, this factor retarded the development of safe ports with swift turn-round for powered ships. For time was not usually of the essence under sail. Most ports along the west coast of South America were open roadsteads, not very convenient for steamships, and bunker coal carried there (in sail) from N.S.W. or Europe was expensive.

At least until the Panama Canal was proven as a useful channel for ships, there was a future for large cargo-carrying sailing-ships; but, before that, losses during the First World War almost decimated them. They were very vulnerable to submarines in European waters and to surface raiders like Count von Luckner's *Seeadler* anywhere. As a former sailing-ship man, the Count had far too good a knowledge of where to find them: most of the ships he sank were big square-riggers, though he treated the crews well and went to considerable trouble to land them. The French firm of A. D. Bordes, deepsea shipowners since the late 1840s—it was founded by Monsieur Antoine Dominique Bordes in 1847—alone lost 22 ships totalling more than 50,000 register tons between 1914 and 1919. A few years later, it had to sell many such ships as still remained for by 1923, in a period of apparently endless recession, there was little work that they could do. Compared with powered ships, the big square-rigged ship was cheap to build and operate and the essential overheads to keep her in commission were not high. If there were cargoes to seek she could seek them, and time was not important when she found them. But if there were virtually no cargoes offering at all on world chartering markets it was no sense to sail her seeking: laid up, both she and her dispersed crews rusted. Neither could be replaced.

Many French sailing-ships which still had years of useful life in them, were laid up in vain hope of better times, in the Canal de la Martinière between St. Nazaire and Nantes. Before that time, of course, bounty legislation having served its purpose had long come to an end. Those ships which survived the war had more than earned their costs. By 1921 or 22, little capital could have been tied up in them: it made sense to keep them to see if any chance of useful employment would return. Except for a few sold foreign—one to Laeisz in Hamburg as the *Pellworm,* another to become the *Suomen Joutsen* (ex-*Laennec,* of 2,260 tons, a Finnish school-ship, still afloat in 1972), a third for a brief career as the German school-ship *Hamburg* —the great majority moved from that lay-up berth to the break-up yards, and that was the end of them.

Three other former French sailing merchantmen also survived into 1972 —the four-masted barque *Champigny* of 3,112 tons gross built at Havre in 1902, later the Finnish school-ship *Fennia* and in the 1970s given back her old name, under the American flag; the small barque *Belem* of less than 1,000 tons, now the Italian school-ship *Giorgio Cini* rigged as a barquentine after many years as a British private yacht; and another large four-masted barque originally named *Ville de Mulhouse* (3,110 tons gross, built in 1899) which has been for some years the Chilean store-ship *Andalucia,* moored off Punta Arenas in the Straits of Magellan.

A few French barques were used in the West Indies logwood trade, with two or three smaller Danes, during the last days of commercial Sail (disregarding a remnant of Finns which survived with difficulty and in the end also without profit until 1950). By 1926, splendid big Cape Horners were being towed out of the Canal near Nantes for breaking-up six or nine at a time, though they were well maintained almost until the knackers got them. In September 1926 the sale for scrap of the well-known 2,000-tonners *Bourbaki, Joinville, MacMahon, Molière, St. Louis, Touraine, Vendée, Versailles* and *Vincennes* was announced together.* All were fine steel barques of around 2,000 tons or more, bounty ships built between 1898 and 1902. Scrap prices were reported at round £2,000 each—nominal value. Apparently, even the Åland Island Finns then had no use for them: within three years things were to become much worse.

France had never taken the view that big sailers were worth retention for their training value, although the fine new four-masted barque *Pola* was accepted as reparations from the German Laeisz Line, renamed *Richelieu* and used briefly as a sort of cargo-carrying school-ship. She was burned out while loading pitch in port in Baltimore in 1927, when she was less than nine years old. She could probably have been salved but was sold for breaking-up, for the French had not shown enthusiasm for the idea of the big square-rigger as a training-ship. Many took the practical view, not only in France, that Sail was Sail and steam was steam, and what was learned in the one was not necessarily of use in the other, though undoubtedly the square-rigged deepsea ship was of the anatomy of the profession. If it were true that experience in real ships of this kind is of no value—I disregard summer-cruising auxiliary vessels of all sorts—there would not be a single qualified master-mariner in any merchant-ship at sea today except possibly some Danes and a handful of Finns and Germans, all elderly. By 1914, even in diehard Britain, not only was powered-ship experience accepted fully (for deck officers' certificates of competence in full-powered ships), but the number of candidates applying with square-rigged experience was already down to half the total. In France it would seem that Sail was almost a world apart, while it lasted. Sailing-ship men did have the privilege of sitting for their master's certificates with 54 months sailing experience: for others the requirement was 60.

Though the sailing-ship men had done naval training, it was as temporary conscript seamen doing their essential national service. According to Henri Picard, the tough Bretons, for the most part, developed little affection for the navy and less for most naval officers.

"Animosity could be real between officers of the French navy and our masters in sail", he says. "These masters were mostly Bretons, sometimes perhaps headstrong, independent men, not at all liking to be 'pushed around'." Contempt for things naval could be so strong that when Captain

---

Sea Breezes, September 1926.

Chevalier of the *Bretagne* was given a commission as a reserve lieutenant in 1917, because the barque was then armed with a couple of small guns and carried seven naval ratings to man them against submarines, he refused to wear the naval uniform (though not to do the job). Why be dressed as a temporary lieutenant—a rank appropriate to the smallest chasseur—when he was an experienced master-mariner in command of a large barque? He had a case, of course: to him the rank was in itself a mark of contempt, and he had no need of it. It was supposed to change the *Bretagne* into a war-ship in action: such points did not bother the old sea dog. But navy ways did. So could some consuls, who were at times recruited from among retired naval officers, and the same Captain Chevalier had a brush or two with them.

"I remember, for instance, that he regarded the Consul at San Francisco as a complete drone, useless from head to foot: but the captain was a hot-headed man." He was also a most competent seaman who sailed his *Bretagne* safely through the war, lieutenant's uniform or no, and a highly capable sailmaker who cut his own sails aboard. His owners and his professional comrades held him in no contempt. The basic salary his owners paid him in 1920-21 was 1,000 francs a month (the exchange then was about 60 to the £ sterling) with approximately another 1,500 francs a month as his percentage on the freights. He was earning about £40 a month on the 15-month voyage, which was from Antwerp to Newcastle, N.S.W. in ballast (no commission), thence coal to Antofagasta, thence nitrates to Bordeaux. So there were two items of substantial master's commission. His emoluments compared very favourably with British.

At the time, monthly rates for others in the *Bretagne* were: —

Mate:	750 F. About £12.10s.	Carpenter:	370 F. About £6.4s.
2nd Mate:	600 F. ,, £10	A.B.:	330 F. ,, £5.10s.
Bo's'n:	385 F. ,, £6.8s.	O.S.:	300 F. ,, £5
Donkeyman:	385 F. ,, £6.8s.	Boy:	150 F. ,, £2.10s.
Cook:	375 F. ,, £6.4s.		

There was a deduction of 5.75 per cent from all salaries and wages for reserve obligations and towards pensions. These were the wages for crews signed on in France. French ships did not sign elsewhere, except unusually, as they had little or no desertion problem. It was not usual to carry a sailmaker signed on as such, because most officers could cut sails and able seamen seam and rope them. The French Cape Horners' sails were always beautifully cut, for the Bretons were thorough workmen.

The wages listed compared favourably with those of other nations still operating sailing-ships. British ships then paid about the same, up to 1921. Joining the *Bellands* of Hull in Melbourne in December 1920, I signed on as ordinary seaman at £5 monthly, but when the ship was to sail from St. Nazaire on her following voyage in mid-1921, able seamen were offered 30

shillings or £2. In the French ships it must be remembered that, except for
the occasional lone *pilotin,* everyone was paid, and reasonably fed too. By
the middle of 1921, the economic state of not only Europe was very bad.

Henri Picard has told me that though masters' wives sometimes sailed
with their husbands on long voyages, it was not the usual thing. In the
Bretagne, Madame Chevalier sailed with her husband until 1921 and had
been with him in the 2,255-ton steel ship *Desaix* before that, since 1912,
and right throughout World War I. Madame Chevalier was a very quiet
woman who spent the voyages in the saloon (which was spacious, comfortable and airy) or walking with her husband on his poop—never anywhere
else, never alone on deck, never in the way. "The crew were very respectful
to her. I have heard of perhaps 40 or 50 such wives who sailed with their
husbands, but some owners, like Bordes, did not like them aboard at all."

Monsieur Picard has made a close study of the careers and performance
of the big French "Bounty" ships, one by one, over the whole fleet insofar
as so formidable an undertaking has been possible. Records now are far
from complete, often non-existent. In the great discard of the deepsea
sailing-ship which followed so closely after the First World War the records
largely went too. No one had regard for the historian who might come along
afterwards seeking facts. When the old-style owners died out, who cared?
The Bretons wrote few books, left no great files of informative correspond-
ence, fostered no maritime historians. The life was above all practical: so
were they, and they still are. It was after an accident put an end to his sea
career that Henri Picard had time to be interested. He found the task
challenging and tremendous: it has kept him busy for years.

One point, long suspected, he soon established, and that was that hear-say
claims of "record" passages were worthless unless they could be verified
from Lloyd's reports or other unquestionable authority. Few could: and
so they are not mentioned. One such claim, as an example, had long been
current for the steel ship *Général Faidherbe,* 2,188 tons, of Nantes, which
was said to have arrived at Vancouver in 1911 after a passage of 29 days
from Hobart, Tasmania, a good 7,500 sailing miles away. Investigation
showed that the *Général Faidherbe* had made no such passage and made
no call at Hobart in 1911 at all, and did not contemplate any, for she was
on passage from Europe to Vancouver direct and, being then just over 10
years old and therefore past the bounty-earning period of the Act currently
in force, to call at Hobart would be a time-wasting diversion. She had sailed
from Europe direct in 135 days. No bounty, no Hobart: it was as simple as
that. But it takes more than cold facts to demolish an old myth.

Results of Monsieur Picard's unique study follow, arranged much as he
prepared them, in alphabetical order, with a special study of the *Bretagne*
in which he sailed. It is an interesting record of an interesting fleet covering
much bravery and adventure.

PART TWO

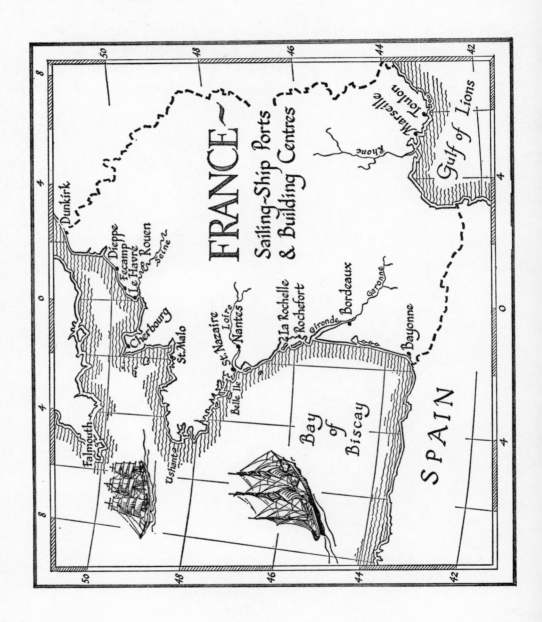

FRANCE

Sailing-Ship Ports & Building Centres

Dunkirk
Dieppe
Fecamp
Le Havre
Rouen
Seine
Cherbourg
St.Malo
Falmouth
Ushant
St. Nazaire
Loire
Nantes
Belle Ile
La Rochelle
Rochefort
Gironde
Bordeaux
Garonne
Bayonne
Bay of Biscay
SPAIN
Marseille
Toulon
Gulf of Lions
Rhône

Henri Picard's List

A. D. Bordes – Iron 4-masted ship, 2,326 gross, 2,155 net tons*.
1884: Built by W. B. Thompson, Glasgow, for A. D. Bordes, Dunkirk.

She was built with a cellular double-bottom holding 450 tons of water. On her outward passage in 1899 she had a great race with her consorts *Madeleine* and *Montmorency,* all three arriving in Valparaiso Bay on May 1 with the *A. D. Bordes* winner. She left Shields on February 18, passed Dover on the 20th and was only 70 days from that point; the *Madeleine* was 71 days from the Downs, and the *Montmorency* 72 days from Prawle Point—all excellent passages.

On October 2 1917, under Captain Joseph Briand, she was attacked by a U-boat, but managed to beat off the enemy with her two guns. Master and crew were subsequently commended for their action. She was still in commission in 1919, in the Chilean trade via Panama Canal, but in 1923 was broken up.

Aconcagua – Iron ship, 1,313 g., 1,194 n.
1880: Built by R. Duncan, Port Glasgow, for C. S. Caird, Greenock, as *Nereus.*

In August 1893 she was sold to Bordes, and renamed *Aconcagua*. On January 1 1917, from Mejillones to Rochefort with nitrate, she was captured by the German submarine *U-70* in the Bay of Biscay, about 300 miles off the French coast, and sunk by gunfire. Capt. Leveque and his crew were saved the following day by the British steamer *Highland Prince,* and landed at Brixham.

Adolphe – Iron barque, 1,169 g., 1,105 n.
1869: Built by Lune Shp. Co., Lancaster, for T. O. Hunter & Co., Greenock, as *Mallowdale.*
1890: Sold by Hunter, Brown & Co. to A. D. Bordes and renamed *Adolphe*.

* Note – Tonnages are 'g'=gross, 'n'=net. 'Mile' means the sea mile of 6,080 feet.

October 1900: Sold for £5,000 to Grimstad, and renamed *Sesa*. On April 9 1904 arrived at Fremantle partially dismasted and was sold at auction there for £450. She subsequently sailed for Bombay where she arrived on October 18 1904. She did not move from here as *Sesa*: and it is most likely that she was hulked at Bombay as she disappears from the records after this.

Adolphe – Steel 4-masted barque, 3,245 g., 2,462 n.
March 23 1902: Launched by Chantiers de France, Dunkirk, for A. D. Bordes.

Here are several of her passages under Captain L. Gosselin:

In September 1902 arrived at Iquique in 105 days from Port Talbot; on May 24 1903 arrived at Iquique 97 days from Dunkirk and returned there in 89 days. On January 27 1904 arrived Iquique in 102 days from Port Talbot, loaded at Caleta Buena, and sailed back to Dunkirk in 88 days. On September 30 1904, arriving at Newcastle (N.S.W.) from Antwerp, 85 days out, commanded by Captain Layec, she was being towed into port in a heavy sea when her towrope carried away while she was approaching the bar, and she went aground on Oyster Bank. Her crew were saved with difficulty but the *Adolphe* became a total loss.

Adolphe – Steel ship, 2,179 g., 1,979 n.
March 1892: Launched by Barclay, Curle & Co., Glasgow, for Thomas Carmichael, Greenock, as *Peleus*.

This beautiful full-rigger of 3,400 tons deadweight, the last of the superb Carmichael fleet, had always made excellent runs under the British flag such as Europe to Australia in 86 and 87 days, California and Oregon to Europe in 110, 112, 113 and 123 days. Her slowest passage was 145 days from San Francisco to Falmouth.

May 1905: Sold by A. & J. H. Carmichael & Co. to A. D. Bordes, Dunkirk, and renamed *Adolphe*, she sailed without incident steadily and reliably for the following 18 years. In October 1923 she was sold to Dutch shipbreakers, as there were then no prospects of further useful employment.

Alexandre – Steel 4-masted barque, 3,205 g., 2,419 n.
June 22 1902: Launched by Chantiers de France, Dunkirk, for A. D. Bordes, Dunkirk.

A regular "bounty" ship, her best passage was in 1903 from Iquique to Dunkirk, 79 days. The same year she went missing while being towed across the North Sea from Dunkirk towards the Tyne. The tow parted some 30 miles off Whitby, in very bad weather, and she was not seen again. As she was in ballast, it was generally considered that she had capsized. Her full crew of 33 went with her.

Alexandre – Steel 4-masted barque, 2,671 g., 2,482 n.
1892: Built by Barclay, Curle & Co., Glasgow, for R. Shankland & Co., Greenock, as *Springburn*.

This famous "bald-header" (ship with no royals) made some excellent sailing performances under the Red Ensign, the best claimed being:

London to San Francisco	103 days
San Francisco to Queenstown	98 „
Cardiff to Capetown	37 „
Newcastle, N.S.W., to San Francisco	42 „

In March 1906 she was sold to A. D. Bordes and renamed *Alexandre*. On July 6 1917 she sailed from La Pallice for Taltal in ballast, commanded by Captain Lebreton. On August 1 at 5 a.m. in lat. 33° 33′ N., long. 23° 15′ W., she was intercepted by the large German submarine *U-155* which opened fire with her two five-inch guns. The submarine kept more than six miles off, beyond the range of the *Alexandre's* small guns which were useless. The barque was becalmed and unable to manoeuvre. The *Alexandre* was captured and abandoned by her crew of 32, who subsequently managed to reach La Palma (in the Canary Islands) about 400 miles away. Her two guns were transhipped into the submarine, and the *Alexandre* was sunk by gunfire.

Alice – Steel ship, 2,630 g., 1,698 n.
November 25 1900: Launched by Chantiers Maritimes du Sud-Ouest, Bordeaux, for Société des Voiliers de St. Nazaire.

She was the only large French sailing vessel rigged with three skysail yards, probably the last steel sailing ship crossing skysail yards. In 1903 she was transferred to Sté. Générale d'Armement, St. Nazaire. The *Alice* had a monkey-poop with a half-round the full width of the ship extending from the stern to just forward of the mizzen-mast, where it was prolonged by a half-poop to forward of the main mast. There was a well-deck from here to the foremast which was stepped through the fo'c'sle. The vessel carried course, double topsails, double topgallant sails, royal and skysail on each mast, and a crew of 27. The skysails, apparently, did her little if any good.

Captain Langlois took her from the builders, and on her maiden voyage she ran ashore at Table Bay but got off without damage. Next voyage, Captain Ferrars in command, she sailed for Vancouver (B.C.), but had to put into Falmouth on the way to restow cargo, and made a slow passage to Vancouver.

In 1907 she was thrown on her beam ends in the South Pacific, but her crew managed to get her upright and continue the voyage. In 1908 the *Alice* loaded a cargo of cement at London for Portland (Oreg.). She arrived at the mouth of Columbia River in January 1909, but could not cross the bar. While she was waiting a gale sprang up which drove her ashore about eight miles north of Columbia River, between Long Beach and Ocean Side, where she soon broke up. Her crew were saved.

Alice – Steel barque, 1,511 g., 1,193 n. (See *Marie-Madeleine.*)

Alice – Steel barque, 2,691 g., 2,270 n.
February 4 1901: Launched by Chantiers de Normandie, Rouen, for the Compagnie Havraise de Navigation (Ed. Corblet & Co.).

Sailed steadily through the First World War, afterwards making several Australian passages with wheat, while freights held, but by February 1922 she was laid up at St. Nazaire, and was sold to be broken up two years later in the general slump.

Alice-Marie – Steel barque, 2,288 g., 1,731 n.
August 31 1901: Launched by Chantiers de la Loire, Nantes, for Pierre Guillon, Nantes, and two years later sold to the Société des Voiliers Dunkerquois, Dunkirk.

On October 4 1908, while on passage in ballast from Birkenhead to Antwerp (in tow), under Captain Cloatre, she was rounding Land's End in dense fog when she struck on the Runnelstone, bumping heavily. At high tide the barque was refloated and her tug tried to tow her to Penzance. Crippled and sinking, she reached Mount's Bay, and though she came two miles to Penzance she could not find her way in and foundered in shallow water off St. Michael's Mount. The crew were landed at Penzance.

Alice-Micheline – Steel barque, 1,124 g., 1,033 n.
1893: Built by Huyghens & Van Gelder, Amsterdam, for W. A. Huijgens of that city, as the *Amsterdam*.

This vessel was French very briefly. The interesting thing is that she survived as late as 1971.

In 1906 she was sold to J. M. Jonasen, Sarpsborg, Norway, and her name maintained for several years. From 1915 until 1923, as the *Sirdal*, she was owned by S. O. Stray & Co., of Christiansand, who owned many large sailing-ships. She became French only in 1923, when bought by Dubosc de Jong & Co., Havre, for the West Indies trade, and renamed *Alice-Micheline*. In

February 1924 she arrived at Havre from Black River with logwood and was then sold to Avv. Pietro Arata fu F., Genoa. Renamed *Piero,* she was again in the campeachy wood trade between the West Indies and Genoa. By 1928 she had been hulked at Leghorn, and it seems that she was damaged there by bombing during World War II. In 1948 she was converted into a full-powered motor-ship, owned by Silvio Bonaso, Genoa, her looks having been altered with a straight stem, bridge, etc. In 1970 the *Piero* was still afloat operating in the Mediterranean, and Dutch sail enthusiasts considered the possibility of buying her and restoring her to her original rig, but these plans failed and she was reported scrapped at La Spezia late in 1970.

The *Amsterdam* was not a famous ship and had a mixed record of passages, though she made Falmouth from Sydney, in 1906, in the creditable time of 97 days.

Almendral – Steel 4-masted barque, 2,126 g., 1,987 n.
March 1889: Launched by Barclay, Curle & Co., Glasgow, for A. & J. H. Carmichael & Co., Greenock, as the *Glaucus.*

She was a very handsome barque and the only four-master in Carmichael's fleet. Among her best passages were the following:

1889:	Liverpool to Calcutta	86 days	
1892:	San Francisco to Queenstown	105	„
1898:	Frederickstad to Melbourne	93	„
1898:	San Francisco to Falmouth	108	„
1899:	Melbourne to Lizard	85	„
1905:	Astoria to Queenstown	109	„
	(last passage under the British flag).		

In June 1905, she was sold to A. D. Bordes, Dunkirk, renamed *Almendral,* and in 1909 made an excellent run of 76 days between the Tyne and Valparaiso. As late as 1921 she was still making good passages in the Chilean trade, sailing from Dunkirk to Iquique via Taltal in 89 days in that year. But she was laid up by the end of the year, and sold for scrap in 1923.

Amérique – Steel 4-masted barque, 2,129 g., 2,017 n.
May 1892: Completed by R. Duncan & Co., Port Glasgow, for the Lyle Shipping Co., Greenock, as *Cape Clear.*

In 1894 she made a good passage of 102 days from Calcutta to Beachy Head as a Britisher. Sold to A. D. Bordes, Dunkirk, and renamed *Amérique* in 1899, she left the Tyne for Valparaiso on August 2 of that year, under Captain Plusquellec, was spoken off Cape Horn on September 22, and not heard of or seen again. It was thought that she could have been sunk by an iceberg.

Amiral Cécille – Steel ship, 2,695 g., 2,293 n.
May 1902: Completed by Chantiers de St. Nazaire, Rouen, for Cie. de Navigation Française, Nantes.

This was a real hard-working bounty-earner, for the big full-rigged ship always appeared fully laden, and rarely figured in the round-the-world-in-ballast mileage voyages, as did many of her contemporaries. In 1904 she was transferred to the Sté. Générale d'Armement, Nantes. On February 8 1910, on a return passage from Seattle, she arrived off Kinsale in 111 days, which was good. Her last voyage was to Australia, returning via the Cape of Good Hope. Here are details:

January 28 1921	:	Arrived Adelaide from Londonderry.
February 11	:	At Port Lincoln.
March 9	:	Sailed Port Lincoln for Nantes, with wheat.
May 31	:	Passed St. Helena.
June 7	:	Passed Ascension.
July 19	:	Arrived St. Nazaire, 132 days out.

In August 1921, the *Amiral Cécille* was drafted to the Canal de la Martinière near Nantes, where she was gutted by fire on January 22 1925.

Amiral Courbet – Steel barque, 2,223 g., 1,969 n.
1900: Built by Chantiers Nantais de Constructions Maritimes, Nantes, for Société des Voiliers Nantais of that port.

On December 15 1911, while on passage from New York to Sydney, in lat. 44° S., long. 37° 41′ E., her steering gear was broken by heavy seas, causing a call at Port Natal for repairs, where she arrived on January 5 1912. She did not last much longer. On October 20, 1915, while bound from Cork to Albany (W.A.) in ballast, Captain Mazurais in command, she became embayed on the Irish coast near Cork, stranded and became a total loss.

Amiral de Cornulier – Steel barque, 2,208 g., 1,946 n.
July 28 1900: Launched by Chantiers Nantais de Constr. Maritimes, Nantes, for Sté. des Voiliers Nantais.

Captain A. Rio took the barque from the stocks and left Nantes for Australia, arriving at Spencer Gulf in only 69 days. Under the same master the *Amiral de Cornulier* later made Portland, Oreg. (from Birkenhead) in 114 days. In September 1908 she had a narrow escape on passage from Limerick to Adelaide when, owing to a very strong gale, she was compelled to anchor with her stern only a few yards from rocks. The tug *Shannon* towed her to Limerick for repairs. Her last passage was in 1921, to Antofagasta from Newcastle, N.S.W., thence to the Azores for orders in 136 days. This last cargo was delivered at Bristol where the *Amiral de Cornulier* was purchased by the Société des Voiliers Français, Havre, and broken up in 1923.

Amiral Halgan – Steel barque, 2,214 g., 1,947 n.
May 28 1900: Launched by Chantiers Nantais de Constr. Maritimes, Nantes, for Société des Voiliers Nantais, Nantes.

On March 2 1912 she left New Caledonia for Glasgow with nickel ore. On March 20 the *Amiral Halgan* encountered a hurricane and was thrown on her beam ends when her cargo shifted. Sails were lost and boats washed overboard. Captain Cloatre decided to turn back and the barque put into Noumea for repairs on April 1.

On her last voyage she arrived at Adelaide from Bordeaux, on February 2 1921. She left Port Victoria at the end of February for Bordeaux; by June the absence of news was causing anxiety until she was spoken off Cape Finisterre early in July. The *Amiral Halgan* arrived in the River Gironde on August 11 1921, about 170 days out. During the voyage she was bought by the Société des Voiliers Français of Havre, and was sold for scrap in 1923.

Amiral Troude – Steel barque, 1,876 g., 1,663 n.
November 1897: Completed by Laporte & Co., Rouen, for R. Guillon & Co., Nantes.

Bought by A. D. Bordes in 1903, she retained her original name. On June 27 1917, she sailed from Iquique to Rochefort with nitrate, under Captain J. B. Forgeard, but on September 30, was torpedoed by the German submarine *U-B-51* in lat. 46° 42′ N., long. 16° 48′ W. Captain Forgeard and his 25 crew were saved by the French barquentines *Raymond* and *Ben Cesari*.

André Théodore – Steel ship, 2,732 g., 2,418 n.
December 1902: Completed by Chantiers de St. Nazaire, Rouen, for Société Navale du Sud-Ouest, Bordeaux, she was sold to Bureau Frères & Baillergeau, Nantes, two years later.

On her third voyage, when the *André Théodore* arrived at Honolulu on July 14 1906, from Barry via Sydney, her master, Captain Robert, reported having felt earthquake shocks south of Australia (in position lat. 46° 50′ S., long. 139° 05′ E.) on April 18, the same date that San Francisco was rocked by its famous quake. During her career under the French flag, she made 13 voyages—five to California, three to Chile, three to Australia, one to Australia and Chile, and one to Chile, Australia and California. On her last Australian voyage in 1920-21, her return passage from Port Victoria to Queenstown took 143 days, but this was a year of many long passages. She was then laid up in the Canal de la Martinière. Sold to Flli. Dufour, Genoa, in January 1924, she was altered to barque rig, and left Nantes for Cadiz in March 1924 as *Lorenzo*. Under the Italian flag she was in the Argentine lumber trade, and made three voyages Cadiz - River Plate and back. At the end of 1927 she was laid up at Genoa, and towed to Savona for breaking up in 1929.

Anjou – Steel barque, 2,069 g., 1,572 n.
November 1899: Completed by Chantiers Dubigeon, Nantes, for R. Guillon & Co., Nantes.

She made an excellent passage in 1903-4 of 98 days from San Francisco to the Lizard, but was lost the following year. On January 20 1905, commanded by Captain Le Tallec, she left Sydney for the Channel for orders, with wheat, but on the evening of February 4, in foggy weather, the barque struck the cliffs on the western side of Auckland Island, and went over on her beam ends. One boat was smashed at once, and the captain insisted that all hands stay aboard until daybreak. It was a terrific night aboard the barque, pounding against the cliffs. However, about 5 a.m. on February 5 they were saved with great trouble. After rowing their three boats for 12 miles they got ashore, and after 12 days arrived at the provision depot on Musgrave Inlet. Here Le Tallec kept his crew alive for three months. At last, on May 7 1905, the New Zealand government steamer *Hinemoa* rescued all. At the subsequent inquiry the captain was commended.

Anne de Bretagne – Steel barque, 2,063 g., 1,571 n.
February 18 1901: Launched by Chantiers Dubigeon, Nantes, for Société Bretonne de Navigation, Nantes (H. Prentout-Leblond & E. Leroux, Mgrs., Rouen).

In November 1905, when off the River Plate, she was part dismasted and disabled in a pampero. The barque was subsequently picked up by the British steamer *Plympton* and towed to Montevideo. Part cargo had to be discharged to pay for repairs, towing and port charges. The *Plympton* claimed £4,000 for salvage and towing. The barque finally arrived at San Francisco on July 22 1906, 280 days from Swansea.

In 1912 she was sold to the Société Générale d'Armement, Nantes, but two years later, in November 1914, while bound from Frederikstad to Sydney with a timber cargo, in lat. 27°S., long. 33°W., she was captured by the German raider *Kronprinz Wilhelm,* to which Captain Picard and his crew were removed. After pillage of her stores over several days, it was decided to sink the barque, but after many attempts by gunfire, dynamite charges and ramming (when the raider got the worst of the impact on her own fore compartment), the *Anne de Bretagne* was left still floating, but waterlogged, on her beam ends, on November 25 1914. She was certainly well-built. She must have sunk in time, as she was not seen again.

Antoinette – Steel 4-masted barque, 2,898 g., 2,612 n.
October 20 1896: Launched by Chantiers de la Méditerranée, La Seyne, for A. D. Bordes, Dunkirk.

From 1897 until 1906 she made eight very good runs on the Europe-Chile route, her best outward and homeward passages being 72 days each. She survived the war, though attacked by U-boats which she succeeded in beating off. This was in October 1917, under Captain P. Lechevanton. On December 21 1919, on passage from Iquique to New York with nitrate, via Panama Canal, she was lost on Serrana Rocks off the coast of Nicaragua.

Antonin – Iron ship, 1,818 g., 1,681 n.
1875: Built by J. Reid & Co., Port Glasgow, for Mackinnon, Frew & Co., Liverpool, as *Killean*.

This old-timer was later owned by McDiarmid, Greenshields & Co., of Liverpool, who sold her in 1893 to A. D. Bordes, who named her *Antonin*. By 1901 she was Norwegian, purchased by C. Zernichas & O. Gotaas & Co. of Christiania, who renamed her *Avanti*. Six years later, on January 21 1907, while on passage from Pensacola to Montevideo with lumber, she was lost on the south-west reef of Tortugas, off the coast of Florida.

Antonin – Steel 4-masted barque, 3,071 g., 2,662 n.
August 24 1902: Launched by Chantiers de France, Dunkirk, for A. D. Bordes, as a more economic replacement for the old ship.

On November 18 1915 she left La Pallice and arrived at Antofagasta on January 29 1916, in 72 days, her best outward passage. On a subsequent homeward passage, she left Iquique for Brest for orders, commanded by Captain F. Lecoq, but was destroyed by another sailing ship—the famous German raider *Seeadler*—in position lat. 7°N., long. 36°W. This was on February 3 1917.

Armen – Steel barque, 2,243 g., 2,016 n.
February 27 1902: Launched by Chantiers Nantais de Constr. Maritimes, Nantes, for Compagnie Celtique Maritime, Nantes.

In 1909 she was sold to the Compagnie Navale de l'Océanie, Paris, and lost the same year while bound from Hamburg to New Caledonia in ballast. Arriving off Noumea she was driven on the rocks by currents in a dead calm, and became a total loss. This was on November 8 1909.

Asie – Steel 4-masted barque, 2,820 g., 2,452 n.
September 11 1897: Launched by Laporte & Co., Rouen, for A. d'Orbigny
& G. Faustin fils, La Rochelle.

Her stability, owing to her sharp lines, was not good when light and she met
with trouble for this reason (see *Europe,* her sister ship). On December 31
1901, for example, she was in Portland (Oreg.), under Captain Ollivaud,
waiting for a cargo of wheat, all her ballast discharged and the barque kept
upright by ballast logs (booms) hung alongside, as was the custom at Portland in those days. In spite of that she fell on her starboard side on to the
wharf, putting her upper yardarms through the warehouses, and went
practically on her beam ends. The ship's hull was little damaged but her
spars and rigging were badly mauled, the jiggermast being the only mast
undamaged. Strangely, and luckily, no person received more hurt than a
few scratches. After this curious misfortune, repairs took seven months.
Here are her passages on her seventh voyage; interesting as perhaps typical:

January 29 1904	:	Left Antwerp with rails.
May 31	:	Arrived Hobart for orders, 123 days out.
June 1	:	Sailed Hobart.
August 23	:	Arrived San Pedro, Cal.; 83 days.
October 8	:	Left San Pedro in ballast.
November 3	:	Arrived Portland, Oreg.; 26 days.
November 30	:	Sailed Portland with grain.
April 25 1905	:	Arrived Birkenhead, 146 days out.

Amount of freights: 182,349 francs, to which the navigation bounty must
be added—124,790 francs for the voyage.
September 13 1908: Bought by A. D. Bordes and retained her original
name.

   She sailed through the 1914-18 War, but in December 1919 while on
passage from Iquique to Nantes, she was lost on Jardinets' Rocks, at the
entrance to St. Nazaire roads. She was then in tow of the tug *Commerce*
which was unable to keep her in the fairway.

Asnières – Steel 4-masted barque, 3,103 g., 2,715 n.
June 7 1902: Launched by Chantiers de la Méditerranée, Havre, for Sté.
des Long-Courriers Français, Havre.

In 1906 the *Asnières* collided with another ship in the River Thames while
on a voyage from Antwerp via London to San Francisco. Later she also
managed to get ashore in Falmouth Bay but was refloated. Her end came
in 1917, under different owners—the Sté. Générale d'Armement of Nantes,
while bound from Bahia Blanca to Bordeaux, with a cargo of wheat, under
Captain E. Ybert. On January 2 1917 the *Asnières* was captured and sunk
by the German raider *Moewe,* in lat. 3°16′N., long. 29°10′W.

Astrée – Steel ship, 2,227 g., 1,987 n.
1890: Built by W. Hamilton & Co., Port Glasgow, for A. C. Le Quellec, Bordeaux.

In September 1901, while on passage Shields for Valparaiso with coal, Captain Jouanjean in command, fire broke out in her cargo. The *Astree* was then off Staten Island and her master decided to crowd all sail for the Falkland Islands. But it was impossible owing to the extent of the fire, and very bad weather. The ship became unmanageable and had to be abandoned, all hands sailing in four boats for Staten Island. Three landed safely near St. John's lighthouse, but the fourth boat was lost with six of the men.

Atlantique – Steel 4-masted barque, 2,970 g., 2,685 n.
April 4 1897: Launched by Chantiers de la Loire, Nantes, for A. D. Bordes.

Going from Iquique to Hamburg with nitrate, on March 20 1904, she took the ground on Zuiderlaaks Banks, near Nieuwdiep, and part cargo had to be unloaded before she refloated. She was then towed to her destination.

In 1905 she was credited with an excellent run of 67 days between Port Talbot and Iquique. She made no more such passages, but survived the war. In 1924, after being idle in port for three years, the *Atlantique* was fitted out again, but for only one voyage to Australia. Arriving at Port Pirie via Adelaide on March 14 1925, she left on April 14 1925 for Falmouth for orders, and so became the last large French sailing ship to round the Horn. The following year she was sold to be broken up.

Atlas – Steel 4-masted barque, 2,070 g., 1,927 n.
1886: Built by Barclay, Curle & Co., Glasgow, for R. Shankland & Co., Greenock, as the 4-masted ship *Bannockburn*.

Her rig was cut down in 1894 to a 4-masted barque without royals—the Jubilee rig. Her figurehead was Robert the Bruce of Scotland, and she was a fine ship like all the *"Burns"*. In 1905 she was sold to Akties. "Bannockburn" (Gundersen & Gjertsen), Porsgrund, Norway, for £5,550. I think she was renamed *Leif Gundersen* between 1914 and 1916. In October 1916, as *Leif Gundersen,* she was reported sold by Akties. "Leif Gundersen" (Gundersen & Gjertsen), Porsgrund, to buyers not named for £53,250. Her name is still *Bannockburn* in Lloyd's Register of 1914-15.

March 24 1917: The Norwegian barque, painted dark green having her name *Leif Gundersen* – Norge, painted in large letters on her sides, was stopped and examined at sea by the French auxiliary cruiser *La Champagne* (ex-British liner *Oropesa*). Suspected letters addressed to Germany were found on board and the barque was taken to Glasgow, where ship and cargo were declared prize, on May 10 1917. The French Government renamed her *Atlas,* port of registry Lorient, and she sailed from Glasgow to the West Indies in ballast on July 17 1917, with a French crew and Captain Le Squeren in command.

There was no further news of the *Atlas* afterwards and, in due course, she was officially posted missing. However, a plausible supposition may be considered. On July 28 1917 an unidentified 4-masted barque, about 2,000 tons, was sunk 200 miles west of the Fastnet by the German submarine *U-30.* It was generally believed that this unknown barque was the *Atlas.*

Babin Chevaye – Steel barque, 2,174 g., 1,930 n.
October 16 1901: Launched by Chantiers Nantais de Constr. Maritimes, Nantes, for Bureau Frères & Baillergeau, Nantes.

On her maiden return voyage from Chile in 1902 she was severely battered off Cape Horn, one man was washed overboard and drowned, five of her crew were hurt seriously. The barque sprung a leak, her main topgallant mast carried away, and her master, Captain Robert, put into Montevideo on August 31 1902. On her second voyage she made San Francisco from Antwerp in 138 days, and Ipswich from 'Frisco in 117 days—more or less average passages. Her third was Swansea to San Francisco in 120 days, thence back to Queenstown in 127 days. In September 1905, while on a passage from Penarth to California, Captain Louis Lacroix in command, the *Babin Chevaye's* rudder was broken off Cape Horn, and the barque put into Taltal for repairs. Arriving at San Francisco on January 13 1906, her charter for grain having been cancelled, she left 'Frisco on February 12 1906 for Sydney where wheat was loaded for Cardiff.

Early in 1908 the *Babin Chevaye* departed from Port Talbot for Iquique, via Hobart again, and arrived back at Antwerp on December 13 1908—a long voyage with two cargoes. She left Antwerp with general cargo for Portland, Oreg., via Cherbourg where Captain Lebeaupin took command. On May 5 1909 the barque was running before a severe storm in the Roaring Forties, when she was swept from stern to stem by a tremendous sea. Two men were lost overboard and her two helmsmen were badly injured. The *Babin Chevaye* called at Hobart on May 29 and arrived at Portland on August 23 1909. In 1910 she passed the Lizard 118 days out from Astoria, Oreg. Her end came in the war, on passage 1917-18 from Antofagasta for Nantes with nitrates, under Captain Bourge. On January 14 1918 she was intercepted by the German submarine *U-84* in the Bay of Biscay, 35 miles west-south-west of Penmarch Head. After a methodical pillage the unarmed barque was sunk by explosive charges and gunfire. Her crew were saved, but it was the last cruise of the *U-84* which was rammed and sunk by the *P.C. 69* on January 26 in the Irish Sea.

Bayard – Steel barque, 2,201 g., 1,970 n.
July 1 1901: Launched by Chantiers Nantais de Constr. Maritimes, Nantes, for Bureau Frères & Baillergeau, Nantes.

In 1904 she made an excellent passage across the North Pacific of 24 days from Hakodate to the Golden Gate. On June 2 1907 she arrived at Falmouth from Portland (Oreg.), 119 days out. While on a passage from Glasgow to Oregon in July 1910, she put into Montevideo with a broken rudder, having been damaged on her winter rounding of Cape Horn. The *Bayard* was partially dismasted by a waterspout off the Columbia River in 1915 and put into San Francisco for repairs. She later made a smart run of 27 days to St. Nazaire from Dakar, in 1918, and the following year to Melbourne from St. Nazaire in 94 days. The homeward passage in 1920 back to St. Nazaire, was 121 days. She made only one more voyage under the French flag, to California, and after a long lay-up was broken up in Germany in 1926.

Bayonne – Steel ship, 2,589 g., 2,241 n.
September 14 1901: Launched by Chantiers de St. Nazaire, for Société Bayonnaise de Navigation, Bayonne.

She was sold ten years later to Société des Voiliers Normands (Prentout-Leblond, Leroux & Co., Mgrs.), Rouen. After a useful career, she was lost during the First World War on passage from New York for Ipswich with 3,300 tons barley and maize, under Captain Thoumyre in the winter of 1917. Arriving at the entrance to the Channel she was delayed by strong head winds several days. When the wind veered to south-west a few days later she sailed before it, but was captured by the German submarine *U-84* 27 miles east of Start Point. Being unarmed, the *Bayonne* was sunk by bombs after her crew had abandoned ship. They landed at Lyme Regis next day. This was on February 18 1917.

Beaumanoir – Steel barque, 1,580 g., 1,395 n.
August 1899: Launched by A. Dubigeon, Nantes, for Louis Bureau & fils, Nantes.

While bound from St. Nazaire to Madagascar in December 1899, she was caught by a cyclone south-east of Madagascar and dismasted. She put into Port Louis (Mauritius) for repairs nine days later. She was dismasted again in a hurricane on September 16 1905, while on a passage from Newcastle, N.S.W., to San Francisco with coal, and was found on October 7 by the Australian steamer *Mona* which towed her to Suva. Later she was towed to Sydney where she was repaired and eventually resumed her voyage to the Golden Gate, arriving on May 31 1906. In 1909 the *Beaumanoir* made a very long passage of 214 days from Saigon to St. Nazaire.

Laid up at Nantes in 1911 she was sold to Rasmus Pedersen & Martin Mosvold, Farsund, Norway, and renamed *Wulff*. In 1916-17 she appears as the *Fixstjerne,* and in 1921 as the *Aristos* owned by Iver Bugge, Larvik. She arrived at Glasgow from Canada in September 1921 and laid up, and was broken up there two years later.

Belen – Steel barque, 2,202 g., 1,987 n. (See *Jeanne d'Arc.*)

Bérangère – Steel ship, 2,851 g., 1,875 n.
October 1902: Completed by Chantiers de St. Nazaire, Rouen, for Société des Voiliers du Sud-Ouest, Bordeaux, and sold to Société des Voiliers Dunkerquois, Dunkirk, 1904.

While on a passage from New Caledonia to Glasgow on September 12 1905, a gallant rescue was effected south of Cape Horn by Captain Beaudouart and his crew. Totally dismasted and on her beam ends since September 7, after struggling for weeks against head winds in her endeavour to round Cape Horn, MacVicar, Marshall's full-rigger *Garsdale* (from the Tyne to Portland, Oreg.) was sighted. Owing to particularly bad weather, saving the British crew by a boat of the *Bérangère* was very difficult. It took all hands 12 hours of skilful and dangerous boatwork, in which the early sea fishing experience of many of the Breton crew greatly helped. The French ship subsequently landed Captain King and 24 of his crew at Greenock. Captain Beaudouart and his crew were highly commended for their action.*

While bound from Buenos Aires to Havre with timber, the *Bérangère* was sunk by the German submarine *U-62* on May 10 1917, 108 miles southwest of the Fastnet.

Biarritz – Steel ship, 2,613 g., 2,252 n.
January 1902: Completed by Chantiers de St. Nazaire for Société Bayonnaise de Navigation, Bayonne.

While on a slow 170 days passage from Cardiff to San Francisco in 1906, scurvy struck the ship, laying low four crew members. She was sold to Sté des Voiliers Normands (Prentout-Leblond, Leroux & Co., Mgrs.), Rouen, in May 1911, and lost in 1917, by fire. She was then on passage from Leith to Montevideo but had to be abandoned about 250 miles from the Brazilian coast on September 30 that year. Her crew were picked up and landed at Rio de Janeiro a few days later, on October 3.

---

*For some account of this rescue, see *The War With Cape Horn,* Alan Villiers (Hodder and Stoughton), pages 51-52.

Barque *Alice*; note very long poop and forecastle-head, typical of the bounty barques. (*National Maritime Museum.*)

French full-rigged ship *Amiral Cécille* alongside in a North American port. (*San Francisco Maritime Museum.*)

The *Amiral Cécille* has set all sail while towing to sea. Note her patent (stockless) anchors. (*Morrison Collection, San Francisco Maritime Museum.*)

Bidart – Steel barque, 2,199 g., 1,917 n.
September 1901: Completed by Chantiers Nantais de Constr. Maritimes,
Nantes, for Société Bayonnaise de Navigation, Bayonne.

When the barque arrived at Tacoma, Wash., on November 22 1906, 178
days from Glasgow, her master, Captain Pinsonnet, reported having lost one
man overboard, and every sail was torn to shreds in a storm. In May 1911
she was sold to Sté. des Voiliers Normands (Prentout-Leblond, Leroux &
Co., Mgrs.), Rouen. On her last passage in 1915, loaded with nickel ore
from New Caledonia for Glasgow, her crew was severely attacked by scurvy
and her master, Captain J. Blondel, decided to put into the Azores for
medical assistance. Approaching landfall the *Bidart* was caught in a gale
with misty weather, and without observations for three or four days the
barque's position became uncertain. With her crew reduced to the half by
illness the *Bidart* was not easy to manage though under little sail, and the
land was sighted too late to avoid. She was embayed, and stranded on Faja
Grande, Fayal, at dawn on May 24, 1915. Shortly after stranding, continuous
heavy seas caused her to break up and three men were lost.

Biessard – Steel barque, 2,701 g., 2,254 n.
June 27 1900: Launched by Chantiers de Normandie, Rouen, for Com-
pagnie Rouennaise de Transports Maritimes (Prentout-Leblond, Leroux &
Co., Mgrs.), Rouen.

Left Havre in ballast for Tchio (New Caledonia) February 3 1914, under
Captain Maréchal. She spent her entire life on this lengthy route, and after
30 wearying passages in 13 years she just disappeared.

Blanche – Iron ship, 1,528 g., 1,414 n.
1877: Built by A. M'Millan & Son, Dumbarton, for W. R. Price & Co.,
London, as *Tilkhurst*.

Joseph Conrad served on board as second mate for a time, under the
British flag. In June 1893 she was sold to A. D. Bordes and renamed *Blanche*.
March 1903, bought by G. Mortola fu G.B., Genoa. Under the Italian flag
her name *Blanche* was maintained until her end. At first she was in the
Pacific voyages, and changed hands during the war. About 1918 she was
converted into an auxiliary, and from 1919 until 1921 made voyages to
Philadelphia and Buenos Aires. In 1921 she was owned by Oleifici Nacion-
ali, Genoa. On November 12 1922 she arrived at Palermo 52 days out from
Havana, and laid up. The following year she was towed to Genoa for breaking up.

Blanche – Steel 4-masted barque, 3,104 g., 2,754 n.
November 29 1898: Launched by Chantiers de la Méditerranée, Havre,
for C. Brown & Corblet, Havre, as *Emilie Siegfried*.

F

Her owners ran her in the New Caledonia nickel ore trade and she made
several very good runs on this route, 74 and 95 days among others. In April
1909 she was bought by Compagnie Navale de l'Océanie, Havre, and renamed *Sainte Marguerite,* and in 1912 came under the ownership of A. D.
Bordes, then acquiring the new name of *Blanche.* Her end came in September 1917 on passage from La Pallice for Iquique in ballast, under the
command of Captain Bailleux. She was sunk by the German submarine
U-151 on September 19 in lat. 47° 10′N., long. 10° 35′W., after a gallant
action lasting two and a half hours, her resistance ceasing only when the
submarine drew right ahead where her guns could not bear. She was torpedoed and sank with Captain Bailleux and 17 of her crew. The 16 survivors, of whom three were wounded, were picked up in their boats four days
later by the French gunboat *Audacieuse* and landed at Rochefort on September 25.

Boiëldieu – Steel barque, 2,208 g., 1,981 n.
August 1902: Completed by Chantiers Nantais de Constr. Maritimes,
Nantes, for Compagnie de Navigation Française, Nantes.

She was transferred in 1904 to Société Nouvelle d'Armement, Nantes, which
became later the Sté. Générale d'Armement, Nantes. Left Sydney for the
Channel for orders on June 3 1904 under Captain Harang on an expensive
voyage. Her quadrant was broken in a storm three weeks later and four
different jury rudders were experimented with more or less successfully until
July 21. During all this time the *Boiëldieu* had been carried south to the
fifty-seventh degree of latitude. Steering north, the New Zealand coast was
sighted on August 8, off Pegasus Bay, and two days after she was picked up
25 miles from Lyttelton by the tug *Ki-Hama* and towed to Lyttelton for
£1,250 (which seems a large sum). The following year she caught fire at
Oakland, Calif., and her poop was badly damaged.

Further misadventures followed. While on a passage from New Orleans
to Nantes in 1919 she was stranded twice before leaving the Gulf of Mexico.
Raised after lighterage she was towed to Key West for repairs, and arrived
in the River Loire 63 days out from the Mississippi. On her last voyage the
Boiëldieu arrived at Granville on March 27 1921, with 3,200 tons of nitrate
from Chile. In May the same year she was the first French sailing-ship to
be laid up in the Canal de la Martinière, near Nantes, and she left this
berth in July 1927 to be broken up at Lorient.

Bon Premier – Steel barque, 1,352 g., 1,266 n.
1891: Built by Act. Ges. "Neptun", Rostock, for H. Mentz of Rostock, as
the *Frieda Mahn.*

She tramped the Seven Seas for many years until 1914, when she left Hamburg for Callao with coke late in July. On August 3 she was stopped and examined by a French vessel of the Calais submarine squadron, but was cleared to proceed to her destination. War began the next day, on August 8, and she was again intercepted off Cherbourg, by the French destroyer *Rapière* and taken to Cherbourg to become the first French war prize. She was renamed *Bon Premier* and given to the managership of Société Générale de Transports Maritimes à Vapeur, Marseilles, with Cherbourg as port of registry. Some three years later, in September 1917, on passage from Fort de France for Bordeaux, commanded by Captain Louis Bré, with a cargo of rum and logwood, she was captured by the German submarine *U-60* and sunk by gunfire in lat. 46° 06'N., long. 11° 25'W., about 220 miles off Cape Finisterre. Her crew were saved after a number of days in their boats.

Bonchamp – Steel barque, 2,193 g., 1,949 n.
May 10 1902: Launched by Chantiers de la Loire, St. Nazaire, for Cie. de Navigation Française, Nantes.

In her maiden voyage she made Iquique from Port Talbot in 95 days, but her return passage to Falmouth was 140 days. In 1904, she was transferred to Sté. Nouvelle d'Armement, Nantes (later Sté. Générale d'Armement, Nantes). She was a big carrier but slow. While on a passage from Port Pirie to Nantes in February 1920, with wheat (via Cape of Good Hope), she was thrown on her beam ends in a storm, in about lat. 27°S., long. 75°E. Several sails were lost and her boats smashed, but she arrived off the Loire 148 days out with no further trouble. Her last voyage was again to Australia, whence she reached St. Nazaire on May 24 1921 from Sydney (via Cape Horn) 134 days out, only to be discharged and laid up in the Canal de la Martiniére.

She was one of the few big barques recommissioned from here, when in September 1925, she was acquired by M. Potet, of Havre, for the West Indies trade. On her last voyage in this she left Calais July 11 1930 with 2,000 tons of cement for Guadeloupe and Martinique, trading in the islands from August 31 until October 3. Afterwards she left Fort de France for French Guiana, loading 1,000 tons logwood at St. Laurent du Maroni from December 3 until December 29 1930, and left the Maroni for Fort Liberty (Hayti) where she loaded 500 tons logwood from January 11 until January 29 1931. Then, after loading 1,100 tons logwood in Jamaica from February 2 until February 18, she sailed for France with a full cargo of 2,600 tons. Back at Havre after a nine months' voyage on April 4 1931, 45 days out, there was bad news for her crew. Her owner was insolvent, and that was the end of the *Bonchamp*. Put up to auction on July 31 at a cost of 30,000 francs, there was no sale. On April 8 1932 she was again put up to auction at the same cost, and sold. On June 7 1932 the old barque left Havre in tow for Bruges, where she was broken up.

Bonneveine – Steel barque (Jubilee rig), 2,617 g., 1,995 n.
September 1902: Completed by Chantiers de la Méditerranée, La Seyne, for Société Marseillaise de Voiliers, Marseilles.

She was sold to Cie. Havraise de Navigation (E. Corblet & Co., Mgrs.), Havre, in 1910. She was in the news a year later, when she was partially dismasted in the South Pacific in a hurricane, and was picked up by the British steamer *Myrtle Branch*, which towed her to Valparaiso. This was expensive salvage.

The *Bonneveine* was not a fast sailer, as typical passages indicate, such as Banana (Belgian Congo) to New York, 75 days in 1919; Cardiff to Port Louis (Mauritius), 88 days, 1921; Port Louis to Adelaide, 41 days same year; Port Lincoln to Falmouth for orders, 142 days, 1922.

Owing to the slump in shipping she was then laid up until 1925, when she was sold to M. Potet, Havre, for the West Indies and French Guiana trade. After four years of this, she sailed from Rotterdam on July 11 1929 with coal for Noumea and took 145 days for the passage to New Caledonia, where she was converted into a nickel ore hulk.

Bossuet – Steel barque (Jubilee rig), 2,204 g., 1,954 n.
January 13 1900: Launched by Chantiers de la Loire, Nantes, for R. Guillon & R. Fleury, Nantes.

She was sold to Sté. Nouvelle d'Armement (later Sté. Générale d'Armement), also of Nantes, eight years later.

She was at first in the California and Oregon grain trade, without incident or noteworthy passages. On August 15 1920 she arrived in the River Loire from Port Pirie, South Australia, 137 days out. Her last voyage to Australia was in 1920-21 when she arrived at Havre on May 22 1921, from Melbourne with wheat. She was then laid up in the Canal de la Martinière until March 12 1926 when she was bought by M. Potet, Havre, for the West Indies trade. Here she made average passages to Hayti, Jamaica, and the Black River for some years until 1929, when she was wrecked outward-bound from Dunkirk towards Fort de France, with cement, under Captain Olivier, in the autumn. On November 8 at 2.45 a.m., she missed stays and, being too near the French coast, went aground about two miles south of Cap Gris-Nez. Her crew were saved by fishermen but the barque drove high on the rocks where she rapidly became a total loss.

Bougainville – Steel barque, 2,248 g., 1,982 n.
July 20 1902: Launched by Chantiers Nantais de Constr. Maritimes, at Nantes, for Bureau Frères & Baillergeau of that port.
In November 1904, while on a passage from New York to New Zealand

laden with a dangerous cargo of case oil, her provision room caught fire near Tristan da Cunha where she anchored, and the fire was put out after several days hard and dangerous work.

The *Bougainville* was a good sailer; the following are some passages she is credited with:

1906:   Hobart to Iquique, 38 days.
1906:   Iquique to Sydney, 37 days.
1906:   Newcastle (N.S.W.) to Portland (Oreg.), 58 days.
1906-7: Portland (Oreg.) to Limerick, 116 days.
1908:   Cardiff to Wallaroo (Australia), 90 days.
1910:   Astoria to Queenstown, 120 days.
1910:   Port Talbot to Hobart, 79 days.
1910:   Hobart to Antofagasta, 41 days.

She became a war casualty in 1916 when, after a passage to Falmouth from San Francisco with wheat, she was ordered to Runcorn. Weighing anchor on February 12, she encountered continual westerly gales which delayed her until March 22. On this day the *Bougainville* was south of the Irish coast when the German submarine *U-70* gave the order to abandon ship immediately. As gunfire took too long to sink the barque, she was then torpedoed and sank. Captain Robert and his crew were rescued by a British trawler and landed in Ireland the following day.

Bougainville – Iron barque, 1,027 g., 976 n.
1863: Built by Pile, Hay & Co., Sunderland.

This is a famous ship which, in fact, was owned by Shaw Savill and Co. (as the *Himalaya*) from 1865 until 1897 and only in her very last years, much later, became French. Between 1865 and 1897, she made 24 round voyages to New Zealand carrying many thousands of emigrants, continuing as a successful passenger-ship until long after steamships had almost entirely taken over the passenger service in the Australian trade. The stout old iron ship was far from worn out when she was sold to Valparaiso in 1897, and later became the *Star of Peru* of the Alaska Packers' fleet of hard-working salmon-packing-accommodation ships, based on San Francisco. These ships made an annual voyage between the Californian port and Alaskan waters.

In 1926, the robust iron hull was still in good condition when she was sold to French owners, the Comptoirs Français des Nouvelles Hebrides, of Noumea, to become a storage hulk at that port. First, renamed *Bougainville,* she loaded lumber in Vancouver for the Fiji Islands, which she delivered safely. Going on to Noumea she was rigged down, then 63 years old. She was still usefully employed as a storage hulk at Noumea until the Second World War reached New Caledonia: in 1972 something of her is still there, well over a century since she went down the ways.

Bourbaki – Steel barque, 2,208 g., 1,957 n.
August 1898: Completed by Chantiers de la Loire, Nantes, for Sté. des Voiliers Nantais, Nantes.

Sold to Sté. Nouvelle d'Armement, Nantes, in 1908 for 150,000 francs. She had a narrow escape in April 1916 while bound from Oregon to Ipswich with barley. She struck a mine in the North Sea but, despite heavy damage to her collision bulkhead, she managed to reach Ipswich, where she was unloaded and repaired. On January 25 1919 she arrived at New York from Grand Bassam; on her return passage she made an excellent run of 14 days between Nantucket and the River Loire. In 1919-20 she made a voyage to Australia, returning Nantes with wheat in 118 days from Geelong. On her last voyage, the *Bourbaki* arrived at Tocopilla from Newcastle (N.S.W.) on January 28 1921. Leaving Chile for Ostend on March 15, she passed Prawle Point on July 17, 124 days out. That September she was laid up in the Canal de la Martinière, which she left again on September 6 1926 for breaking up, but she was converted into a barge and foundered in a gale on December 19 1938 in Quiberon Bay.

Brenn – Steel barque, 2,187 g., 1,950 n.
March 17 1900: Launched by Chantiers de la Loire, St. Nazaire, for Cie. Celtique Maritime, Nantes.

1909: Sold to Cie. Navale de l'Océanie, Paris. A. D. Bordes bought her in 1912, retaining her original name, until January 14 1917, when she left La Pallice in ballast for Taltal for orders, under Captain F. Bernot, only to be captured two days later in the Bay of Biscay by the German submarine *U-59*. After pillage of her stores the unarmed barque was sunk by bombs and gunfire. Her crew landed safely on the Spanish coast near Vivero, after three days in the boats.

Story of the *Bretagne*

There were two large steel barques named *Bretagne,* the first lost very early in her career, the second much longer lived and distinguished by the fact that, as he served a voyage aboard her, Henri Picard has made a special study of her career. As this is now a unique record of the career of such a vessel, it follows here in full, preceded by the very brief summary of the short career of her predecessor.

Bretagne – Steel barque, 2,064 g., 1,567 n.
September 16 1898: Launched by A. Dubigeon, Nantes, for Raoul Guillon, Nantes.

Her maiden voyage was made with coal for San Francisco, returning to
Antwerp with wheat. On her second voyage, sailing from Antwerp on April
5 1900 for San Francisco with cement, Captain Guillon in command, the
Bretagne struggled for six weeks to round Cape Horn, but having had her
rudder quadrant broken, was disabled and leaking badly. On August 26
1900 a gallant rescue of her crew and masterpiece of seamanship was
effected in heavy weather by the master of the British full-rigged ship
Maxwell (bound from Iquique for Shields), and the water-logged barque
was abandoned sinking off Cape Horn. The crew were landed at Calais by
the *Maxwell* on October 29 1900.

Bretagne – Steel barque, 2,197 g., 1,914 n., 3,100 tons deadweight.
Length 227', breadth 40' 4", depth 22' 5", poop 52', forecastle 39'. Signal
letters: H.N.P.J.

She was built to the order of Raoul Guillon & Co., Nantes, in place of his
barque of the same name lost off Cape Horn. Launched on September 27
1901 by Chantiers Nantais de Constructions Maritimes, Nantes, she was
completed in October.

Maiden Voyage (Commander: Captain Canevet)

On November 7 1901 she left St. Nazaire roads in tow of the British tug
Flying Eagle for Barry to load coal. Two other new barques left St. Nazaire
on the same day, the *Gael* for Cardiff, and the *Alice Marie* also for Barry
and Table Bay.

November 9	: Arrived Barry: left December 1 for Table Bay.
December 9	: Put into St. Nazaire with her main-mast cap damaged.
December 23	: Left St. Nazaire repaired.
January 18 1902	: Spoken 187 miles S., 65°W of Lisbon by the British liner *Suevic,* with her foretopgallant and fore-topmast carried away at topmast cap, and hanging. Everything intact on main and mizzen. Steering about east-north-east; foresail, two jibs and everything on main set. Asked for longitude check.
January 25	: Towed into Lisbon for repairs: cost 12,000 francs.
March 20	: Sailed Lisbon May 21, arrived Table Bay, 62 days out (171 days from Barry).
July 22	: Left Table Bay.
September 5	: Arrived Hobart, 45 days out: left September 10.
November 14	: Arrived Tacoma, 65 days from Hobart.
December 30	: Sailed Seattle.
May 17 1903	: Spoken in lat. 36°N., long. 39°W.

June 1 1903   : Arrived Falmouth, 152 days out.
June 13   : Arrived Limerick.

This 19 months' long voyage was not satisfactory and, probably dissatisfied with it, her owners sold the *Bretagne* to Louis Levesque & Co., Nantes. She seemed slow, and could have been imperfect aloft at the time.

Second Voyage (Commander: Captain Ferlicot)

September 5 1903: Left Limerick.
September 8   : Spoken in lat. 46°N., long. 7°W.
October 12   : Arrived Philadelphia, 36 days out.
November 13   : Sailed Philadelphia.
November 15   : Spoken in lat. 38°N., long. 71°W.
March 1 1904   : Arrived Hobart, 108 days out: left March 5.
May 3   : Arrived Kobe, 59 days from Tasmania.
June 11   : Sailed Kobe.
Early November   : Called at Taltal for orders.
November 7   : At Antofagasta, 149 days from Kobe.
November 16   : At Pisagua.
December 28   : Left Pisagua.
May 14 1905   : Spoken in lat. 14° 43′N., long. 26°W.
May 27   : Left Falmouth: possibly touched only, for orders.
May 30   : Arrived Dunkirk, 153 days from Pisagua.

Third Voyage (Commander: Captain Jean Henry)

July 5 1905   : Left Dunkirk.
July 9   : Spoken in lat. 48°N., long. 6°W.
July 23   : Spoken in lat. 19°N., long. 21°W.
September 26   : Arrived Hobart, 83 days out: sailed September 28.
November 19   : Arrived Honolulu, 52 days from Hobart: sailed same day.
December 3   : Arrived Portland (Oreg.), 14 days from Honolulu.
January 7 1906   : Sailed Portland.
January 10   : Left Astoria.
May 16   : Arrived Falmouth, 126 days out: sailed May 20.
May 23   : Arrived Antwerp.

Fourth Voyage (Commander: Captain J. Henry)

August 12 1906   : Left Antwerp.
October 4   : Spoken in lat. 34°S., long. 47°W.
December 22   : Arrived San Francisco (via Cape Horn), 131 days from Zeebrugge.

March 14 1907   : Left San Francisco with grain.
July 21   : Off Falmouth, 129 days out.
July 28   : Arrived Ipswich, week from Falmouth.

Fifth Voyage (Commander: Captain J. Henry)

August 18 1907   : Left Ipswich.
September 10   : Sailed North Shields: touched at Brest September 16.
September 17   : Left Brest.
December 14   : Arrived Hobart, 88 days from Brest. Left Hobart December 16.
February 23 1908: Arrived San Francisco, 69 days.
April 2   : Sailed San Francisco.
April 20   : Arrived Astoria, 18 days from San Francisco.
May 19   : Left Portland (Oreg.).
May 22   : Left Astoria.
June 25   : When 7 miles off Pitcairn Island, a sudden squall wrecked foretopgallant and royal masts, and blew away several sails. The *Bretagne* was thrown on her beam ends. The first mate, Emile Thebaud of Nantes, aged 41, washed overboard and drowned. No one saw him go while heavy seas were constantly coming aboard.
September 5   : Spoken in lat. 34°N., long. 30°W.
September 21   : Passed Dungeness, 122 days out.
September 23   : Arrived Ipswich.

Sixth Voyage (Commander: Captain J. Henry)

October 19 1908 : Left Ipswich, under Captain Jouanjean, ship's husband, for North Shields.
November 4   : Sailed North Shields, under Captain Henry.
November 8   : Passed Dover.
November 14   : Spoken in lat. 44°N., long. 9°W.
January 22 1909 : Arrived Hobart, 75 days out from Dover: left January 24.
April 6   : Arrived San Francisco, 72 days from Hobart.
June 16   : Sailed San Francisco for Italy.
November 21   : Passed Cape Camarat, 158 days (not reported when passing Gibraltar).
November 25   : Arrived Savona.

Seventh Voyage (Commander: Captain J. Henry)

March 10 1910   : Left Savona for Genoa, which she left March 19.

March 29 1910   : Passed Tarifa.
June 17   : Arrived Newcastle (N.S.W.), 80 days from Tarifa.
August 10   : Sailed Newcastle.
October 27   : Arrived San Francisco, 78 days.
December 15   : Left San Francisco.
February 10 1911: Off Cape Horn.
April 17   : The *Bretagne* experienced very bad weather in lat. 47°
                      58′N., long. 22° 36′ W., and she was thrown on her
                      beam ends through part of cargo shifting; several sails
                      cut away.
April 22   : Off Falmouth, 128 days out.
April 25   : Arrived Harwich.

Eighth Voyage (Commander: Captain J. Henry)

May 16 1911   : Left Harwich.
June 14   : Sailed North Shields.
September 11   : Arrived Hobart, 88 days from Walmer: left 14th.
November 14   : Arrived Astoria, 61 days from Hobart.
December 21   : Sailed Portland (Oreg.).
December 31   : Left Astoria.
May 2 1912   : Arrived Queenstown, 123 days out: ordered to Belfast.

Ninth Voyage (Commander: Captain J. Henry)

May 25 1912   : Sailed Belfast for Port Talbot.
June 29   : Left Port Talbot.
October 19   : Arrived Iquique, 112 days out.
December 22   : Sailed Iquique.
April 14 1913   : Arrived Falmouth, 113 days out, ordered to Hamburg,
                      reached in 5 days.

Tenth Voyage (Commander: Captain Henri Lelièvre)

June 13 1913   : Sailed Hamburg.
June 14   : Left Cuxhaven.
June 24   : Spoken in lat. 43°N., long. 10°W.
July 14   : Spoken in lat. 14° 14′N., long. 25°W.
November 7   : Arrived Honolulu, 144 days from Dungeness.

The cabin boy of the *Bretagne* deserted and stowed away aboard the small
British steamer *Kestrel* of Ottawa, bound for Fanning Island, but as she was
short of a fireman, the cabin boy was assigned to stoking, which he regretted,
for this was a very hard life compared with his duties in the cabin of the
barque.

December 9 1913 : Sailed Honolulu with 1,200 tons rock ballast.

December 26   : Arrived in Columbia River, 17 days.

December 28   : Arrived Portland (Oreg.). While in port all the crew deserted except master, officers and cook.

February 2 1914 : Left Portland with 114,515 bushels barley, valued at $74,200, and 18,715 bushels wheat, valued at $16,850.

May 4   : Spoken in lat. 3°N., long. 30°W.

June 13   : Passed the Lizard, 131 days out.

June 19   : Arrived Ipswich, 137 days.

Eleventh Voyage (Commander: Captain Abel Chevalier)

(After the desertions, which were unusual in a French ship, one wonders whether the master had been replaced.)

July 18 1914   : Left Ipswich.

July 20   : Arrived Rotterdam.

October 20   : Sailed Rotterdam.

October 26   : Arrived Barry: left December 9.

March 3 1915   : Arrived Fremantle, 84 days out.

March 20   : Sailed Fremantle.

March 29   : Arrived Adelaide, 9 days.

May 4   : Left Adelaide for Newcastle (N.S.W.) in ballast, and passed Bass Strait 6 days later. She was delayed by head winds south of Cape Howe for several days, then caught off Cape Howe in a storm in which several sails were lost. The sand ballast shifted causing a list of 33 degrees. Experienced seamen were uncommon then owing to the war, and the crew clamoured to abandon ship. With only a handful of determined men aboard and the drifting barque near to capsize in a mountainous sea, Captain Chevalier managed to reach a position 25 miles south of Newcastle where the *Bretagne* was picked up by a tug and towed to port, 17 days from Adelaide. Repairs took more than two months.

August 5   : Left Newcastle.

October 5   : Arrived Taltal, 61 days out.

November 19   : Sailed Taltal.

March 1 1916   : Arriving off the entrance to the English Channel in 103 days, she was then delayed by strong head winds for 18 days. Submarines were very bad, but she safely reached Le Havre on March 19, 121 days out from Chile.

Twelfth Voyage (Commander: Captain A. Chevalier)

May 5 1916   : Left Havre.
May 13   : Arrived Liverpool, 8 days.
June 29   : Sailed Garston for New Caledonia.
November 3   : Arrived Noumea, 127 days: left December 16.
May 15 1917   : Arrived Nantes, 150 days.

Thirteenth Voyage (Commander: Captain A. Chevalier)

By June 1917 it was the peak of the German submarine campaign and nearly all merchant vessels were armed. Two 90 millimetre guns were fitted on the poop of the *Bretagne* and a brand-new wireless set installed aboard. Six gunners and a telegraphist of the French Navy were embarked at Nantes. On July 23 1917 she left Nantes for St. Nazaire.

After target practice the barque anchored in St. Nazaire roads for 41 days owing to submarines, and waiting for good wind.

September 3 1917: Sailed in company with a French barque bound for Melbourne and a large U.S. schooner bound for New York. The three sailing-ships were convoyed to Belle-Ile by armed steam-trawlers.
December 13   : Arrived Sydney, 101 days out.

Fourteenth Voyage (Commander: Captain A. Chevalier)

January 24 1918 : Like many other French sailing vessels the *Bretagne* was then chartered by the U.S. Government.
February 23   : Left Sydney.
June 1   : Arrived San Francisco, 98 days out.
July 10   : Sailed San Francisco.
September 12   : Arrived Sydney, 64 days.
October 22   : Left Sydney.
December 30   : Arrived San Francisco, 69 days, where she waited about three months for a grain cargo.
March 31 1919   : Sailed San Francisco.
August 22   : Arrived Ipswich, 145 days.

Fifteenth Voyage (Commander: Captain A. Chevalier)

November 9 1919: Sailed Ipswich.
December 5   : Passed Fernando Noronha.
February 5 1920 : Arrived Taltal, 86 days from Dungeness.
February 26   : Left Taltal.
June 19   : Passed Dungeness, 114 days out.
June 20   : Arrived Ostend.

Sixteenth Voyage (Commander: Captain A. Chevalier)
Mate: P. Grouhel; Second mate: J-B. Bruneau; Apprentice: H. Picard.

July 31 1920 : Left Ostend.
August 2 : Arrived Antwerp.
September 1 : Sailed Antwerp in ballast.
October 25 : Crossed the Equator, 45 days from the Lizard.
November 17 : "I remember that day. In the morning the barque was scudding before a furious storm in lat. 44° 26'S., long. 17°E., foggy and rainy weather when, about 10 a.m., the Captain observed suddenly that we were steering towards a capsized big iceberg. Collision was avoided only by a few yards after a swift manoeuvre. In the afternoon it blew a hurricane, and in a sudden veering of the wind from north-west to south-west, the barque falling off the wind was thrown on her beam ends through her sand ballast shifting. All our efforts to bear away were useless, and the foresail and the two lower topsails were lost in the twinkling of an eye and furled sails torn from their yards. After exhausting work in the hold and aloft the *Bretagne* was straightened again in 72 hours." (Loss of sails was estimated at a cost of 50,000 francs.)
December 24 : Arrived Newcastle (N.S.W.), 105 days from the Lizard.
February 21 1921: Left Newcastle with coal.
April 5 : Spoke French barque *Bourbaki,* bound from Tocopilla to Channel for orders.
April 20 : Arrived Antofagasta, 59 days. Two months here discharging coal and loading nitrate.
June 10 : Left Antofagasta.
June 27 : Starboard life-boat crushed by a sea (lat. 49° 41'S., long. 80° 02'W.).
June 30 : Fore upper-topsail lost and foresail damaged (lat. 49° 54'S., long. 81° 43'W.).
July 8 : Off Cape Horn, strong squalls with hail and snow, starboard boat crushed by a sea, and fore lower topgallant sail lost.
August 11 : Crossed the Line.
September 14 until
    September 24 : Becalmed near Azores.
October 6 1921 : Off Wolf Rock, 118 days out.
October 9 (6 a.m.): Arrived Falmouth 121 days from Antofagasta.
October 11 : Left Falmouth.
October 17 : Arrived in River Gironde under sail: beating all day.

		At 5 p.m. clewed up all sails for the last time and anchored near Royan.
October 19 1921	:	In tow of the tug *Gallus* in River Gironde, stranded near Blaye, heavy list to port.
October 20	:	Freed by four tugs; arrived Bordeaux in the evening, 9 days from Falmouth.

During this 14 months' voyage the barque had been under sail for 294 days. October 22 1921, the *Bretagne* was laid up in Bordeaux in the big slump, with a number of other sailing vessels, including the old colonial clipper *Tamar*. The *Bretagne* was idle at Bordeaux until November 1922, when she was sold to H. H. Schmidt of Hamburg and renamed *Wilhelmine*.

Looking back in 1971, M. Picard writes: "This voyage of fourteen months made an unforgettable impression on me, and I look upon this period of my life as the most happy one. I lived among the sailing-ship men with pleasure, and found them a fine breed. It was good to have lived in such times and know such ships!"

Seventeenth Voyage
(Commanders: Captain Meyer, later Captain O. F. Borgwardt)

December 17 1922	:	Left Bordeaux in ballast under Captain Meyer: anchored off Le Verdon (mouth of River Gironde) owing to storms in Biscay.
January 2 1923	:	Sailed Le Verdon.
April 14	:	Arrived Callao, via Cape Horn, 102 days out.
May 16	:	Left Callao for Chinchas islands (no report of an arrival or sailing Chinchas islands): loaded guano.
August 11	:	Arrived Callao to clear ship.
August 14	:	Sailed Callao for New York, via Panama Canal.
September 6	:	Arrived Panama, 23 days: clear of Canal September 11.
October 25	:	Arrived New York, 44 days. Captain Meyer left.
January 3 1924	:	Sailed New York, under Captain O. F. Borgwardt: coal ballast.
February 21	:	Arrived Hamburg, 49 days out.

Eighteenth (and last) Voyage
(Commanders: Captain O. Heinatz, later Captain F. Dutack)

May 8 1924	:	Left Hamburg for Iquique: Captain O. Heinatz.
May 14	:	Put into Cuxhaven, ballast coal heating.
May 16	:	Arrived Hamburg to discharge ballast. Captain O. Heinatz landed, injured by an accident in the North Sea.

May 24 1924	:	Sailed Hamburg for Iquique with new ballast; Captain F. Dutack.
July 4	:	Spoken in lat. 0° 59′S., long. 31° 26′W.
July 13	:	Spoken in lat. 3° 59′S., long. 34° 36′W.
September 8	:	Put into Cabedello (Brazil), 107 days out.

Captain Dutack seemed to be an inexperienced sailing-ship master and did not succeed in rounding Cape San Roque—although he would not be the only master who failed to weather this Cape. The *Bretagne* was not good to windward in ballast trim, and the bottom was foul. The *Wilhelmine's* charter for nitrates was cancelled and she went to Australia for grain.

September 24	:	Left Cabedello for Cape Borda for orders.
September 30	:	Spoken in lat. 3° 30′S., long. 32° 30′W.
End November	:	Arrived Port Adelaide.
December 6	:	Arrived Port Pirie, 73 days from Cabedello.
January 17 1925	:	Left Port Pirie for U.K./Continent with grain.
February 23	:	Having encountered very bad weather, discovered ten inches of water in the hold: altered course for Talcahuano.
March 16	:	Put into Talcahuano, 58 days out.

Found 12 inches of water in after hold and 250 tons of cargo damaged. Pumped out March 17 and 300 tons damaged cargo plus 750 tons undamaged discharged by April 16. Several rivets found to be loose and some damage to rudder and to hull below waterline. Drydocked: and hull in poor condition.

July 28	:	Sailed Talcahuano for Iquique in ballast. (Cargo presumably sold.)
August 6	:	Arrived Iquique, 9 days.
September 4	:	Left Iquique, with nitrate cargo.
December 9	:	Passed the Lizard, 96 days out via Cape Horn.
December 14	:	Arrived Delfzijl.
March 11 1926	:	Left Delfzijl for Bremerhaven in tow.

She was afterwards broken up at Blumenthal, north of Bremen. So ended the long life of a good ship which rounded Cape Horn 20 times.

The maiden voyage and the last voyage of the barque were equally unsuccessful and took 19 months each. She was thrown on her beam ends at least four times during her career, as far as I know. She was not at all a "flyer" such as many Bordes ships were, but only a good *"navire de compagnie"*, as we said in those vanished days.

There was yet another *Bretagne,* an iron barque of 1,049 g., 977 n. tons,

built by Williamson & Co., Harrington, U.K.. in 1872 for Peter Iredale &
Co., Liverpool, as *Ada Iredale*. She survived her share of accidents under
three flags—British, American and French—over half a century. On October 15 1876, while bound from Ardrossan towards San Francisco with coal,
she caught fire and was abandoned by her crew about 2,000 miles east of
the Marquesas Islands. Her master, Captain Lenton, with his wife and the
crew, spent several weeks in their boats before arriving at San Francisco.
The barque was written off and paid for as a total loss. After an eight-
months' drift unseen in the Pacific, she was found by a French cruiser and
towed into Papeete, Tahiti, arriving on June 9 1877. Her coal cargo was
still smouldering, her masts and iron-wire rigging lay a snakish mess fes-
tooned around her, but the hull was still tolerably sound. The coal smoul-
dered on until May of the following year, when the *Ada Iredale* was sold
"as is" to Captain I. E. Thayer of San Francisco. Using local labour, he
took on the immense task of re-riveting over 100 plates, straightening out
twisted frames and deck beams, and laying completely new decks. That
done, he re-rigged her and sailed her to San Francisco where he sold her
to Crawford & Co., who renamed her *Annie Johnson* and put her in the
Cape Horn trade, which was good at the time. Here she made at least 13
voyages and is credited with a run from the Golden Gate to off Diamond
Head in 8 days 9 hours, in 1903. She must have been an excellent sailer
as well as a very strong and well-built vessel. She appears in Lloyd's Register
for 1914-15 under the Johnson name, ex-*Ada Iredale,* but by that time
rigged as a 4-masted schooner, owned by the Matson Nav. Co. The change
of rig was made in 1912. In 1921 she appears in the Register as an auxiliary
4-masted schooner, and in 1926 she was sold by the Matson Nav. Co. to
Captain L. Ozanne, Papeete, who gave her the name *Bretagne.* Under Captain Ozanne she was in the Pacific French Islands subsidised trade, with two
voyages a year between Tahiti and San Francisco.

On October 4 1929, when she was 57 years old, she sprang a leak, was
abandoned, and sank south of Cape Flattery, Oregon, when on passage from
British Columbia to Suva with a cargo of canned salmon and lumber. The
master, his family and crew were picked up by the U.S. steamer *Whitney
Olson* and landed at San Francisco. This time the old *Ada Iredale* really
had gone.

Two last "Bs" complete this section. First is the *Brizeux,* a steel barque
of 2,197 g., 1,963 n. tons.
January 21 1901: Launched by Chantiers de la Loire, St. Nazaire, for the
Sté. Bretonne de Navigation, Nantes.
She was a good sailer, on her maiden voyage reaching Europe from San
Francisco in the creditable time of 107 days. She was sold to Sté. des Voiliers,
Dunkerquois, Dunkirk, in October 1902, and was chiefly in the North

The beautiful barque *Alexandre* is about to be sunk: a photograph taken from a First World War U-boat. (*Dr. Jürgen Meyer Collection, Hamburg.*)

The big French square-riggers had distinctive sail-plans—the *Boiëldieu* of Nantes shows hers off well near the Lizard. (*James Randall.*)

Pacific grain trade to North Europe. The First World War claimed her, when on passage in late 1916 from Havre to Buenos Aires, with Captain Louis Bourgneuf in command and Monsieur Chasseboeuf as first mate.

In the morning of October 21 1916, the unarmed barque was captured by the German submarine *U-B-18* about 12 miles north-north-west of the Casquets, and sunk by bombs and gunfire. Her crew were saved by a Dutch steamer and landed in a British port. Captain Louis Bourgneuf was a competent ship-master, and when he left sailing-ships had been 23 times round Cape Horn. Long since retired in Brittany, he was still alive and well in 1971, aged 94.

Last is the *Buffon*, a steel barque, 2,609 g., 1,972 n. tons.

July 11 1902: Launched by Chantiers de la Loire, Nantes, for Cie. Maritime Française, Nantes.

Sold in 1913 to Sté. Générale d'Armement, Nantes. She never made very good passages and was rather a slow-coach. A typical passage:

March 9 1919 : Arrived San Francisco from Melbourne.
April 29   : Left San Francisco for Nantes with flour in bags.
July 26   : Off Cape Horn.
October 27   : Arrived off River Loire, 181 days out.

On March 28 1921, she passed the Lizard for the last time, bound from Portland (Oreg.) to Bordeaux with wheat. On May 26 of that year she was laid up in the Canal de la Martinière. There she stayed until February 15 1927, when she left, only to be broken up.

Cambronne – Steel barque, 1,863 g., 1,633 n.

1896: Launched by Laporte & Co., Rouen, for Sté. des Voiliers Nantais.

Her best voyages were from Astoria to Falmouth in 116 days during 1902-3, and from Antwerp to Puget Sound in 128 days (first passage, passed the Lizard on January 28 1903 in 116 days, while the British 4-masted barque *Semantha* passed the Scillies on the same day, also from Astoria, 115 days out).

April 13 1905: Arrived Queenstown 153 days out from Astoria— the slowest passage of the grain fleet that year.

1907: Bought by A. D. Bordes, and retained her original name.

December 28 1916: Left Antofagasta for France, commanded by Captain A. Mathieu.

March 21 1917: In lat. 20°10′S., long. 28°05′W., she met the German raider *Seeadler* but was not destroyed, as the latter was packed with crews of captured ships. To rid his vessel of them, von Luckner's prisoners—263—were placed aboard the unarmed *Cambronne*, which had been well provisioned. The barque's topgallant masts were sawn off, and all spare sails and spars thrown overboard, so that with only her lower sails she could not make port

G

in a hurry. With a British master in command—Captain John Mullen of the late four-masted barque *Pinmore*—she was ordered to shape course for Rio de Janeiro.

March 30 1917: Arrived Rio and disembarked her "guests", when Captain Mathieu recovered his command.

April 14 1917: Left Rio for Nantes.

July 8 1917: The *Cambronne* was captured by the German submarine *U-C-72* in 47°35′N., 10°W., and sunk by bombs and gunfire. On July 10 her crew landed at Sein Island, but a wounded man died in the boat.

Cannebière – Steel barque, 2,454 g., 1,983 n.

May 26 1900: Launched by Chantiers de la Loire, Nantes, for the Sté. Marseillaise de Voiliers, Marseilles.

Captain A. Lefeuvre took the barque from the stocks and left Nantes for New Caledonia at the end of August 1900, arriving at Noumea 100 days out. On her return passage the *Cannebiére* arrived at Havre in 100 days again, on May 7 1901. In 1902 she made Fremantle from Barry in 84 days.

March 15 1905, bound from Glasgow to New Caledonia with coal, she stranded and sank on the bar of Dundrum Bay (Ireland). Her crew were saved with the exception of the cook. A salvage agreement was subsequently established on a "no cure no pay" basis for £3,000.

May 21: the *Cannebière* was refloated and beached on a sandy bottom for temporary repairs.

May 24 1905: Towed to Belfast, and drydocked from June 5 until June 19. She resumed her voyage several days later.

May 1910: Sold to Compagnie Havraise de Navigation (E. Corblet & Co., Mgrs.), Havre.

April 1916: Left Havre for Buenos Aires.

October 24 1916: While on her return passage from Buenos Aires to Havre, under Captain Rihouet, she was sunk by the German submarine *U-B-18,* 20 miles south-south-west of Bishop's Rock.

Canrobert – Steel barque, 1,789 g., 1,594 n.

March 1897: Completed by Laporte & Co., Rouen, for Sté. des Voiliers Nantais, Nantes.

Here are a few lines from her maiden voyage log: "June 4 1897: Noon posion 19°38′S., 37°05′W. In company with the beautiful British 4-masted barque *Queen Margaret,* 35 days out from Barry Dock. Kept neck and neck with us all day. The Englishman passed us the following morning." The *Canrobert* was not a "flyer" like the *Queen Margaret*. In 1908 she was sold to Actieselsk. "Glitre" (O. Gotaas & Co.), of Christiana, Norway, and renamed *Glitre.*

1923 : Bought by H. Diederichsen, Kiel.
1926 : Broken up at Hamburg.

Cap Horn – Steel 4-masted barque, 2,675 g., 2,492 n.
1888 : Built by Russell & Co., Port Glasgow, for A. D. Bordes.

She was the first steel four-poster built for them, and had a capacity of 601 tons of water in her cellular double-bottom and another 1,200 tons in tanks. Despite the idea that use of water ballast was somewhat dangerous for sailing-ships, the *Cap Horn* is said to have been the first sailing vessel to round Cape Horn depending solely on water ballast for stability. She had other troubles, though she proved a good ship in general. On February 7 1892, arriving from Iquique with nitrate, she grounded in a fog near Calais, but was refloated without aid. Again, on January 28 1910, she collided at the mouth of the River Elbe with the German steamer *Heinrich Horn,* cutting off the steamer's funnel and mainmast with her bowsprit, which had to be replaced at Hamburg. July 3 1919: Left Antofagasta for La Pallice with 4,200 tons nitrate.
November 1919: Posted overdue: reinsured twice, but eventually turned up at La Pallice on November 29, 149 days out—a very long passage. In 1923 she was broken up in Belgium.

Carmen – Iron 4-masted barque, 1,716 g., 1,612 n. Later *Nemrac.*
1877: Built at Barclay, Curle & Co., Glasgow, for R. & J. Craig, Glasgow, as *County of Inverness.*

Was one of the famous Craig's "Counties" until the end of the century, at first ship-rigged, altered to 4-masted barque in the early 1900s.

April 28 1899	: Arrived Dundee from Chittagong with jute, 105 days out, her last voyage for R. & J. Craig: acquired by Shaw, Savill & Co., Glasgow.
1911	: Sold by Shaw, Savill for £2,250; hulked at Buenos Aires, named *Dora* (Argentine flag).
1916	: Rerigged and refitted for £5,000. Sold to R. Boussac, Bordeaux, for £30,000 and renamed *Carmen.*
1917	: Owned by Société d'Importation du Nord et de l'Est (Ramet), Bordeaux.
1920	: Converted to a steamer.
1921	: She appears as the S.S. *Carmen* owned by Compagnie Franco-Atlantique de Transports, Bordeaux.
1925	: Sold to Esthonian interests, renamed *Nemrac.*
1940	: Bought by Soc. Anon. Emanuele V. Parodi, Genoa: renamed *Amicizia.*

| April 10 1945 | : Sunk in an air-raid at Hamburg. |
| 1947 | : Refloated: broken up. |

Caroline – Steel 4-masted barque, 3,026 g., 2,392 n.
November 1895: Completed by Chantiers de la Loire, Nantes, she was one of the first French-built sailing ships for A. D. Bordes Co.

August 12 1900	: Left Dunkirk commanded by Captain Louvet.
October 24	: Arrived Iquique, 73 days out.
November 3	: Sailed Iquique.
January 16 1901	: Arrived Dunkirk, 74 days.

It seems that this five months and seven days' round voyage was the shortest ever made to Chile by a French sailing vessel.
September 3 1901: While on a passage from Iquique to Dunkirk, stranded in foggy weather on Magdalena Point, west coast of Pico Island (Azores), and lost. Crew saved.

Caroline – Steel 4-masted barque, 2,309 g., 2,131 n.
1891: Built by Richardson, Duck & Co., Stockton, for "Muskoka" Ship & Co. (F. C. McMahon), Windsor, N.S., as *Muskoka,* with typical down-easter rig of short hoisting single topgallantsails, royals, and skysails.

She was perhaps the fastest modern steel sailing-ship ever built; sailed by her noted Blue-nose skipper, Albert Crowe. Among other smart passages she made Cardiff to Hong Kong in 85 days and from Oregon and California to the Channel in 99 and 96 days.

June 1909: Bought by A. D. Bordes, renamed *Caroline.* The following are her best passages under the French flag:

1912	: Iquique to La Pallice, 91 days (Captain Gautier).
1912-13:	Port Talbot to Iquique, 87 days (Captain Le Mentec).
1916	: Nantes to Taltal, 69 days, and St. Nazaire to Antofagasta, 70 days (Captain Langhetee).

The *Caroline* survived the war, but she had fire in her cargo of coal on July 18 1920, in Antofagasta Bay, and became a total loss.

Cassard – Steel barque, 2,289 g., 1,719 n.
June 1899: Completed by Chantiers de la Loire, St. Nazaire, for Sté. des Armateurs Nantais, Nantes.

On her maiden voyage she left Nantes in July 1899 for Swansea, arriving at San Francisco on January 2 1900, and at Antwerp in July 1900 with grain. Amount of freights 174,527 francs; to this the navigation bounty 103,113 francs must be added. Her following passage from Antwerp to Astoria was made in 120 days.

May 20 1906: While bound from Sydney towards Falmouth with wheat, after rounding Cape Horn, she encountered a strong east-north-easterly gale with foggy weather and was wrecked on Bleaker Island (Falklands). Captain Lemoine and his crew were saved. On June 29 the wreck was sold for £99.

Cerro Alegre – Iron ship, 1,592 g., 1,436 n.

1883: Built by R. Duncan & Co., Port Glasgow, for the "Skelmorlie" S.Co. (T. O. Hunter & Co.), Greenock, as *Skelmorlie*.

Sold July 1894 to A. D. Bordes and renamed *Cerro Alegre*.

1914: Bought by Chilean interests, renamed *Puerto Montt*.

1917: Sold to Rederiaktieb. Othalia (H. Stenberg, Mgr.), Helsingborg, Sweden, and renamed *Transocean,* one of several ships of that name.

1924: Broken up.

We come now to another well-known and well-documented sailing-ship, the *Champigny,* a steel 4-masted barque of 3,112 g., 2,728 n. tons, completed June 1902 by Chantiers de la Méditerranée, Havre, for the Société des Long Courriers Français of that port, and in 1972 is still in existence. She was a typically French-built vessel with a forecastle which came well abaft the foremast and a poop 115 feet long, and modern rig. Her first master was the well-known Captain Jacques Boju, who was succeeded by Captains Castex, Guerguin, Gicquel, Noël, Couédel, Malbert and Sevin.

The following is a record of her career:

Maiden Voyage

June 18 1902	: Sailed Havre.
June 21	: Arrived Penarth: sailed August 1.
December 10	: Arrived Honolulu, 131 days: sailed December 20.
January 10 1903	: Arrived San Francisco, 21 days.
February 25	: Sailed San Francisco.
May 11	: Arrived Melbourne, 75 days: sailed July 5.
July 9	: Arrived Newcastle (N.S.W.): sailed August 11.
October 13	: Arrived San Francisco, 63 days.
November 24	: Sailed San Francisco.
March 23 1904	: Arrived Swansea, 120 days.

Second Voyage

May 4 1904	: Sailed Swansea (in tow).
May 8	: Arrived Brest.

May 12 1904 : Sailed Brest. She was weathering the Horn from July 14 to August 15, winter weeks.

October 9 : Arrived San Francisco, 150 days: sailed November 24.

January 23 1905 : Arrived Sydney, 60 days: sailed March 10.

July 12 : Arrived Falmouth, 124 days: at Cardiff in tow July 23.

Third Voyage

September 11 1905: Sailed Cardiff, sailed from Cherbourg four days later.

January 31 1906 : Arrived Honolulu via Cape Horn, 138 days.

February 20 : Sailed Honolulu.

April 15 : Arrived Newcastle (N.S.W.), 54 days.

May 14 : Owing to the French barque *Bayard* being struck by a heavy squall in Newcastle, her moorings gave way and she fouled the French sailing ships *David d'Angers* and *Champigny*. All three vessels sustained slight damage.

May 26 : Sailed Newcastle.

About the end of July 1906, the *Champigny*, while trying to get out of Valparaiso, came against the Chilean barque *Nelson* and the British steamer *Madura*. The *Champigny* and the *Madura* sustained no damage, but the *Nelson* suffered some to the bowsprit which cost £200.

About August 1 : Arrived Antofagasta.

November 16 : Sailed Caleta Coloso.

March 20 1907 : Passed Lizard, 124 days.

March 21 : Arrived Falmouth: sailed for Brake 4 days later.

April 1 : Arrived Brake.

Fourth Voyage

June 8 1907 : Sailed Brake in tow.

June 17 : Sailed Cherbourg, and rounded Cape Horn in 12 days, 50°S. to 50°S.

November 14 : Arrived San Diego, 150 days.

December 23 : Sailed San Diego.

January 19 1908 : Arrived Tacoma, 27 days.

January 29 : Sailed Tacoma.

May 1 : Touched at Pernambuco to land sick man.

June 17 : Passed Fastnet, 140 days.

June 18 : Arrived Queenstown. Left June 21 in tow.

June 23 1908 : Arrived Belfast.

Fifth Voyage

August 1 1908	: Sailed Belfast: at Cherbourg August 4 and sailed again August 6.
November 13	: Arrived Hobart, 99 days.
November 15	: Sailed Hobart.
January 20 1909	: Arrived off Honolulu, 66 days: sailed same day.
February 10	: Arrived Vancouver (B.C.), 21 days from Hawaii.
March 30	: Sailed Vancouver.
May 24	: Arrived Noumea, 55 days.
August 11	: Sailed Noumea.
December 12	: Passed Lizard, 123 days; and week later arrived at Dieppe.

Sixth Voyage

January 30 1910	: Sailed Dieppe.
May 23	: Arrived New Caledonia, 113 days.
August 6	: Sailed New Caledonia.
December 6	: Passed Prawle Point, 122 days.
December 13	: Arrived Hamburg.

Seventh Voyage

January 29 1911	: Sailed Hamburg: at Cherbourg February 1 and sailed next day.
June 28	: Arrived San Francisco, 146 days.
August 21	: Sailed San Francisco.
January 31 1912	: Arrived Queenstown, 163 days.
February 12	: Sailed Queenstown: at Hull 5 days later.

Eighth Voyage

March 24 1912	: Sailed Hull: touched at Cherbourg March 27 and sailed same day.
June 22	: Arrived Newcastle (N.S.W.), 87 days.
August 18	: Sailed Newcastle with coal.
October 12	: Arrived Valparaiso, 55 days.
November 30	: Sailed Valparaiso.
December 8	: Arrived Taltal to load nitrates.
February 1 1913	: Sailed Taltal.
May 31	: Arrived Dunkirk, 119 days.

Ninth Voyage

June 28 1913   : Sailed Dunkirk for Rotterdam, in tow.
July 25   : Sailed Rotterdam.
November 27   : Arrived San Francisco, 125 days.
January 19 1914   : Sailed San Francisco. The *Champigny,* under Captain
                      P. Nöel, is credited with an exceptional run from the
                      Golden Gate to the mouth of the Columbia River in
                      52 hours, averaging about 10 knots.
January 28   : Arrived Astoria.
February 27   : Sailed Portland (Oreg.).
March 8   : Sailed Astoria.
July 4   : Passed Prawle Point 118 days: thence to Ipswich.

Tenth Voyage

March 12 1915   : Arrived Tyne.
April 28   : Sailed Tyne.
October 9   : Arrived San Francisco, 164 days.
November 18   : Sailed San Francisco.
April 6 1916   : Arrived Falmouth, 140 days.
April 17   : Sailed Falmouth (in tow) and arrived Sharpness five
                      days later.

Eleventh Voyage

May 27 1916   : Sailed Sharpness for Port Talbot, whence sailed on
                      June 28 for Antofagasta, arrived October 16, 110 days.
December 26   : Sailed Antofagasta.
May 20 1917   : Arrived Bordeaux, 145 days.

She was then sold to the Société Générale d'Armement of Nantes, which at that time was the most important sailing ship firm in France.

Twelfth Voyage

September 4 1917 : Sailed Bordeaux.
December 30   : Arrived Melbourne, 117 days.
February 6 1918   : Sailed Melbourne.
June 4   : Arrived San Francisco, 118 days (long passage).
August 3   : Sailed San Francisco.
October 15   : Arrived Melbourne, 73 days.
November 30   : Sailed Melbourne.
February 15 1919 : Arrived San Francisco, 77 days.
March 28   : Sailed San Francisco.
August 29   : Arrived St. Nazaire, 154 days.

Thirteenth Voyage

April 4 1920	:	Arrived Buenos Aires from St. Nazaire.
June 4	:	Sailed Buenos Aires.
July 4	:	Arrived Table Bay, 30 days out, and sailed again July 30.
September 19	:	Arrived Newcastle (N.S.W.), 51 days.
December 1	:	Sailed Newcastle.
January 25 1921	:	Arrived Coquimbo, 55 days.
March 18	:	Sailed Coquimbo for Junin, whence she sailed on May 7 1921 for Queenstown for orders, reached in 137 days on September 21, sailing four days later.
October 11	:	At Bruges, with her nitrate cargo damaged by sea-water.
November 22	:	Arrived Falmouth and left on November 28 (in tow of tug *Plover*).
November 30	:	Arrived Falmouth again (in tow), put back through stress of weather.
December 4	:	Sailed Falmouth (in tow of tug *Plover*).
December 5	:	Passed Ushant.
December 7	:	Arrived St. Nazaire.
December 8	:	Arrived Nantes.

This was her last voyage under the French flag. The *Champigny* was laid up in the Canal de la Martinière on February 28 1922, but she was one of the comparatively few big ships which went to sea again. In 1923 the Finnish School Ship Association was looking for a vessel to replace the first *Fennia* (built as the *Goodrich* in 1892 at Belfast for Boyd, Bros. & Co., she was a steel four-masted barque of 2,262 tons), and in the *Champigny* found an ideal ship. She was modern as sailing-ships went, and her build made her easy to fit out as a cadet-ship since there was plenty of space in her extensive superstructure for the boys' quarters. So, in July 1923, she was bought by A/B. Finska Skolskeppsrederiet (Lars Krogius, Mgr.) of Helsingfors, and renamed *Fennia*. She was put into trading with a crew and cadets, under the command of Captain Orvar Blom, and towed to Lorient. Subsequent voyages are under the Finnish flag, bearing her new name.

The former *Champigny* sailed as the ordinary tramp Cape Horner until 1927, when she took shelter in the Falkland Islands after being dismasted while outward-bound from Cardiff towards Valparaiso with a cargo of patent fuel and coke. During a round-the-world voyage in 1923-24, she crossed the Atlantic from Lorient to Campbellton, N.B., in 35 days, was 105 thence to Melbourne with timber, loaded coal at Newcastle, N.S.W., and was 58 days (which was poor) thence to Iquique. Here she loaded nitrates for Ardrossan, Scotland, which she reached in 110 days on January 12 1925, having been some 16 months on the whole voyage and handled three full cargoes. The times were bad and became no better. During the following voyage in 1925-26, the *Fennia* sailed from U.K. to Santos, Brazil (49 days), thence round the Horn to Taltal and Iquique (82 days) seeking a nitrates cargo, thence (still in ballast) across the Pacific to Melbourne (100 days) seeking grain for Europe—again in vain. After a four months' wait, the former Frenchman crossed the South Pacific eastwards for Antofagasta. A passage of 53 days saw her there, and at last she loaded another cargo—nitrates for Delfzijl, a mainly rough passage which took her 126 days with loss of a boy, some expensive sails, and costly deck damage. The freight was not good, and the voyage-loss must have been considerable.

But she remained in commission as a school-ship cargo-carrier: her next voyage was her last—to date, anyway, for the old *Champigny* even in 1972 may not be finished yet. On February 10 1927, she hauled out of Cardiff's Bute dock bound on that classic old Cape Horner run, for Valparaiso direct. It was winter then, but with luck Captain Christerson hoped that he would be past the Horn well before the southern winter began. He might have managed this but in the event it made no difference, for the four-master was so seriously dismasted before she got to the Horn that she had to stagger in distress back to the Falkland Islands. The whole of the main and mizzen-masts came out of her and half the fore, and the jigger topmast as well. This near-fatal accident was the climax of a long fight with violent storms with squalls of Force 10, always from the direction in which the heavy-laden ship had to go. Vital running rigging began to go, then far more vital standing rigging, then swiftly afterwards the masts, while the 3,000-ton hulk of the great ship rolled and floundered in the tumult of the sea and her twisted shambles of fractured steel masts and yards, held to her remorselessly by the heavy iron-wire rigging, writhed about her torn decks and flailed her sides. How much of this could she stand? There was a limit, obviously. The Captain did miraculously to keep the barque afloat, headed for the Falklands, for she was practically unmanageable. He wanted to get into Port Stanley but, unable to make this, had to let his anchors go as soon as the land gave him a bit of a lee. This soon became a situation more dangerous than the open sea, for if the anchors did not hold she would smash on the rocks, fast. Captain Christerson reflected grimly that at least she had little windage, in her dismasted state. A local steamer approached, offering "assistance", claiming salvage. The Captain knew about Falklands salvage: he paid out all his chain and hung on.

"I am not 'salvage' while I have one mast left," said the Captain: but he knew the situation was perilous enough. He induced the steamer to accept a towage agreement—costly but not ruinous—and was moved to safe anchorage. This was mid-May 1927: there the *Fennia* ex-*Champigny* stayed as store-ship and hulk until on a day in 1966 Mr. Karl Kortum (former A.B. in the barque *Kaiulani*, second mate of the barque *Carthaginian*, saver of the ship *Balclutha*, Director of San Francisco's Maritime Museum and Old Ships Sanctuary) happened by. Mr. Kortum liked the looks of the old four-master and liked her story. And so, in November 1967, this last survivor of the battered veterans of the Horn was towed away from the Falkland Islands, for Montevideo. There in early 1972 she awaits refit for the passage onwards towards San Francisco, where the plan is to restore her to her stately rig, in permanent place by the veteran ships already there. In this enterprise many have assisted, chief among them Mr. William G. Swigert Jr. and Captain Fred Klebingat.

(For inspiration and example, they have the old Scots four-masted full-rigged ship *Falls of Clyde*, being restored in Honolulu Harbour by the enterprise of the Bishop Museum there and the skill of Master-Rigger Jack Dickerhoff, aided by James Kleinschmidt.)

Chanaral – Iron ship, 1,420 g., 1,184 n.
1875: Built by J. E. Scott, Greenock, for R. W. Jamieson (C. S. Caird, Mgr.), Greenock, as *Martin Scott*.
Sold to A. D. Bordes October 1893 and renamed *Chanaral*.

January 28 1902: Left River Loire in ballast in tow for Port Talbot, and three days later she was caught in a severe easterly gale. Her tow-rope parted and her master, Captain Loreau, tried to set her lower topsails, but the *Chanaral* was capsized by ballast shifting in a few minutes and went down 70 miles north-west of Ushant. There was only one survivor, the first mate, Monsieur Legrand, who was rescued by the Norwegian steamer *Victoria* after 12 hours in the water. The master and 20 men were lost.

Chanaral – Steel 4-masted barque, 2,423 g., 2,258 n.
1892: Built by R. Duncan & Co., Port Glasgow, for Thom & Cameron, Glasgow, as *Achnashie*.

A good vessel, under the British flag she made a passage of 57 days from Newcastle, N.S.W., to San Francisco, which was the best of the year. In April 1907, she was sold to A. D. Bordes for £10,500 and renamed *Chanaral*. January 11 1916: Left Mejillones for Fayal (Azores) for orders. Captain Y. Bernard in command. Arriving at Fayal on April 6, 86 days out, she was ordered on to Falmouth a week later but did not arrive. It was discovered that she was torpedoed by the German submarine *U-67*, 60 miles off the Scillies. Her crew were later saved on April 22.

(See account of Captain Krage's voyage from Chile to France in this ship.)

Charlemagne – Steel ship, 2,326 g., 1,728 n.
April 30 1901: Launched by Chantiers de la Loire, Nantes, for Cie. Maritime Française, Nantes.

Captain A. Codet took her in command on the stocks, and her maiden passage was from Nantes to New Caledonia in ballast. She arrived safely and, on December 11 1901, left for Havre with nickel ore. She was neither seen nor heard of again.

Charles Gounod – Steel barque (Jubilee rig), 2,199 g., 1,960 n.
January 13 1900: Launched by Chantiers de la Loire, St. Nazaire, for N. & C. Guillon, Nantes.

On her maiden voyage she made Newcastle, N.S.W., from St. Nazaire in the creditable time of 73 days (in ballast). Her return passage from San Francisco to Queenstown with wheat was made in 106 days—two very good runs indeed. In 1912, she was sold to Sté. Générale d'Armement, Nantes.

While bound from Durban to Nantes with grain, January 21 1917, under Captain Rault, she was captured by the German raider *Seeadler* and sunk by bombs in a position lat. 8°N., long. 26°W. (See *Cambronne*). From the *Charles Gounod*, Count von Luckner captured the sailing instructions for sailing vessels, which were instrumental in the raider intercepting other ships.

Châteaubriand – Steel ship, 2,247 g., 2,029 n.
January 26 1901: Launched by Chantiers Marit. du Sud-Ouest, Bordeaux, for Sté. Bretonne de Navigation, Nantes (H. Prentout-Leblond & E. Leroux, Mgrs., Rouen).

She was sold in 1912 to Sté. Générale d'Armement, Nantes.

Arrived in South Australian waters from Montevideo in December 1912, in ballast. The ship hove-to off Cape Borda on the afternoon of December 16, signalled her number and asked for orders. The lightkeeper had no orders and so the ship set off for the Semaphore Anchorage (Port Adelaide) to request them there. But she kept too far to the north-west, and at about 2 a.m., on December 17, went ashore in Sturt Bay, on the west side of St. Vincent Gulf not far from the Troubridge Island lighthouse. The stranding was reported and tugs dispatched from Port Adelaide. First attempts to refloat the vessel were unsuccessful but, on December 29, the tug *Wato* succeeded in refloating the ship. She had sustained damage to her forefoot and bottom plates, and was towed to Melbourne for repairs. On April 8 1915, while on passage from London to New York, under Captain Grondin, she was torpedoed by the German submarine *U-32*, 25 miles south-east of Beachy Head.

Château d'If – Steel barque, 2,450 g., 1,980 n.
June 26 1900: Launched by Chantiers de la Loire, Nantes, for Sté. Marseillaise de Voiliers, Marseilles.

In 1904, she made a good run from Liverpool to Fremantle in 77 days, the best passage of the year to West Australia. She was sold to Cie. Havraise de Navigation (E. Corblet & Co., Mgrs.) Havre, in May 1910.

From May 1920 until February 1921, she made a voyage from Nantes-Baltimore-Malmö-Christiania, thence to Melbourne from Christiania, arriving in Australia on June 23 1921 and sailing again on August 8. She was 120 days from Melbourne to Falmouth, discharged her grain at Cardiff and, in February 1922, was laid up in the Canal de la Martinière and broken up in 1924.

Chili – Iron barque, 1,318 g., 1,202 n.
1885: Built by W. B. Thompson, Glasgow, for A. D. Bordes.

Had a narrow squeak in February 1912, when the Lizard lifeboat *Admiral Sir George Back* went to her help after nearly running ashore in fog. The lifeboat passed a tow rope to her from a tug, and she was towed to safety. Her end came when homeward bound from Iquique for Nantes with nitrate in 1917, under Captain J. Ollivier, when she was captured on the evening of December 13 by the German submarine *U-B-54* in lat. 47°49′N., long. 7°11′W., and sunk on December 14.

Circé – Iron ship, 1,619 g., 1,481 n.
1885: Built by A. Stephen & Sons, Glasgow, for A. C. Le Quellec, Bordeaux.

Her first 16 years of service were in the nitrate trade from West Coast of South America under the French flag. On September 29 1901, while bound from the Tyne to Caleta Buena with coal, she caught fire off Staten Island. On October 5 1901 she put into Port Stanley, Falkland Islands, where she was scuttled. When the fire was put out she was raised, and left Port Stanley on January 30 1902. Her return passage was excessively hard and slow, and the *Circé* arrived at St. Nazaire only on September 3 1902. She was immediately sold to Norwegian owners: O. G. Gjessen & Co., Skudesnaes, and renamed *Karmö*. In 1921 she was owned by the A. S. "Karmö" (Jacobsen & Thon), of Fredrikstad, who sold her in 1924 to Jerman Oelckers y Cia, Puerto Montt, Chile, renamed *Calbuco*. Under the Panamanian flag in 1943, operating during the Second World War. Her last overseas passage was from Buenos Aires to Marseilles in 111 days, in 1945. She was then laid up until towed to Genoa in 1948 for breaking up. So ended a 63 years' long career with the old ship still in reasonable condition.

Colbert – Steel barque, 1,551 g., 1,419 n.
December 15 1894: Launched by Chantiers de la Loire, Nantes, for A. Viot, Nantes.

Sold to Natterqvist, Hernösand (Sweden), 1904, and renamed *Danae*. In 1909 she appears as the Norwegian *Ketty,* owned by G. C. Brövig, Farsund. By 1916 her name is *Sirius,* still under the Norwegian flag. On March 22 1917 she was sunk by bombs by the German submarine *U-57*, about 150 miles east of Duncansby Head.

Colbert – Steel ship, 1,566 g., 941 n.
1909: Built by Blohm & Voss, Hamburg, for Deutscher Schulschiff-Verein, Oldenburg, as *Prinzess Eitel Friedrich*.

She was a smart training ship until she was allocated to France as war reparations in 1919. Unfortunately France made little use of her: towed to St. Nazaire she was left idle in port, abandoned and neglected, for about ten years. In 1922 she was sold by the French government to the Société des Armateurs Français for 136,450 francs with a view to sailing her as a school ship, but plans did not materialise. On May 23 1925, she was renamed *Colbert* under the ownership of the Sté. de Navigation "Les Navires Ecoles Français" —a new subsidiary company of the Sté. des Armateurs Français—and registered at Nantes, but she remained laid up in St. Nazaire. At the end of 1926 she was sold to the Baron de Forest and it was reported that he intended to convert her into a yacht, but nothing seems to have been done in this direction and the *Colbert* remained idle. On December 26 1929, having been sold at a low price to the Polish Government and renamed *Dar Pomorza,* she left St. Nazaire for Nakskov in tow. On December 29, when off Ushant, her tow-rope parted in a westerly gale and she was driven close to rocks; she was anchored for 48 hours with a clearance of only six yards from a rock off the Brittany coast until she was picked up again by her tug, the Dutch *Poolzee*. Finally, the *Dar Pomorza* arrived safely at her destination on January 9 1930.

After extensive repairs she was given small auxiliary oil engines, and arrived at Gdynia on August 13 1930. Until the outbreak of war in 1939 she was in regular commission, making the usual round of the sailing training-ship to the West Indies and back, "showing the flag". Her normal complement was from 150 to 200 cadets. During World War II she sheltered in Swedish waters, and returned to Poland after it was over.

In 1972 the *Dar Pomorza* was still in service, operated by Wyzsza Szkola Morska, of Gdynia. In April 1971, on a courtesy visit to Dover with 150 cadets on board, she went aground near the Signal Station on the Eastern Arm of Dover Harbour. However, on the next rising tide, the *Dar Pomorza* refloated with no apparent damage, and sailed for Cadiz.

Colonel de Villebois-Mareuil – Steel barque (Jubilee rig), 2,187 g., 1,926 n.
November 26 1900: Launched by Chantiers Nantais de Constructions Maritimes, Nantes, for the Cie. Maritime Française, Nantes.

Arriving at Astoria (Oreg.) from Newcastle-on-Tyne, with general cargo, on December 3 1911, Captain R. Vivier reported his vessel had a narrow escape coming round Cape Horn. One exceptionally dark night as the *Colonel de Villebois-Mareuil* was skimming along at a good rate, she suddenly sighted a big 4-masted barque coming head-on a short distance away. Both vessels threw their helms hard over in order to clear, but as they shot by, the *Mareuil* struck the stranger's taffrail a glancing blow. The *Mareuil*'s jib-boom was cracked and her bob-stay and martingale were carried away, but the hull was not injured. It was believed that the other vessel was not damaged, as the hull was not touched. The identity of the other barque was never learned as the two ships rushed by one another so rapidly, each with her people fully occupied.

Sold 1913 to Sté. Générale d'Armement, Nantes.

January 14 1919 : Left Wellington, N.Z., for San Francisco.
March 16 : Arrived San Francisco, 61 days out.
April 16 : Left San Francisco for Nantes.

On her last voyage in 1921 she reached Port Adelaide from Dublin in 95 days, loaded wheat at Port Lincoln and sailed June 11, arriving Queenstown October 7 1921, 118 days out. She was towed thence to Sligo Bay where she had a narrow escape from being blown ashore when the tow-line parted. She survived this, to be laid up in the Canal de la Martinière in January 1922, leaving the Canal for Lorient to be broken up at the end of January 1927.

Commandant Marchand – Steel barque, 2,313 g., 1,731 n.
March 16 1900: Launched by Chantiers de la Loire, Nantes, for the Cie. Maritime Française, Nantes.

This was a most unfortunate vessel. On February 25 1903, she left Leith in tow of the Watkins' tug *Oceana,* bound for Antwerp to load cement for San Francisco, under Captain Arnaud. Her tow-rope parted off Whitby in rough weather, and the tug lost sight of her in a squall and proceeded to Middles-brough. There was no firm news of the *Commandant Marchand* again, though the Norwegian steamer *Oscar Fredrik* arrived Liverpool on March 20, where it was reported to have seen, on March 13 in lat. 63°15′N., long. 2°32′E., a vessel resembling the barque, carrying only three storm sails, heading west but making no signals. The tug *Cruiser* was at once engaged to search for her and sailed from the Mersey on March 26, but was compelled to put into Stornoway on the 29th on account of rough weather. Although she searched as far north as Hammerfest, the tug was unsuccessful. The barque was officially posted missing on June 10 1903.

Commandant Posth – Iron ship, 2,093 g., 1,879 n.
1874: Built and owned by M. Wigram & Sons, London.

She was first registered as the auxiliary steam screw barque *Durham*. By 1889, she appears as the full-rigged ship *Durham*, owned by Sailing Ship "Durham" Co. (J. Herron & Co.), Liverpool. In 1909, her registry was changed to Argentine and her name to *La Argentina*, under the ownership of E. Meincke of Buenos Aires. In 1911 and 1913 the ship was owned by Remonda, Montserrat & Co., of Rosario. She was probably bought by French interests in 1917 and in 1919 her name was *Marakech*, owned by Cie. Chérifienne de Navigation, Casablanca. By 1920, she appears as the *Commandant Posth*, under the ownership of Bienhoa Industrielle et Forestière, Bordeaux, and was briefly in the West Indies trade before being sold for scrap a year or two later, in 1924.

Connétable de Richemont – Steel barque, 2,297 g., 1,732 n.
April 30 1901: Launched by Chantiers Nantais de Constr. Maritimes, Nantes for Sté. Bretonne de Navigation, Nantes.

She was another unlucky ship, for on her maiden voyage from Swansea to San Francisco and Liverpool, her master, Captain Thoreux, and several of her crew died at sea. On her second and last voyage, commanded by Captain J. Rault, she left Liverpool for New York where she loaded case oil for Hong Kong. She delivered this safely and sailed from Hong Kong in ballast for Port Cassal, Chile, on July 17 1903. The voyage was beset by calms and head winds for many weeks, and the barque bought $60 worth of victuals from the American liner *City of Peking* which she chanced to meet. In September she was again delayed by calms and head winds. Captain Rault decided to steer for Honolulu to renew provisions and water, but she stranded on the French Frigate Shoals, 85 days out, on October 10. On October 11, owing to the bad situation of the barque, the master and his crew of 23 decided to abandon ship. Three boats were lowered and they set off together for the Hawaiian Islands. On October 17, at 10 p.m., the master's boat sighted a small island near Niihau, where they landed the following day. All hands were ultimately saved.

Captain Rault assumed that the wreck was caused by chronometer error. At considerable expense two expeditions were assembled to attempt salvage, the first in November 1903, and the second with the steamer *Ada* in January 1904, but without success.

Coquimbo – Iron barque, 1,015 g., 834 n.
1876: Built by Aitken & Mansel, Glasgow, for J. Guthrie, Cardiff, as the *Cochrina*.
Sold 1890 to A. D. Bordes and renamed *Coquimbo*. Sold 1903 to Norwegian interests but her name was maintained. She left Gulfport on January 20 1909 for Buenos Aires with lumber and steel, but went ashore 12 days later on Boynton Beach (near Palm Beach, Fla.) and became a total loss.

Above: The flush-decked *Bonneveine* in light ballast. (*Marius Bar Photos, Toulon.*)

Right: Big French barque *Buffon* running with a good fair wind. In 1905 there were over 200 such French Cape Horners in commission. (*Alan Villiers Collection.*)

Below: With an ineffective ballast-log resting by the turn of her bilge, the capsized French ship *Asie* at Portland, Oregon. She was raised again. (*San Francisco Maritime Museum.*)

The *Bretagne* in the Derwent, Hobart, Tasmania. (*Beattie.*)

After ballast shifting, the *Bretagne* is in a little trouble. (*Henri Picard Collection.*)

Captain Abel Chevalier of the *Bretagne*. (*Henri Picard Collection.*)

Henri Picard aboard the *Bretagne* at Newcastle, N.S.W., January 1921, when he was a *pilotin*. (*Henri Picard Collection.*)

The first *Bretagne*, ex-*Ada Iredale*, has lost her square-rig to become a four-masted schooner, at the end of her career. (*San Francisco Maritime Museum.*)

Colonel de Villebois-Mareuil towing across the Columbia River Bar, October 1912; view taken from the tug across a big sea. (*Henri Picard Collection.*)

Châteaubriand stranded in St. Vincent Gulf, South Australia, December 1912. Ashore she stayed. (*A. D. Edwardes, South Australia.*)

Coquimbo – Steel ship, 1,759 g., 1,615 n.
1890: Built by Russell & Co., Port Glasgow, for Foley & Co., London, as *Burmah*.

Sold January 1907 to A. D. Bordes and renamed *Coquimbo* to replace the other.

In August 1913, while bound from Iquique to Nantes, she was partially dismasted off the Falklands, arriving under jury rig in the River Loire in 122 days.

While on a passage in July 1917 from Antofagasta to La Pallice, arriving off the French coast near Rochebonne Shoals on the night of July 9, 105 days out, she was becalmed, drifting slowly towards the Rochebonne minefield laid by the German submarine *U-C-21*, on May 23 1917 (33 miles west-south-west of Ré Island). On July 11 she was still becalmed, and at 1 p.m. a mine was sighted drawing steadily nearer. Captain Le Saux immediately gave orders to abandon ship but, before her boats had been lowered, she struck the mine and sank in the twinkling of an eye with her master, the second mate and five men. The survivors were saved by a fishing boat and landed next day at La Rochelle.

Cornil Bart – Steel barque, 2,242 g., 1,998 n.
June 1902: Completed by Chantiers de la Loire, St. Nazaire, for Sté. des Voiliers Dunkerquois, Dunkirk.

Her passages were rather good. She made Portland (Oreg.), from St. Nazaire in 119 days, and once New York from San Francisco in 85 days, a prodigious run indeed, although it cannot be verified. But between June 1915 and May 1916, she made Portland (Oreg.) from Dublin in 152 days, coming back to Falmouth in 156 days, and was ordered to Nantes. Perhaps she was then some time out of dry-dock. In December 1919 she reached Dungeness from New York in 18 days.

On February 15 1921 she arrived at Adelaide from Dunkirk (voyage days not given). The next passage on the record is her last under the French flag —111 days from Port Victoria, South Australia, to Plymouth, also in 1921. In April 1923 she was sold to Skibs. A/S "Anitra" (Erling Stray A/S), Kristiansand, Norway, and renamed *Anitra*. She was broken up at Genoa in 1926.

Corumoc – Steel barque, 1,072 g., 996 n.
1892: Built by Fevigs Jernskibsbyg, Arendal, for Actieselskabet "Ragna" (Chr. Moller), Christiana, as *Ragna*.

From 1909 until 1922 she was owned by Acties. Seilfart (John P. Pedersen & Son, Mgrs.), Christiana, and retained her original name. In 1922, she was bought by the Compagnie des Rhums Purs, Havre, for the West Indies

H

trade, and renamed *Corumoc*. She made several West Indies voyages in 1923/24, and was sold to M. Potet, Havre, in 1924 or 25 and renamed *Trielen,* still in the West Indies trade. She remained in this until April 7 1926, when she reached Havre 45 days out from Hayti, and laid up. She was soon after sold to Belgium for scrap.

Crillon – Steel ship, 2,256 g., 1,979 n.
August 1902: Completed by Chantiers de St. Nazaire for the Cie. Maritime Française, Nantes.

Her best passage was made from Europe to Australia in 69 days, a splendid run indeed for such a ship: but the year is not stated. She was sold to the Sté. Générale d'Armement, Nantes, in 1913 and made her last long voyage in 1921, to Port Adelaide from Southampton, thence with grain back to Falmouth, 134 days. She discharged at Cardiff that September, and in the absence of further employment, was towed off to the Canal de la Martinière and broken up in 1928.

Croisset – Steel barque (Jubilee rig), 2,700 g., 2,257 n.
September 20 1899: Launched by Chantiers de Normandie, Rouen, for Cie. Rouennaise de Transports Maritimes (Prentout-Leblond, Leroux & Co., Mgrs.), Rouen.

She distinguished herself by an unusual and expensive accident before she got to sea at all. On December 30 1899 she suddenly capsized in port while fitting out afloat, but was straightened up again after cutting off her masts, which then had to be renewed. She was chiefly in the nickel ore trade from New Caledonia, but she did not last long.

On July 17 1908 she left New Caledonia for Glasgow with 3,500 tons nickel ore, commanded by Captain A. Kervégan, picked up the North Irish coast 117 days out in November, and got on it to stay. The date was November 13 1908, the weather misty. She stranded on South Rock, Cloughey Bay, and became a total loss. Her crew were saved by the Cloughey lifeboat.

Daniel – Steel ship, 2,790 g., 1,819 n.
April 1902: Completed by Chantiers de St. Nazaire, for Sté. des Voiliers de St. Nazaire, and in 1903, transferred to Sté. Générale d'Armement, St. Nazaire.

Another fine ship with a short life. She sailed from Bellingham (Wash.) for Delagoa Bay with timber on July 3 1906, under Captain David, and went missing. It is thought that she was lost off Cape Horn because many floating baulks of timber similar to her cargo were sighted between Diego Ramirez

Islands and Staten Island about the time she should have reached those waters.

David d'Angers – Steel ship, 1,981 g., 1,739 n.
December 1901: Completed by A. Dubigeon, Nantes, for Sté. des Armateurs Nantais, Nantes.

While bound from Iquique to Hamburg on March 4 1904, she grounded on a sand bank near Horta (Azores), and was refloated. Her last voyage under the French flag was made to Australia, and in 1912 she was sold to Akties. "Geysir" (O. Gotaas, Mgr.), Christiania, and renamed *Geysir*. In 1916, while still operating under the same company, her managing owners became Sigurd Bruusgaard and her home port Drammen. In 1917 she passed to Danish colours when purchased by A. Olsen & Co., of Copenhagen, but they kept her for only 18 months before selling her to Rechnitzer, Thomsen & Co. (Limfjorden Rederiselskabet) of Aalborg.

In 1924 she made her fourth and final change of flag, this time to Swedish colours when she became the cargo-cadet ship *Manhem* owned by A/B Skolskepp of Gothenburg and managed by S. G. Jansson. By 1925 it was difficult to find employment for her, and the ship was sold to the breakers.

Desaix – Steel ship, 2,255 g., 1,979 n.
July 1902: Completed by Chantiers de St. Nazaire for Cie. Maritime Française, Nantes.

She carried 2,950 tons of nickel ore, and was engaged in the tramp sailing-ship trades. On June 3 1912 she arrived at Caleta Coloso, 100 days out from Barry, South Wales, and returned to Ardrossan in 106 days, via Falmouth. On March 8 1913 she sailed from Port Talbot for Caleta Coloso, and arrived June 27, 111 days—rather a slow passage, as also was her 112 days homewards. During this voyage she was sold to Sté. Générale d'Armement, Nantes.

Her last voyage was unlucky. Arriving at Port Adelaide on March 6 1921 from Dublin, her return passage was made via the Cape of Good Hope. Sailed Port Lincoln on April 25 and arrived at Table Bay on July 28, in 94 days. Left Table Bay on August 5 for Falmouth. Her master died at sea on September 18. Spoken October 21 in position lat. 39°10′N., long. 38°05′W., short of provisions. Arrived Falmouth on November 6 in 93 more days, 195 days out from Port Lincoln. In a year of poor passages hers was the worst.

Arrived Canal de la Martinière on January 8 1922, and left to be broken up five years later.

Dieppedalle – Steel barque, 2,702 g., 2,253 n.
March 8 1900: Launched by Chantiers de Normandie, Rouen, for Cie.

Rouennaise de Transports Maritimes (Prentout-Leblond, Leroux & Co., Mgrs.), Rouen.

In 1902 she sailed from Havre to New Caledonia in 82 days and returned in 86 days, but the following year she made a slow passage of 176 days from Hamburg to Santa Rosalia (Western Mexico). (This was a much more difficult passage.)

On her last voyage she left Garston on January 26 1921 and arrived at Sydney, via Hobart, on June 3 in 128 days. Sailed from Sydney with wheat on August 24 and arrived at Falmouth on December 6, 104 days out. Reached Bremen on January 4 1922, where she was burnt out on January 16 1922, and scrapped.

Du Couëdic – Steel barque, 2,297 g., 1,732 n.
May 15 1901: Launched by Chantiers Nantais de Constr. Maritimes, Nantes, for Sté. Bretonne de Navigation, Nantes.

She also went missing, for she left San Francisco in ballast for Sydney on December 22 1902, under Captain Pignorel, and was never heard of again. On May 6 1903 the master of an American schooner arrived Sydney and declared that he had seen a wreck seemingly French-built near the Marshall Islands, and it was supposed she was the *Du Couëdic*. The French Government sent a vessel to search but no wreck was seen. On July 9 1903 she was officially posted as missing.

Duc d'Aumale – Steel barque, 2,189 g., 1,944 n.
December 27 1900: Launched by Chantiers Nantais de Constr. Maritimes, Nantes, for Cie. Maritime Française, Nantes.

Was in collision June 22 1902 with the British steamer *Camrose,* and put into Calais for repairs. Sailed Rotterdam September 19 1907 with pig-iron and coke for San Francisco. After crossing the Line she was found to be leaking slightly. This became worse during heavy weather east of Staten Island (five feet of water in the hold) and, to prevent sinking, she was beached on a muddy bottom in Roy Cove, Falkland Islands, on the evening of November 25 1907. She was eventually refloated and towed into Port Stanley on February 17 1908. She left Port Stanley for Montevideo on April 5, arriving there 13 days later. She was drydocked at Buenos Aires and the leak was repaired. She resumed her voyage on July 18, arriving at San Francisco on November 20 1908, 14 months from Rotterdam. She was sold to Sté. Générale d'Armement, Nantes, in 1913, and on passage in 1917 from Bahia Blanca to Pauillac with wheat, commanded by Captain Doublecourt, was captured by the German submarine *U-43* and sunk by bombs in 45°21′N., 8°50′W. on January 22 1917. Her crew were taken on board the submarine and the day after were handed over to a Norwegian steamer bound to Portland, Me. The latter vessel gave them to a Spanish trawler, which took them to Corunna, whence they reached France.

Duchesse Anne – Steel barque, 1,324 g., 1,114 n.

1891: Built by A. Dubigeon, Nantes, for L. Bureau & Fils, Nantes.

February 8 1901: While on passage from Iquique to Falmouth, she was dismasted about 300 miles north-east off the Bermudas. Jury rigged, the *Duchesse Anne* sailed on to Falmouth without aid, whence she was towed to London. Repaired in France, she left Swansea with coal on August 8 1901, and on January 4 1902 arrived at San Francisco, 149 days out.

February 13 1902: Sailed San Francisco.

June 7 1902: Arrived Falmouth in 114 days. However, the late Captain Lacroix, who was serving as first mate aboard the barque at that time, has always asserted that this passage had been made in only 89 days "land to land". Perhaps his interpretation of that rather vague term was that of a true seaman in love with his ship. The 114 days was itself quite good. "Clipper" or not, after this she arrived at St. Nazaire and laid up in July 1902, and was subsequently sold for 115,000 francs to G. C. Brövig, of Farsund, and renamed *Andrea,* probably because she was rather small for deepwater trades. She sailed from St. Nazaire on March 21 1903, under the Norwegian flag, and arrived at Barry in only 38 hours; she tramped the seven seas for the next decade. Then, on October 8 1913, she sailed from the River Tees with 1,400 tons of coal, under Captain Ellertsen, for Gregory Bay in the Straits of Magellan, which she reached in 84 days, but fire in her coal cargo spread rapidly and she burned out. Here she disappears from the records.

Duchesse Anne – Steel ship, 1,260 g., 721 n.

March 1901: Launched by J. C. Tecklenborg A.G., Geestemunde, for Deutscher Schulschiff-Verein, Oldenburg, as the training ship *Grossherzogin Elisabeth* and became French after World War II.

She was the first school-ship owned by the German School-Ship Association which was founded in 1900 by a number of leading German ship-owners, particularly those from Hamburg and Bremen. Early in 1932 she was transferred to the Deutsche Seemanns-Schule, and was permanently moored at Finkenwarder, Hamburg. She remained under the German flag until 1945, when she was allocated to France as reparations. Renamed *Duchesse Anne* and towed into Lorient, she was left idle in port. In 1948, in spite of her age, she was still a particularly smart ship.

In 1951 she was taken to Brest, partially rigged down and converted to a floating barracks, for naval ratings, to relieve the shortage of shore accommodation. At the beginning of 1972 she is still at Brest but reported not to be in good condition, serving as a hulk for a mine-sweeping flotilla.

Duchesse de Berry – Steel ship, 2,572 g., 1,941 n., the ship that could not pass Cape Horn.

March 1902: Completed by Chantiers Maritimes du Sud-Ouest, Bordeaux, for R. Guillon & Co., Nantes.

Sold to Société d'Armement l'Océan, Nantes, in 1904. During her short career she was engaged, on three outwards passages, in fighting Cape Horn gales, but on no occasion could she get the best of that promontory. Her maiden voyage in 1902 was from Penarth to San Francisco, coal-laden. But, unfortunately, she could not manage it round the "corner". Quitting, she faced about and headed for the Good Hope route, limping into Table Bay on September 10 1902, leaky, with cargo shifted, bulwarks gone, and three boats carried away. Several months were spent effecting repairs, and the *Duchesse de Berry* arrived at San Francisco a very long time later with more damage, having continued eastwards.

Her second voyage—from Swansea to San Francisco—meant another attempt to round the Horn: again she could not make it, turned back, proceeding via the longer haul, arriving at San Francisco on November 2 1905. On May 9 1906, on her return passage to Leith, she was in collision with the Dutch steamer *Waterland* in a dense fog, three miles off Whitby, and put into South Shields. She was towed to Leith on May 16.

On her third and last voyage, sailing from the Tyne on July 12 1906, and from Cherbourg on July 21 for San Francisco again, the *Duchesse de Berry*, in her final attempt, struck Penguin Rocks near St. John Bay on the east coast of Staten Island in a fog and foundered, on October 19 1906. Captain Gautier de Kermoal and his crew were saved and landed at Punta Arenas.

Duguay Trouin – Steel ship, 2,557 g., 1,932 n.
February 1902: Completed by Chantiers Maritimes du Sud-Ouest, Bordeaux, for Sté. Bretonne de Navigation, Nantes (H. Prentout-Leblond & E. Leroux, Mgrs., Rouen).

During the fierce "norther" which swept the Bay of Valparaiso in June 1903, when the British full-rigged ship *Foyledale* was lost, the *Duguay Trouin* was driven ashore with the loss of several lives and abandoned, but was eventually refloated and repaired. She made some good passages, for example to New Caledonia from Havre in 84 days in 1910, and back to the Clyde from New Caledonia in 93 days. Sold to Sté. Générale d'Armement, Nantes, in 1912, on her last voyage she arrived at Ipswich on March 30 1921 from San Francisco, thence to the Canal de la Martinière, which she left July 9 1927 for breaking up.

Duguesclin – Steel barque, 1,488 g., 1,332 n.
December 1894: Completed by A. Dubigeon, Nantes, for L. Bureau & Fils, Nantes.

She was another good sailer. On her maiden voyage she reached Saigon from St. Nazaire, via Sunda Strait, in 112 days, and on her second voyage she made the same passage in 118 days. In 1896 she had a good race with the British 4-masted barque *Pinmore*. She left Astoria for Queenstown 36 hours behind the *Pinmore,* and the two vessels sailed in company for three days off Cape Horn. Finally, the *Duguesclin* arrived at Queenstown on January 30 1897 in 120 days, beating the *Pinmore* by over three days. On another occasion, on passage in 1897, she left Cardiff for Hong Kong, sailed five days in company with the famous British 4-masted barque *Queen Margaret,* a noted fast ship. An accident off the Java coast when the Dutch steamer *Speelman* ran into her spoiled *Duguesclin's* chances but, in spite of rigging damage which delayed her for several days, she arrived at Hong Kong only 102 days out. Leaving Hong Kong on September 17 1897, the *Duguesclin* arrived at Portland, Oreg., in 47 days. On her return passage she made the English Channel from Astoria in 117 days, but was sold to Herman Jacobsen & Co., of Sarpsborg, in 1905 and renamed *Lysglimt*. During the First World War, in 1916, she was bought by A/S Excelsior (S. O. Stray & Co., Mgrs.), of Christiansand, and renamed *Semedal*. She survived the war and was broken up in 1925. (There was another *Lysglimt* under the Danish flag.)

Dunkerque – Steel 4-masted barque, 3,152 g., 3,094 n.
1889: Built by Russell & Co., Port Glasgow, for A. D. Bordes.

She had a very short life. Leaving Cardiff for Rio de Janeiro with coal on June 23 1891, under Captain J. Voisin, she went missing. On June 27 one of her boats was discovered off the entrance to the Channel empty, and her loss was attributed, rightly or wrongly, to a fire-damp explosion in her cargo.

Dunkerque – Steel 4-masted barque, 3,203 g., 2,873 n.
August 11 1896: Launched by Laporte & Co., Rouen, for A. D. Bordes.

She was a powerful vessel, a 5,000 deadweight tonner, with cellular double bottom and a 1,200-ton deep tank amidships. The *Dunkerque* was also a very fine ship and made many excellent passages to Chile. She is said to have broken the Shields-Iquique record in 1905 with a 63 days' passage, but this cannot be verified. It must have been "land-to-land", not "port-to-port": in which case it was also very good.

On April 19 1906 she rescued part of the crew of the full-rigged ship *Comte de Smet de Naeyer,* a Belgian training ship which had foundered off the Bay of Biscay that day with the loss of 33 lives. A rather mysterious affair: the *Dunkerque* came upon a boat of survivors a few hours after the Belgian school-ship had quietly gone down with no apparent damage.

She survived the war, and when the slump came was laid up at Dunkirk until March 1924 when she left in tow, with an Italian crew, for Swansea, where a coal cargo was loaded, and she was towed to Italy where the coal was discharged and the *Dunkerque* broken up.

Dupleix – Steel barque, 2,206 g., 1,939 n.
July 1900: Completed by Chantiers de la Loire, St. Nazaire, for Sté. des Armateurs Nantais, Nantes.

In 1908 her nitrate cargo caught fire at Bilbao and she had to be scuttled. Eventually refloated, 1,500 tons nitrate were lost, but she was repaired. On February 7 1910 she arrived at Port Adelaide, 81 days from Beachy Head. On the return passage from Port Victoria with wheat on June 4 1910, she was in the south-east trade winds when she was involved in collision with the British 4-masted barque *Eclipse*. It was dark and impossible to avoid the shock, but the two ships escaped more or less damaged. The *Dupleix*, with only her jib-boom smashed, was able to proceed but the *Eclipse* was compelled to put into a Brazilian port. In London Courts the French barque was found at fault. During World War I, while bound from Tocopilla to Queenstown commanded by Captain Charrier, she was captured by the German raider *Seeadler* and sunk by bombs, in 1°30′N., 28°W., on March 5 1917.

Duquesne – Steel ship, 2,174 g., 1,926 n.
June 15 1901: Launched by Chantiers de la Loire, Nantes, for Cie. Maritime Française, Nantes.

In 1907 she had a race from San Francisco to Runcorn with the British full-rigged ship *Wray Castle*, but the *Duquesne* was beaten by four days. In 1913 she was sold to Sté. Générale d'Armement, Nantes. After the war, she made several voyages in the Australian grain trade and for a brief period in 1924-25 was in the trade to French Guiana. Loaded with logwood she arrived at Bordeaux on February 6 1925, 27 days out. It was her last voyage, and she was laid up in the Canal de la Martinière on May 28 1925. Towards the end of 1928 the *Duquesne* was towed to Arcachon where she was converted into a coal hulk, and broken up at Bayonne 20 years later.

Edmond Rostand – Steel barque, 2,203 g., 1,951 n.
November 6 1900: Launched by Chantiers de la Loire, St. Nazaire, for N. & C. Guillon, Nantes.

Sold to Sté. Générale d'Armement, Nantes, in April 1912. In 1919 she made Nantes from New York in the creditable time of 20 days, and in June 1920 sailed from Geelong with wheat in 106 days back to Nantes. On May 10

1921 she sailed from Melbourne with wheat loaded at Geelong, and arrived Queenstown, 111 days out, leaving for Cardiff on September 8. By October 15 1921 she was laid up in the Canal de la Martinière. Sold to M. Potet, Havre, five years later for the West Indies trade, she left the Canal on May 3 1926, but within a year was laid up again. She was broken up in 1928.

Edouard Bureau – Steel ship, 2,228 g., 2,075 n.
January 1892: Launched by J. Blumer & Co., Sunderland, for Ship *Wiscombe Park* Co. (G. Windram & Co.), Liverpool, as the "Limejuicer" *Wiscombe Park*.

She was a big carrier without any pretensions to speed, but profitable with her 3,450 tons deadweight. Sold in 1909, she was then owned by Alexander Black Sailing Ship Co. (Chadwick, Wainwright & Co., Mgrs.), Liverpool, until 1919 when she was bought by Bureau Frères & Baillergeau, Nantes, to take the place of one of their torpedoed vessels. The big "slump" was not then foreseen. Renamed *Edouard Bureau,* she made only two voyages under the French flag, arriving at Falmouth on March 20 1921 from San Francisco, and at Ipswich on March 25 where her grain cargo was unloaded.

Sold in 1923 for scrap, the *Edouard Bureau* arrived at Rotterdam from St. Nazaire on June 29, but was reprieved by Vinnen Gebrüder G.m.b.H., Hamburg, to take up the role of training ship. Renamed *Greif*—the name means "as a bird in flight"—in 1925, she got on the overdue list during a 143 days' passage from Plymouth to Callao in ballast. The following year she did a very good run from Valencia (Spain) to Adelaide in 69 days, 67 days from Tarifa. Her luck did not last; on June 7 1927, she arrived at Falmouth from Port Pirie in 126 days, with her decks swept, all boats lost and two men reported washed overboard off Cape Horn. The *Greif* left Falmouth under sail for Belfast on June 10, but struck on the Twin Rocks, Irish Sea. She managed eventually to reach Belfast where she was condemned and bought for £2,500, to be broken up. There was no second reprieve.

Edouard Detaille – Steel barque (Jubilee rig), 2,185 g., 1,920 n.
January 19 1901: Launched by Chantiers de la Loire, Nantes, for N. & C. Guillon, Nantes.

Sold in 1912 to Sté. Générale d'Armement, Nantes. On September 25 1917, while on passage from Sydney to Rochefort with wheat, she was torpedoed by the German submarine *U-60*, 144 miles north-north-west of Cape Ortegal.

Elisabeth – Steel barque, 2,061 g., 1,859 n.
May 10 1899: Launched by Chantiers de Normandie, Rouen, for Ch. Tiberghien & Fils, Dunkirk (H. Prentout, Leblond & E. Leroux, Mgrs., Rouen).

On her maiden voyage she left Rouen for Melbourne in September 1899, and made her homeward passage in 93 days, arriving at Dunkirk on May 23 1900. She made other quite good Australian voyages, e.g. from Christiania (Oslo) to Melbourne in 1903-4 in 90 days, and the return passage to Falmouth with wheat in 92 days. Later in 1904 the *Elisabeth* sailed from Fredrikstadt laden with a full cargo of flooring boards to Melbourne in 91 days.

After years of useful tramp voyaging (such as London-Capetown-Port Pirie-Falmouth-Antwerp in 1905-6), she had serious scurvy aboard in 1912 while on a passage from New Caledonia homewards. Three men died at sea, and her master, Captain J. Blondel, put into Pernambuco for medical assistance.

While bound from Pisagua to Havre with nitrate on June 3 1917 the *Elisabeth* was sunk by the German submarine *U-C-29* in a position about six miles south-east of the Lizard.

The *U-C-29* was sunk by the Q-ship *Pargust* four days later, on June 7 1917, south-west of the Irish coast.

Emile Renouf – Steel 4-masted barque, 2,924 g., 2,425 n.
March 1 1897: Launched by Chantiers de la Méditerranée, Havre, for Cie. Havraise de Navigation à Voiles (E. Corblet & Co., Mgrs.), Havre.

On her maiden voyage she made Noumea from Havre in 97 days, but on February 6 1900, while on passage from New Caledonia towards Glasgow with nickel ore, under the orders of Captain Boju, she was wrecked near Mare Island (Loyalties). Having struck a sunken reef of doubtful position, the barque managed to get off the reef, but foundered immediately. Her crew were saved by the schooner *La Perle* and landed at Noumea. (There were many reefs on the South Pacific charts marked "Position Doubtful" and others even "Existence Doubtful". For deep-draught Cape Horn ships, sailing in such waters was dangerous.)

Emilie Galline – Steel barque, 1,944 g., 1,698 n.
March 10 1899: Launched by Chantiers de la Loire, Nantes, for Sté. des Voiliers Français, Havre.

She was credited with an exceptional passage from Antwerp to Chile in 59 days, and another from San Francisco to Newcastle (N.S.W.) in 31 days. Unfortunately I am unable to give her sailing dates, and I cannot guarantee the veracity of these alleged runs, rather surprising in my opinion*. Her master was then the late Captain L. Arnaudtizon, a hard-driver of wide experience, who was in command of the *Emilie Galline* from 1906 until 1915.

---

* They must be regarded as unproven, at best.—A.V.

On January 24 1901 she was driven ashore by a cyclone at Tchio (New Caledonia), but was refloated on April 3 by the Australian tug *Champion,* and towed to Sydney for repairs. Some verified passages follow, none particularly fast, e.g. Seattle to Sharpness, 1906, 163 days; London to Portland (Oreg.), 1906-7, 141 days (from Prawle Point), and Portland to Queenstown 131 days.

February 7 1908 : Arrived Portland (Oreg.), 123 days from Dover.
July 6 : Arrived Queenstown, 116 days from Coos Bay.
November 11 : Arrived Hobart, 90 days from Dungeness.
January 5 1909 : Arrived San Francisco, 51 days from Hobart.

On May 1 1917 she left Taltal for Havre with 2,500 tons nitrate, commanded by Captain J. Frostin and was captured on August 13 by the German submarine *U-C-79,* about 25 miles south-south-east of Eddystone, and sunk by explosive charges.

Emilie Siegfried – Steel 4-masted barque, 3,104 g., 2,754 n. (See *Blanche*).

Emma Laurans – Steel barque, 2,152 g., 1,907 n.
February 7 1902: Launched by Chantiers de la Méditerranée, Havre, for Sté. des Voiliers Français, Havre.

Another war casualty—on December 9 1916, while on passage from Bordeaux to New York under Captain Garnier, she was captured by the German submarine *U-52* off the Canary Islands and sailed eastward in company with the U-boat. She was sunk close to the shore on December 10.

Empereur Ménélick – Steel barque, 1,977 g., 1,744 n.
September 22 1900: Launched by A. Dubigeon, Nantes, for Société des Armateurs Nantais, Nantes.

In 1912 she was sold for £5,000 to Akties "Buland" (Pedersen & Mosvold), Farsund, and renamed *Buland,* and resold in 1915 for a much higher price to A/S Christiansand (S. O. Stray & Co., Mgrs.), Christiansand, acquiring the name of *Svarvarnut.* This was one of the Bounty ships which were sold foreign when their bounty-earning days were over. In 1925 she was owned by A/S Norsk Rutefart (S. O. Stray & Co., Mgrs.), Christiansand, but was sold for scrap for £2,000 the same year at Stavanger.

Ernest Legouvé – Steel barque (Jubilee rig), 2,246 g., 1,868 n.
February 1 1901: Launched by Chantiers de la Loire, Nantes, for N. & C. Guillon, Nantes.

In 1905 she sailed to Hobart from Liverpool in the excellent time of 66 days, but a few years later, in 1912, was sold to Sté. Générale d'Armement, Nantes. In September 1915 the *Ernest Legouvé* left Sharpness with salt, under Captain Le Creurer, and arrived at Sydney on January 11 1916, 120 days out. Thence she loaded coal at Newcastle (N.S.W.) for Iquique, and arrived at London with nitrates from Chile in October 1916. On April 2 1917 she left Northfleet for Buenos Aires with cement, commanded by Captain Le Pannerer, and three days later while still in tow by the British tug *Joffre* was torpedoed by the German submarine *U-B-32* and sank in a few minutes. Her second mate and three men were saved by the tug but her master and 19 men were lost.

Ernest Reyer – Steel barque (Jubilee rig), 2,300 g., 1,730 n.
December 22 1900: Launched by Chantiers de la Loire, Nantes, for N. & C. Guillon, Nantes.

Captain Pilliwuyt took command from the stocks, and the barque was freighted for Madagascar and Portland (Oreg.). Arrived Hobart from Madagascar in September 1901 having experienced very bad weather and having lost two boats and several sails. On December 4 1901. arriving at the entrance to the Columbia River in a strong north-westerly gale, the bar was found impassable and, in spite of the great efforts of her crew, she was thrown ashore at the mouth of the Qui-Ni-Hult River (Wash.), about 30 miles north of Grays Harbor. The crew were rescued with great difficulty, but the *Ernest Reyer* became a total loss in a few days. Her wreck was sold for $1,300 in January 1902. It was said that seven other vessels were lost in the general area during this one storm.

Ernest Reyer – Steel ship, 2,708 g., 2,278 n.
February 24 1902: Launched by Chantiers de St. Nazaire, Rouen, for N. & C. Guillon, Nantes.

On her maiden voyage she reached Hobart from the Channel in 69 days. Later, while on passage from Port Victoria to Limerick, she was caught in a furious storm. Her master decided to take shelter in Galway Bay but anchored in a bad place. She was in distress there from February 26 until March 1 1908. However, on March 2 the *Ernest Reyer* managed to clear herself from her dangerous anchorage and reach Limerick.

In 1912 she was sold to Sté. Générale d'Armement, Nantes. In 1915-16, she made a passage to Cape Town from Seattle in 99 days. In February 1916 she left Table Bay for Falmouth (f.o.) with a maize cargo. Her master, Captain Jules Rioual, had a presentiment that he would never arrive at his destination, and before sailing gave to Lieut.-Col. H. L. Jones, R.M., of Cape Town, a letter to post to his wife when he heard of his loss. Captain

Rioual was right. The *Ernest Reyer* was posted missing in July 1916. A few years after the war it was learned that the ship was sunk on April 17 1916 by the German submarine *U-69* in lat. 49°N., long. 8°10′W.

About 1921-22 the obsolete corvette *Bayonnais,* completed in 1887 by the Government yard at Brest for the French Navy and condemned in 1920, was bought by three sailing-ship masters and renamed after their unlucky old friend of the *Ernest Reyer* as the *Capitaine Jules Rioual.* After repairs the old ship was re-rigged as a barquentine, and disappears from the register about 1930. She was probably sold for scrap.

Ernest Siegfried – Steel 4-masted barque, 3,104 g., 2,754 n. (See *Seine.*)

Eugène Pergeline – Steel barque, 2,203 g., 1,953 n.
September 20 1900: Launched by Chantiers Nantais de Constr. Maritimes, Nantes, for Sté. des Voiliers Nantais, Nantes.

In December 1915, while bound from Havre to New Caledonia with plaster, she encountered very bad weather in the Bay of Biscay and was partially dismasted. She put into Lorient for repairs. On March 15 1917, while on a passage from New Caledonia to Glasgow, she was sunk by the German submarine *U-54* about 25 miles south-south-east of the Fastnet.

Eugène Schneider – Steel barque, 2,218 g., 2,039 n.
April 5 1902: Launched by Chantiers Nantais de Constr. Maritimes, Nantes, for Cie. de Navigation Française, Nantes.

In 1904, transferred to the Société Générale d'Armement, Nantes. On July 12 1910 she left Liverpool for Callao with coal; on September 22 the Horn was in sight but her cargo was afire, and precautions were taken. Matters grew worse each day, and on September 27 Captain Le Meilleur decided to put back to Port Stanley. It was impossible to reach the Falklands owing to head winds, so the barque altered course for Montevideo where she arrived on October 12. The *Eugène Schneider* was rapidly beached and scuttled; raised when fire was put out, she was found considerably damaged, but was repaired. Brought before the London Prize Court at the beginning of World World I, she was apparently carrying nitrates belonging to a German firm when she arrived at Queenstown for orders. The cargo was condemned and ordered to be discharged at Liverpool. Her owners were subsequently paid compensation for the delay incurred while the law took its leisurely course.

After this she sailed successfully throughout the war and for a few years afterwards. On September 3 1921 she arrived at Falmouth, 151 days out from Australia. A few days before, she had been involved in a collision with the French steam trawler *Coucy* and had had several plates damaged. From the autumn of 1921 until February 1924 she was laid up, like many of her colleagues. Her owners having decided to put her in the log West African Trade, she left St. Nazaire in ballast on March 5 1924 for Kamerun, and continued these voyages until Christmas night 1926 when she was run down about 30 miles south-west of St. Catherine's Point by the British steamer *Burutu*. The *Eugène Schneider* sank in two or three minutes with her master, Captain Govys, and 23 of her crew. The remaining four managed to scramble on board the *Burutu,* which was practically undamaged.

(The English Channel and its vicinity was a notorious danger spot for collisions between steam and Sail, one reason being that it could be difficult to see a square-rigged ship by night, especially from an enclosed bridge.)

Eugénie Fautrel – Steel barque, 2,212 g., 1,945 n.
September 18 1899: Launched by Chantiers de la Loire, St. Nazaire, for G. Ehrenberg, Havre.

In 1909 she was owned by the Banque pour la Marine et l'Industrie which sold her to the Sté. Générale d'Armement for £6,600 in August, 1912. On September 29 1917, while bound from Geelong with grain for Bordeaux, she was captured by the German submarine *U-60*, and sunk by gunfire in 46°06'N., 11°25'W.

Europe – Steel 4-masted barque, 2,839 g., 2,459 n.
May 17 1897: Launched by Laporte & Co., Rouen, for A. d'Orbigny & G. Faustin Fils, La Rochelle.

She was a "tender" ship like her sister ship *Asie*. During the night of August 14-15 1897 she was alongside the fitting-out wharf of her builders when she was caught by the sudden rising of the river level with the incoming tide, and capsized. She was raised on September 18, having suffered no hull damage, but all rigging had to be renewed. Completion was delayed eight months and she did not sail until April 25 1898, from Havre to New Caledonia. Here are several of her best passages:

1902: Astoria to Longships, 113 days.
1903: Astoria to Falmouth, 106 days.
1904: Cuxhaven to Hobart, 77 days.

Under the ownership of d'Orbigny & Faustin she made ten voyages, eight of them to Oregon or California. The *Europe* was a hard-working bounty-earner as well as a good ship. For example, on her seventh voyage, from May 31 1904 until April 16 1905, she collected 89,395 francs freight and 122,433 francs bounty, having carried one cargo during that time. She made the outward passage in ballast, Hamburg-Hobart-Portland (Oreg.) and the call at Hobart of course increased the mileage. For the return passage she loaded grain from Portland to Ipswich. The whole voyage took one year. Passages made on this seventh voyage were: Hamburg-Hobart, 78 days; Hobart-Portland, 80 days; Portland-Ipswich, 131 days.

On September 13 1908 she was sold to A. D. Bordes, and made several voyages to Chile, with good runs, until the war. On July 3 1915, while bound from Iquique to Horta (Azores) she was reported on fire and abandoned for a few hours, but the crew returned and the fire was eventually put out, and the barque managed to reach her destination under sail. On June 25 1917 she left Sydney for Pauillac with wheat, under the command of Captain Adolphe P. Nicolas, on her last voyage. On September 24 1917 she was captured by the German submarine *U-C-63* in 45°15′N., 10°50′W., and sunk by bombs and gunfire. Her crew were picked up in their boats on September 28.

Faulconnier – Steel barque, 2,585 g., 1,715 n.
July 9 1902: Launched by Chantiers de la Loire, St. Nazaire, for Sté. des Voiliers Dunkerquois, Dunkirk.

Her maiden voyage was also her last. She first loaded case-oil at Philadelphia for Hiogo (Japan), via Hobart. From Hiogo she crossed to California to load wheat at San Francisco for Limerick. But on January 1 1904, caught in a heavy gale off the Irish coast, she was driven ashore in a critical position at Travera, near Seven Heads.

Shortly after the stranding continuous heavy seas caused the vessel to break up, submerging her entirely. Captain Hermic and his crew of 25 were safely landed at Courtmacsherry.

Faulconnier – Steel 4-masted barque, 3,076 g., 2,914 n.
1891: Built by Ramage & Ferguson, Leith, for Eckenstein & Mead, Liverpool, as *Wilhelm Tell*.

From 1899 until 1919 she appears in Lloyd's Register as the *Edmund* owned by G. J. H. Siemers & Co., Hamburg. Throughout the war she was idle at Iquique, and was allocated to France as reparations about 1919.

The *Edmund* passed Prawle Point on January 8 1921, from Iquique. Arriving at Dunkirk on January 11, 103 days out, she was laid up until sold in June of that year by the French Government to the Société des Voiliers Dunkerquois for 135,057 francs, and renamed *Faulconnier*. She made no voyage for her new owners and was broken up in 1923. She was not put in commission under the French flag.

Fédération – Steel barque, 1,145 g., 972 n.
1889: Towards the end of this year she was launched by A. Dubigeon, Nantes, for Charles & Fernand Brunellière Frères, Nantes.

Her maiden, second and third voyages took 33, 26 and 29 months. On her fourth voyage she was chartered from St. Nazaire with patent fuel for Madagascar, and was then commanded by Captain H. Prévost. After unloading at Diégo Suarez and Nossi Bé, she left Madagascar in ballast for False Point (near Calcutta), but was caught in a cyclone and thrown on Providence Island (north-north-east of Madagascar) on February 20 1898. The *Fédération* rapidly became a total loss, and her crew were saved a few weeks later by a passing vessel.

Fervaal – Steel barque, 2,300 g., 1,705 n.
November 4 1899: Launched by Chantiers de la Loire, St. Nazaire, for Cie. Celtique Maritime, Nantes.

On April 19 1901 arrived Antwerp from San Francisco with wheat on her maiden return voyage, and on June 3 of that year left Cherbourg for Portland (Oreg.), under Captain Mabon. She wrecked on Staten Island, near St. John's lighthouse, on August 1 1901. Her crew were saved by the Argentine warship *Primero de Mayo,* but two were lost. She was then some 60 days out on the passage and was having the usual difficulty in beating past Cape Horn.

The First Five-Master, *France I*

France – Steel 5-masted barque, 3,784 g., 3,624 n.
September 2 1890: Launched by D. & W. Henderson & Son, Glasgow, for A. D. Bordes.

The largest ship of their fleet, she was also the largest sailing vessel in the world at the time of her launch—a 5,900-deadweight tonner with a 921-ton cellular double bottom and a 1,236-ton main tank. Her sail area was 49,000 square feet, and her crew numbered 46 hands. She had the grace and beauty of line which is such an important factor in the general appearance of a sailing-ship, which was not always evident in the big 20th-century sailers. The *France* is reputed to have been a tender ship in spite of her water ballast tanks, in fact just a little crank even when loaded. Her best passages to Chile were made in 63, 71, 73, 75, 76 and 78 days—all good, most very good.

On January 25 1897 H.M.S. *Blenheim* ran into her while she was anchored at night in Dungeness Roads. A curious conflict ensued; the *France* carried two riding lights instead of the one which was then required by international regulations. The cruiser thought they were the lights of two ships at anchor and went between them. Although she was badly damaged the *France* was repaired, but she was found to blame. In fact she was just a bit ahead of regulations, as later ships of 150 ft. or upwards were required to carry two riding lights.

The massive four-masted barque *Champigny* is still afloat, though not yet (1972) fully restored. Here she is in dry-dock in Oakland, California, more than 50 years ago. (*San Francisco Maritime Museum.*)

The big four-masted barque *Champigny* makes her number off Sydney while the pilot-boat approaches. (*From the Nichols Collection, Mitchell Library, Sydney.*)

Down with her sails set, the *Duc d'Aumale* was sunk by *U-43* in January 1917. (*Photograph by* U-43: *from Dr. Jürgen Meyer Collection.*)

Figurehead of the French barque *Europe*. (*Mrs. G. O. Wilson Collection, San Francisco Maritime Museum.*)

Eugène Schneider: view taken the day before her loss. She was knocked down by a steamer in the **English Channel.** (*Henri Picard Collection.*)

Bow view, *France II* in ballast. Note patent anchor. She is towing to sea. Though huge, the *France II* was not as attractive as *France I*. (*Alan Villiers Collection.*)

On March 14 1901 she left North Shields for Valparaiso with coal, commanded by Captain Forgeard. On May 10 the *France* was struck by a violent
pampero off the coast of South America, when she took a list of 45 degrees
and sprang a serious leak due to her cargo shifting. On May 13, in approxi-
mate position 34°S., 48°W., she had to be abandoned by her crew, all of
whom were picked up by the German 4-masted barque *Hebe* which was just
in sight. They were landed at Valparaiso on June 9 1901. Meanwhile, the
Spanish barque *Josefa* arriving on May 22 at Montevideo, reported that on
May 13 she had seen the half-capsized *France* abandoned as a drifting
derelict about 500 miles off the River Plate. The tug *Hurracan* was then
sent to search for her, but was compelled to return on May 29 after an
unsuccessful search. The five-poster was never seen again.

The Second Five-Master, *France II*

France – Steel 5-masted barque (Jubilee rig), 5,633 g., 5,010 n.
November 9 1911: Launched by Chantiers de la Gironde, Bordeaux, for
Société des Navires Mixtes (Prentout-Leblond-Leroux & Co.), Rouen.

The second *France* was built with a cellular double-bottom, having sections
designed to form water ballast tanks, in which she could take a total of 2,685
tons. In her early days she was an auxiliary with twin-screws driven by two
eight-cylinder single-acting two-stroke engines of 295 n.h.p. Her tonnage
has never been exceeded in a sailing-ship: the *France* was really the largest
sailing vessel ever built. She was an 8,000-deadweight tonner. Her sail area
was 68,350 square feet (32 sails), and her crew all told numbered 45. She
was intended for the French ore trade from New Caledonia, and was fitted
with every modern device to save labour, as well as wireless and an electric
lighting plant. Her accommodation was very good.

The vessel was a long time completing, and her trials were made only in
August 1913 off La Pallice, under the command of Captain Lagnel. The
France is best described as imposing and impressive, but could hardly be
called beautiful. She did not look her size at a distance, but close to she was
truly enormous. Many considered that she represented the final development
of the big square-rigged sailing vessel.

"I remember vividly the big five-poster when she was at St. Nazaire in
June 1920," writes M. Picard, "I was then looking for a ship, so I went
aboard and met the famous Captain Le Port, but his answer was rather
abrupt—'No apprentice here, you know!' I remember too that the first
mate—an Englishman—was much more pleasant than his master . . . "

Here is the complete record of the second *France's* career:

November 1913   : Arrived Clydebank, under Captain Lagnel.
December 5 1913 : Left Clydebank for New Caledonia with coke and coal.

I

March 6 1914   : Arrived Tchio, 92 days.
April 24   : Left New Caledonia with 7,300 tons nickel ore.
August 3   : Arrived at Rothesay Dock, Clydebank, 102 days.
October 29   : Left for New Caledonia.
February 25 1915 : Arrived Tchio, 119 days.
July 28   : Touched at La Pallice for medical assistance, 109 days.
August 18   : Arrived Greenock.
February 4 1916 : Left Clydebank, commanded by Captain L. Gaude.
May 16   : Arrived Tchio, 81 days from the Irish coast.
July 9   : Sailed New Caledonia with nickel ore.
October 1   : Off the Tuskar, 83 days out, and arrived Clydebank on October 5.

The *France* was then sold to Cie. Française de Marine et Commerce, Rouen. Two 90-millimetre guns were fitted on the poop.

February 21 1917 : Left the Clyde for Montevideo with coal.
February 28   : In the evening, about 150 miles west-north-west of Cape Finisterre she was attacked by a German submarine, but the big barque managed to escape carrying a press of sail with engines full speed, and the aid of night.
April 15   : Arrived Montevideo, 53 days out.
June 11   : Sailed River Plate, arrived Santos 21, and left June 25.
August 5   : Arrived New York, 41 days, and left October 2, with case oil.
December 27   : Arrived Port Adelaide, 86 days.
May 4 1918   : Left Sydney for Tchio; arrived on May 16.
July 7   : Left New Caledonia for Dakar, arrived there on September 21, 76 days.
January 2 1919 : Sailed from Dakar, and arrived Le Verdon Roads (River Gironde) under sail, on February 17; 46 days.
March 31   : Sailed Bordeaux, under Captain L. Caplain.
April 18   : Arrived Havre Roads.
April 29   : Arrived Havre. Her engines were subsequently removed for they had not given satisfaction for a long time, and the *France* became a true sailing vessel.
September 10   : Arrived Shields from Havre, towed by the French tug *Abeille No. 2;* commanded by Captain Le Port. When in the Tyne, extensive repairs were carried out, including the fitting of a large new donkey-boiler for burning oil fuel.
December 1   : Left the Tyne bound for Baltimore, with coal, in tow of several tugs. As soon as an offing had been made these left her, except the British tug *Joffre,* which was

engaged to tow her as far as the Lizard. But her tow rope parted during a strong gale in the North Sea on December 2. On December 3 the *Joffre*, having lost her tow, signalled the incident to Flamborough Head and stated that she had left the *France* at midnight off the Yorkshire coast, that the big ship was then on her beam ends and making bad weather of it. The report caused considerable anxiety; the *France* was listed overdue at Lloyd's and reinsurance quoted at 10 guineas per cent.

On December 9 the *France* was reported at noon in 53°55′N., 0°40′E., waiting for a tug from Grimsby. Finally she was reported safe and arrived in Leith Roads on December 19. Her subsequent movements were:

February 13 1920 : Sailed Leith for Baltimore.
February 27 : Anchored in Dungeness Roads and sailed February 28.
April 18 : Arrived Baltimore 50 days from Dungeness.
April 29 : Left Baltimore.
May 21 : Arrived St. Nazaire, 22 days.
June 15 : Sailed St. Nazaire in ballast.
July 23 : Arrived Baltimore, 38 days.
November 5 : Left Baltimore.
December 2 : Arrived St. Nazaire, 27 days.
February 17 1921 : Sailed St. Nazaire, towed.
February 22 : Arrived Newport, Mon.
March 7 : Sailed Newport with 7,600 tons of coal.
June 25 : Arrived Lyttleton, 110 days. Her best day's run on this passage was 285 miles.
September 5 : Left Wellington with the largest cargo ever shipped in Sail from New Zealand—11,000 bales of wool and 6,000 casks of tallow. She arrived London early in December after a good passage of 90 days. On the way to the Horn she made the following runs on consecutive days: 266, 240, 276, 322, 286 and 243 miles. On her way from the Horn the *France* struck some very bad weather, and one big sea created havoc on her main deck besides washing two of the crew overboard.
February 5 1922 : Left London with cement, steel rails and trucks, for the ore mines in New Caledonia.
May 19 : Arrived Tchio, 103 days.
July : Sailed Tchio in ballast for Pouembout (New Caledonia) to load 8,000 tons of nickel ore. On the night of July 11-12 she drifted in calm with current on a coral reef, where she bumped heavily all night long.

The *France* was aground near a spot named Coya, about 60 miles from the entrance to Noumea. Early on July 12 her S.O.S. signals were picked up by the British steamer *Canadian Transporter,* which was 220 miles away. The latter immediately replied—"Keep a stout heart. Stokers doing their damnedest." But by this time the crew of the *France* had already abandoned the wreck which was hard and fast, and nearly dry at low water.

There is no doubt that the *France* could have been salved without much difficulty if her wreck had not occurred at a time when shipping was in a very low state, and her refloating was found unnecessary by her owners. The hull was sold for £2,000, in December 1922. So ended the career of the largest sailing-ship ever built.

France Marie – Steel barque, 1,994 g., 1,673 n. (carrying petroleum in bulk). January 17 1900: Launched by Chantiers de la Méditerranée, Havre, for A. Vimont & Co., Marseilles.

From 1900 until 1908 she made 28 outward passages between Marseilles and Philadelphia, and 27 homeward passages at an average of 36 days, the best passage 23 days and the slowest 70. She was a fine barque, and her career was the uneventful one of the good ship under the French flag. In 1911 she was sold to Belgian interests (Continental Petroleum Co.). Transferred in 1912 to the "Texas Co.", Port Arthur (U.S.A.), she was then converted into a three-masted schooner barge and renamed *Tampico.*

Although reported as foundered in 1937, she was still in use as a floating wharf at New Orleans in 1943.

François – Steel barque, 2,212 g., 1,945 n.
August 25 1900: Launched by Chantiers de la Loire, St. Nazaire, for G. Ehrenberg, Havre.

On her maiden voyage, commanded by Captain Arnaudtizon, she left St. Nazaire in ballast on October 19 1900, crossed the Line 18 days out, and arrived at Newcastle (N.S.W.) on January 8 1901, in 80 days. Arrived at San Francisco in 45 days from Newcastle with coal, left Port Costa for Ipswich with 3,000 tons of barley in bags, arriving Straits of Dover 94 days out—a very good round voyage. In 1906 while on a passage from San Francisco to Queenstown, under Captain Bellini, she was posted overdue and reinsured at a very high rate, but turned up in the slow time of 202 days. She had been delayed by 100 days of dead calm in the Atlantic. In 1909 she was sold to the Sté. des Armateurs Nantais, Nantes. On August 10 1915, while bound from Portland (Oreg.) to Queenstown with wheat, she was sunk by the German submarine *U-35* about 60 miles south-west of the Fastnet.

François Coppée – Steel barque (Jubilee rig), 2,289 g., 1,728 n.
November 6 1900: Launched by Chantiers de la Loire, Nantes, for N. & C. Guillon, Nantes.

Her maiden voyage was to San Francisco where she arrived on December 5 1902. She did not last much longer. On November 20 1903, when on passage from Newcastle (N.S.W.) for San Francisco, and without solar observation for three days, she was making land by night in a fog, when she went ashore near Tomales Bay, about 35 miles north-north-west of the Golden Gate. Shortly after the stranding heavy seas submerged the barque. Her master, Captain Irruye, and 11 men were drowned.

Françoise d'Amboise – Steel barque, 1,973 g., 1,741 n.
May 18 1901: Launched by A. Dubigeon, Nantes, for Sté. Bretonne de Navigation, Nantes.

On her maiden voyage, in the summer of 1901, she was at Swansea loading coal for San Francisco with the barque *Duchesse Anne* and the new full-rigged ship *Hoche*, also chartered for the same port. The three-masters laid a bet for the best passage, but the *Duchesse Anne* arrived in the Californian port in 110 days, a fortnight before the two other vessels. In 1912, she was sold to Sté. Générale d'Armement, Nantes. On June 21 1916, while on a passage from Leith to Valparaiso, she was sunk by the German submarine *U-22* about 68 miles north-west of Fair Island.

Gaël – Steel barque, 2,198 g., 1,949 n.
September 13 1901: Launched by Chantiers de la Loire, St. Nazaire, for Cie. Celtique Maritime, Nantes.

In 1906, she is credited with a fast passage of 43 days from San Francisco to Sydney.

May 22 1909: Left London for Portland (Oreg.) via Cherbourg and Hobart, with cement, under the orders of Captain D. Métayer, well-known for "cracking-on". The barque experienced gale upon gale after rounding the Cape of Good Hope and, perhaps too hard driven, suffered considerably. On August 17 1909, the carpenter found four feet of water in the hold, and the master decided to alter course for the Australian coast. In spite of her steam pump working continually, matters grew worse day by day, and on August 21 1909, the *Gaël* was abandoned sinking in 36°44'S., 114°07'E., about 160 miles off Cape Leeuwin. After sailing for five days in their boats the crew landed safely on the Australian coast.

(Note: It must have been hard driving indeed which caused an eight-year-old steel hull to open up, if this were the real cause of the sinking. But cement is notoriously a heavy, "dead" cargo.)

Galathée – Iron barque, 1,235 g., 1,086 n.
1884: Built by A. Stephen & Sons, Glasgow, for A. C. Le Quellec, Bordeaux.

When under the French flag she was chiefly in the nitrate trade. On January 13 1893, in collision with an iceberg, the forward part and some rigging were damaged, and she put into Rio de Janeiro for repairs. In another serious accident in October 1894 she parted her cables and stranded on Hills Bank in the North Sea, but was refloated by Dunkirk tugs. She was sold in October 1903 to B. A. Olsen & Son, of Lyngör, and renamed *Nebo*. October 24 1913: Left Risör for Cardiff with timber, under Captain D. Christiansen, and ran ashore a month later on the Horn Reef (Danish Coast), about 200 metres from the shore at Blaavanshuk. The *Nebo* was abandoned by the crew and became a total loss.

Général de Boisdeffre – Steel barque, 2,195 g., 1,960 n.
August 3 1898: Launched by Chantiers de la Loire, Nantes, for R. Guillon & R. Fleury, Nantes.

Sold 1908 to Sté. Générale d'Armement, Nantes. On January 14 1917 she left Mejillones, Chile, for Brest, under Captain Pireau, and went missing. Although she was officially recorded as a war loss by French maritime authorities, her fate is a mystery, so much the more as the German Navy declared that there were no German records about her. There is also the possibility that she was sunk by a German submarine which herself later went missing.

Général de Charette – Steel barque, 2,297 g., 1,711 n.
May 5 1898: Launched by Chantiers de la Loire, Nantes, for Leon Guillon, Nantes.

Her maiden voyage was made to San Francisco and she made few others. In July 1900 she left Swansea for San Francisco with coal, commanded by Captain Rehel. By September she was fighting her way past the Horn, but went aground in a snow-storm near Cape Good Success (Lemaire Straits), about four o'clock on the morning of September 3, and became a total loss. Two men were lost, the rest of her crew being rescued by the schooner *Elena*. (If she were in the Straits of Lemaire at all, she could easily be in serious trouble.)

Général de Négrier – Steel barque, 2,196 g., 1,946 n.

May 10 1901: Launched by Chantiers Nantais de Constr. Maritimes, Nantes, for N. & C. Guillon, Nantes.

Sold in 1912 to Sté. Générale d'Armement, Nantes. In 1913 she made a voyage to Antofagasta, Chile.

August 11 1921: Spoke British liner *Cluny Castle* in 24°04′S, 0°33′W., 125 days out from Australia and short of provisions. Revictualled.

October 9 1921: Arrived Queenstown 184 days out: thence to Hull—a poor passage by any standards. She was soon laid up like her colleagues; however she was the first vessel to be fitted out again, and was put in the West African log trade. She left St. Nazaire in ballast for Kamerun on November 27 1922, and made six voyages to Kamerun. On her seventh and last voyage she left Ghent on December 5 1926 and arrived in 63 days. Loaded with sleepers at Manoka and Duala in about three months, she left Kamerun for Sète on May 4 1927, but was much delayed by calms. She spoke the British steamer *Baron Sempill* on August 13 in 39°03′N., 17°48′W., short of provisions, and was revictualled. Passed Gibraltar on August 23 and put into Almeria for three days: she was picked up by the tug *Tourbillon* 50 miles off Toulon on September 20 and arrived at Sète the next day, 140 days on passage. She was broken up in 1928 at Marseilles. (This was a difficult trade for heavy metal square-rigged ships, with a great deal of calm.)

Général de Sonis – Steel barque, 2,190 g., 1,943 n.

November 7 1901: Launched by Chantiers Nantais de Constr. Maritimes, Nanes, for Cie. de Navigation Française, Nantes.

On her maiden voyage in 1902 she covered the 6,160 miles between Table Bay and Hobart in 25 days in spite of two days of calm, a splendid ten knots' average. In 1904 she was transferred to Sté. Générale d'Armement, Nantes. Early in February 1913 arrived at Port Victoria to load wheat, and completed loading 35,920 bags of grain on March 8. On March 6, the French barque *Jean Bart,* bound for Wallaroo from Antwerp, struck the west coast of Wardang Island. Two days later her crew, with the exception of the second mate who remained on board, was taken in lifeboats to the *Général de Sonis* and accommodated. On the evening of March 12 a violent south-westerly gale swept into Spencer Gulf. A coastal schooner was wrecked off Port Victoria, and the *Général de Sonis* dragged both anchors and was driven aground (the *Jean Bart*'s crew was wrecked for the second time in a week).

The *Général de Sonis* was leaking only slowly, and on March 15 the tug *Euro* refloated her. Unfortunately there was a mistake in signals; when the French master signalled for the tug to slow down while the barque picked up her anchors, the tug stopped towing. A strong breeze was blowing and the barque took charge and drifted ashore, this time on rocks. The *Général de Sonis* now had several holes; most of her cargo became saturated, and thousands of bags of putrefying grain were jettisoned. On June 17 the small coaster *Jessie Darling* attempted to refloat the barque, but succeeded only in breaking several hawsers. Two days later the little steamer made another attempt, breaking more hawsers but succeeding in moving the barque a short distance. The following day, June 20, at high tide a kedge was run out and with the aid of sails the unlucky French master finally succeeded in refloating his command. She was found to have two small holes under the fore hatch and a larger one in the fore-peak. These were patched temporarily and on July 9 1913 the *Général de Sonis* was towed to Wallaroo by the *Jessie Darling*, after which she proceeded to Melbourne for repairs—near four months after her stranding.

This was not the end of the big barque's adventures. On April 8 1915 she was being towed up Channel by the South Shields tug *Homer* bound for Sunderland, when off St. Catherine's Point they were ordered to stop by the German submarine *U-32*, commanded by Oberleutnant Baron Von Spiegel. What Captain H. Gibson, the tug's master, did was something quite unexpected on the part of the German, as he slipped his towing hawser and swung the tug round her heel, making straight for his antagonist under a hail of bullets. The windows and woodwork of the wheel-house were smashed, but the captain escaped injury. The *Homer* missed the stern of the enemy by three feet, then turned and made for the Owers Lightship. In the mêlée the unarmed French barque made her escape by clapping on all sail and fled before the wind. She was afterwards picked up by the Dover tug *Lady Crundall* and anchored in the Downs. Captain Bénard was in command.

In 1919 she made a good passage from Saigon to Nantes with rice, rounding the Cape of Good Hope and being off Ushant 110 days out. Her last voyage to Australia was made in 1919-20, arriving at Nantes from Geelong on May 6 1920 in 101 days—again, a good run. She left Nantes in June 1920 for San Francisco via the Panama Canal, and arrived back at Ipswich on March 21 1921 to be laid up in the Canal de la Martinière. Here she was bought by M. Potet, Havre, for the West Indies trade, in which the *Général de Sonis* made seven voyages (West Indies and French Guiana). On January 5 1928 arrived Havre after a slow 76 days' passage, during which Captain Rault and three of his crew fell ill and died at sea.

On her last voyage in this trade, she sailed from Havre on December 2 1930, but on March 2 1931, when entering port, grounded on the bar of the River Maroni (French Guiana), but was refloated. Arriving at Havre on June 29 1931 from Savannah-la-Mar (44 days), she was laid up.

Like the *Bonchamp* under the same ownership, she was put up to auction on July 8 1932 at a cost of 20,000 francs, but there was no sale. On September 9 she was again put up at the greatly reduced cost of 1,000 francs. This time she was sold, and on November 5 1932 the *Général de Sonis* left Havre in tow for Bruges to be broken up. She was the last of the large sailing-ships flying the Tricolour: with her ended the French bounty ships era.

Général Faidherbe – Steel ship, 2,188 g., 1,904 n.
May 18 1901: Launched by Chantiers de la Loire, Nantes, for Cie. Maritime Française, Nantes.

Among her passages are the following:

March 9 1910   : Arrived Falmouth, 119 days out from Astoria.
April 20 1911   : Arrived Ipswich from San Francisco, 140 days.
November 15   : Arrived Vancouver, 153 days from London.

In 1913 she was sold to Sté. Générale d'Armement, Nantes. Some later passages are:

July 4 1919   : At Nantes from Adelaide, 112 days.
June 12 1920   : Arrived off River Loire from Geelong, 128 days.
April 10 1921   : Sailed from San Francisco.
September 6   : Arrived Falmouth from San Francisco, 149 days, and
                    left on September 8 for Ipswich.

Then came the end—lay-up in the Canal de la Martinière, which she left on June 19 1927 to be broken up.

Général Foy – Steel barque, 2,192 g., 1,973 n.
August 9 1900: Launched by Chantiers de la Loire, Nantes, for Sté. des Voiliers Français, Havre.

On her maiden voyage she reached New Caledonia from St. Nazaire in 90 days: and on March 20 1902 arrived at San Francisco from Europe in 108 days. She then sailed back to Ipswich, England, in 117 days.

In 1903 another passage to San Francisco was made in 104 days. After a last voyage to Australia in 1921 she was laid up, and on July 20 1923 arrived at Rotterdam to be broken up.

Général Mellinet – Steel barque, 1,943 g., 1,491 n.
March 1895: Completed by Laporte & Cie., Rouen, for Sté. des Voiliers Nantais, Nantes.

She had an uneventful career under the French flag and was sold in 1905 for 120,000 francs to G. C. Brövig, of Farsund, Norway, and renamed *Gunvor*. On April 11 1906, while on a passage from New York to Melbourne, she put into the Bermudas, leaking. On November 29 1911 she left Caleta Buena with nitrate for Falmouth (f.o.), under Captain Salvesen, to become one of the many fine ships lost by bad landfalls in the English

Channel. On April 6 1912, making the land by night in hazy weather, 129 days out, she stranded at Beagle Point, Coverack, near Black Head, and became a total loss. So close inshore was she that her bowsprit overhung the rocks, and her crew of 19 lowered a rope ladder over the bow to gain the shore dry-footed.

The *Gunvor*'s cargo was insured for £25,000.

Général Neumayer – Steel barque, 1,858 g., 1,640 n.
August 1897: Completed by Laporte & Co., Rouen, for Norbert Guillon, Nantes.

January 1900	: Arrived San Francisco from Swansea, 187 days out.
December 8 1903	: Bound from Algoa Bay to New Caledonia, put into Sydney with a leak and drydocked.
June 1907	: Sold for 150,000 francs to A. D. Bordes: sailed without further incident in peace and war.

Laid up in 1921, she was scrapped in Belgium in 1924.

Geneviève – Steel barque, 1,101 g., 987 n.
August 8 1894: Launched by Anciens Etablissements Cail, St. Denis, for Cie. Nationale d'Armement, Havre.

She was sold to Norway nine years later as already too small to earn in the deep-water trades, after her ten bounty-earning years expired. In 1903 she was sold to Aas & Cappelen of Fredrikstad, and renamed *Erling*. In 1917 she made a passage from River Plate to Glasgow. In 1921 she was owned by Z. Moller & Aas, Fredrikstad, and was broken up in 1925.

Geneviève Molinos – Steel barque, 1,972 g., 1,729 n.
January 8 1899: Launched by Chantiers de la Loire, Nantes for Sté. des Voiliers Français, Havre.

She was rather a good passage maker in her early days. In 1906, under Captain J. Delignac, while on passage from London to Portland (Oreg.), she was off Dungeness when she fell in with the British four-masted barque *Inverness-shire* which was bound from Antwerp to Portland (Oreg.). The French barque arrived in the Columbia River 12 days before her colleague. On her return passage the *Geneviève Molinos* reached Falmouth in 111 days. (But the *Inverness-shire* was no flyer.) On another passage she left Seattle with the skysail-yarder *Clyde*, then under the Norwegian flag. The two vessels arrived at Queenstown on the same day, but the French barque was an hour before the famous full-rigged ship, the Norwegian master having lost his £4 bet. In fact the two ships must have been rather well matched.

The *Geneviève Molinos* arrived at Portland (Oreg.) on September 30 1907, with 2,500 tons of cement from London, and cleared from the port on October 10 with 95,470 bushels wheat for the United Kingdom. Some of her passages follow: —

February 17 1910 : Arrived Dublin from Puget Sound, 136 days.
October 1 : Arrived San Francisco from Swansea under Captain Carméné, 149 days.
April 11 1911 : Passed Dover, 146 days from San Francisco.
September 12 : At Mejillones, 103 days from Penarth.

Later, the *Geneviève Molinos* loaded general cargo at New York for Manila in 1918. Her last passage was slow. Leaving Port Lincoln on July 25 1921, she was posted overdue and reinsured for five guineas per cent, finally arriving at Queenstown (for the last time) in 150 days, and reached London on December 20 1921. The barque was sold to Dutch shipbreakers in September 1923.

She was a good-looking vessel, as pretty as her poetic name when deep-loaded in good trim.

Germaine – Steel barque, 1,930 g., 1,695 n.
May 1 1900: Launched by Chantiers de la Méditerranée, Havre, for Sté. des Voiliers Havrais, Havre, as *Ville de Belfort*.

On July 10 1901 she arrived at Noumea partially dismasted and was subsequently repaired at Sydney. A year later she was sold to Cie. Havraise de Navigation (E. Corblet & Co., Mgrs.), Havre, and renamed *Germaine*. She was a good sailer and never known as a "slow poke". In 1903 she made Hobart from Havre in 74 days. It was reported that she had overtaken 33 sailing-ships while running in the Roaring Forties. On March 17 1921 she left Port Lincoln for Bordeaux. It was her last voyage for she was eventually laid up in Canal de la Martinière, and broken up at Bilbao in 1925.

Gers – Steel 4-masted barque, 2,128 g., 2,030 n.
August 1890: Completed by Barclay, Curle & Co., Glasgow, for the Lyle Shipping Co., Greenock, as *Cape York*.

She was a passage-maker under the British flag. Among other good runs she reached Adelaide from Barry Docks in 72 days in 1893, and sailed from Newcastle N.S.W., to Mollendo in 38 days in 1899. In November 1899 she was sold for £14,500 to A. D. Bordes and renamed *Gers,* but did not last long. In October 1904 she left Tocopilla for La Pallice with nitrate, commanded by Captain Delépine, but when making the land in heavy and hazy weather in mid-January 1905, she stranded on Chanchardon Point, Ré Island. The sea was very rough, but the crew managed to hold on in the rigging all night and were saved the day after with great difficulty and splendid seamanship by the French steam trawler *Georgette*. The *Gers* became a total loss.

The skipper of the trawler, Monsieur Fernand Castaing, was commended for his courageous action. He subsequently became owner of the "Steam Trawlers Co." of La Rochelle. The figurehead of the *Gers* is well looked after to this day in the grand-children's home of the late and well-remembered Fernand Castaing.

Gers – Another steel barque, 2,137 g., 1,981 n.
1885: Built by Harland & Wolff, Belfast, for S. Lawther, Belfast, as *Queen's Island*.

About 1890 she was sold to G. Thompson & Co., Aberdeen, and renamed *Strathdon,* which also became a well-known ship. In 1903 she was owned by Sir William Henderson of Aberdeen and, in November 1905, was bought from the Aberdeen White Star Line by those good judges of good ships Messrs. A. D. Bordes, and renamed *Gers*. There followed the unpublicised career of the hard-working, well-behaved ship, never in the news, until 1922 when she was laid up at Nantes, to leave in January 1924 for Bruges where she was scrapped. Basil Lubbock pays a tribute to her as both *Queen's Island* and *Strathdon* in his *Last of the Windjammers,* Vol. I (Brown Son and Ferguson, Glasgow).

Gipsy – Iron ship, 1,519 g., 1,447 n.
1874: Built by W. Pile & Co., Sunderland, for Devitt & Moore, London, as *Rodney*.

This was another famous old ship. In her early days she was a record-maker, and her passenger accommodation was well-known for its luxury. Most of her life then was spent between London and Melbourne or Sydney and, in 1888, when taking part in the annual wool race, the *Rodney* arrived second off Gravesend after a passage of 78 days, just an hour behind the *Cutty Sark*. Her best passage was to Sydney in 1887, when she ran from off the Lizard to Sydney in 67 days. Her best homeward passage was 77 days Sydney to London. Her best run to Melbourne was 71 days in 1882, and to Adelaide 74 days in 1880, according to Lubbock.

In 1896, when sailing clippers had been pushed out by steamers, Devitt & Moore sold the *Rodney* to F. Boissière of Nantes. Renamed *Gipsy,* late in the summer of 1901 she left Iquique for Falmouth with nitrates. She did well until early December when, nearing the Scillies 81 days out, the weather was thick and squally with freshening wind. The *Gipsy* ran on before the south-westerly gale until, realising that he had passed Falmouth, her master, Captain Warneck, decided to run for Plymouth for shelter. The wind backed and increased until it was blowing a hard gale, and forcing the ship nearer into the land. She was sighted off Looe, still making up the coast, frequently hidden in rain squalls. At six o'clock distress rockets were seen from Downderry, and soon the lifeboat was away to her rescue. The *Gipsy* was on the rocks, while the French crew tried to pump her dry and get clear. This was unsuccessful, and it was soon obvious that they must abandon her. This was on December 7 1901. Captain Warneck said later that probably he could have got into Plymouth Sound if he had not identified the lights of Whitesand Bay as those of Plymouth. So the splendid *Rodney* did not sail long for France. Perhaps she did not care for her new name.

Grande Duchesse Olga – Steel barque, 1,981 g., 1,748 n.
July 2 1898: Launched by A. Dubigeon, Nantes, for Sté. des Armateurs Nantais, Nantes.

On April 29 1900 she left San Francisco for Europe, but arrived at Tahiti partially dismasted on August 1. She left again on January 4 1901 after extensive repairs. In June 1911 she was sold for £4,000 to Skibsaktieselskapet Mosvold (Pedersen & Mosvold) of Farsund, and renamed *Mosvold*. Resold in 1915 to Christiansand interests, she acquired the name *Sagitta*, but on April 2 1917 she was sunk by explosive charges put aboard her by the German submarine *U-78* in the North Sea, about 85 miles east-south-east of Lerwick (Shetlands).

Guerveur – Steel barque, 2,596 g., 2,048 n.
May 1902: Launched by Chantiers de la Loire, Nantes, for Cie. de Navigation Française, Nantes.

Sold in 1904 to Sté. des Voiliers Nantais. On August 23 1908, while on passage from Eureka (Calif.) to Europe, she collided with an iceberg off Cape Horn and was badly damaged. The *Guerveur* succeeded in reaching Montevideo for repairs by September 14. She left on October 14 and arrived at Liverpool on December 21, 68 days from Montevideo. On December 20 1909, while bound from Glasgow to New Caledonia, she was thrown on her beam ends through ballast shifting off Cape Finisterre. After four days in the hold her crew got her upright, and continued the voyage. Again, on November 18 1910, she had a narrow escape near Cherbourg, when almost cast ashore through her tow rope parting. Only a sudden veering of the wind allowed the barque just to clear the rocks.

On December 29 1913 she left New Caledonia for Havre, but her passage was delayed by calms and head winds. On January 30 1914 she was partially dismasted and her cargo shifted; rounding Cape Horn on March 7 under jury rig, she finally arrived at Havre in 186 days—a long and trying passage. Her end came in 1917 on a passage from Glasgow for New Caledonia with coal. She was attacked by the German submarine *U-48* on March 12 and, despite the French gunners' action, the third shell of the submarine made a hole below the waterline and the barque sank rapidly, about 84 miles north-north-west of Tory Island. The crew abandoned her, while the *U-48* continued to fire. Luckily not a man was injured. Captain Huet and his crew landed safely on the Irish coast three days later, thanking God for His mercies.

Guéthary – Steel barque, 2,178 g., 1,930 n.
September 1 1901: Launched by Chantiers Nantais de Constr. Maritimes, Nantes, for Sté. Bayonnaise de Navigation, Bayonne.

On February 11 1909, while anchored at Poro (New Caledonia) loading nickel ore, she was thrown ashore in a cyclone, but was subsequently refloated. In May 1911 she was sold to Sté. des Voiliers Normands (Prentout-Leblond-Leroux & Co., Mgrs.), Rouen. On October 21 1914, while bound from New Caledonia to Glasgow, she stranded at Port Ellen Bay and became a total loss. (It will be noted that, like several others, she changed ownership when the ten-year bounty-earning period was up. One thinks that there was some good economic reason for this.)

Gustave et Paul – Iron ship, 1,458 g., 1,399 n.
1876: Built by Bowdler, Chaffer & Co., Liverpool, for R. Nicholson & Son, Liverpool, as *Corby*.

Bought by H. O. Morgan of Liverpool about 1890. She became French in April 1898, when sold to G. Dor, Marseilles, and renamed *Gustave et Paul*. Again in April 1900, she was sold (for £5,500) to Flli. A. & G. Semidei, Genoa, acquiring the name of *Caracciolo*. Under the Italian flag she made several voyages to the Pacific. On June 27 1908 she left Marseilles with a cargo of bricks and arrived at Auckland after a passage of 87 days. In July 1910, while on passage from New Caledonia to Antwerp, she was severely battered south of Chatham Island. With her cargo shifted and her rigging badly damaged, she put into Auckland, where she was condemned and sold for scrap.

Haudaudine – Steel ship, 2,393 g., 1,734 n.
1902: Built by Chantiers de St. Nazaire for Sté. des Armateurs Nantais, Nantes.

Arriving in New Caledonia in ballast from Nagasaki in the fall of 1904, under Captain Allaire, she loaded 3,200 tons of nickel ore at Kataviti (west coast of the island). Leaving New Caledonia on January 3 1905 in tow of the French steamer *Saint Pierre,* her tow rope parted just before the pair cleared the narrow fairway. The *Haudaudine* struck the coral reef and sank rapidly. Her crew were saved.

Hautot – Steel barque, 2,789 g., 2,020 n.
September 26 1900: Launched by Chantiers de Normandie, Rouen, for Cie. Rouennaise de Transports Maritimes (Prentout-Leblond-Leroux & Co., Mgrs.), Rouen.

On July 4 1906, commanded by Captain Guerpin, she left New Caledonia for Glasgow and went missing. It was assumed that she probably struck an iceberg, and there was a strange report that she was seen wrecked in the middle of a huge and dangerous ice-field but could not be approached. This was a very bad ice season in the vicinity of Cape Horn and towards the Falkland Islands.

Hélène – Steel 4-masted barque, 3,456 g., 3,194 n.
1892: Built by W. Pickersgill & Sons, Sunderland, for Andorinha Sailing Ship Co. (E. F. & W. Roberts), Liverpool, as *Andorinha.*

She was a powerful 5,150 deadweight tonner, originally crossing three sky-sail yards. In 1900 she reached Newcastle (N.S.W.) from Cape Town in the creditable time of 24 days and some hours. From 1903 until 1909 she was owned by S. Goldberg & Sons of Swansea who sold her in 1909 to A. D. Bordes, when she was renamed *Hélène.*

The lofty barque had the honour of being the biggest vessel in the fleet during the time under the Bordes' house-flag. But on February 22 1919, while bound from Baltimore to Nantes with steel, under Captain Maison-neuve, she sank off the Virginia coast after being in collision with the Norwegian steamer *Gansfjord.* It was night and the *Hélène* went down in a few minutes, with the loss of 17 lives.

Hélène Blum – Steel ship, 2,767 g., 1,757 n.
September 12 1901: Launched by Chantiers Maritimes du Sud-Ouest, Bordeaux, for Sté. des Voiliers de St. Nazaire.

Mr. Blum was a ship-chandler of San Francisco and an important shareholder in the Sté. des Voiliers de St. Nazaire. The ship was named in honour of his wife. On her maiden voyage she left Bordeaux on November 17 1901 for Cardiff and the Pacific. Her homeward passage was from Iquique to Havre. In 1903 she transferred to Sté. Générale d'Armement, St. Nazaire.

The *Hélène Blum* made several voyages to the North Pacific, but she had not a long life.

April 1 1908: Left Bristol for Port Stanley (Falkland Islands) in ballast, commanded by Captain F. Hervé. Owing to head winds, anchored about midnight near Lundy Island, sailing again three days later. On April 13 she passed Madeira and on the 19th sighted St. Vincent, Cape Verde Islands.
April 26: Crossed the Line.
May 8: Spoke the German full rigger *Parnassos* of Hamburg, from Hamburg to Coquimbo, 47 days out.

On the night of May 19-20, the ship's position was 180 miles from the north coast of the Falklands, 45 days from Lundy Island. But the *Hélène Blum* was then delayed by strong head winds, and Cape Bougainville was sighted only on May 24. By May 26 she was within sight of Cape Pembroke lighthouse (entrance to Port William and Port Stanley), but about 10 p.m. she struck on Seal Rocks. After an hour she began to founder rapidly and her crew of 28 had to abandon her. They were saved by the tug *Samson*.

Hoche – Steel ship, 2,211 g., 1,941 n.
May 4 1901: Launched by Chantiers de la Loire, Nantes, for Cie. Maritime Française, Nantes.

On August 19 1909 she had a narrow escape while bound from Newcastle (N.S.W.) to Portland (Oreg.) with coal. She was making the land 19 miles south of Tillamook Head, 63 days out, when a dead calm set in for several days until August 22. In the meantime she was driven slowly by currents to within about 900 yards of the dangerous Arch Rock (1.5 miles south of Tillamook Head). Fortunately she was able to anchor in 27 fathoms. When a light breeze arose she was compelled to slip her foul anchor and four shackles, sailing within a few yards of Arch Rock to get clear.

She arrived safely at Astoria on August 23 and was sold to the Sté. Générale d'Armement four years later: but she was not to avoid fatality. Her end came in 1915 when she was chartered for a voyage from Ipswich to Valparaiso via Leith—a roundabout beginning. On October 22 1915 she left Ipswich for Leith in ballast, under tow, but her tow rope parted in a gale. She was sighted for the last time on October 28 in the evening, adrift in stormy weather, about eight miles off Carnoustie. The next day, her four boats, some life-belts and wreckage were found on the Scottish coast between Arbroath and Carnoustie: nothing else was ever found.

The *Hoche* was officially posted lost with all hands four miles east-south-east of Carnoustie on October 29 1915.

Horizon – Iron barque, 1,078 g., 1,007 n.
1888: Built by C. J. Bigger, Londonderry, for H. Estier of Marseilles.

The first five-masted barque *France* leaving Greenock, 1890. (*Adamson, Rothesay.*)

France II leaving St. Nazaire, 1920. She had tremendous sheer.
(*Neurdein Frères, Paris-Corbeil.*)

Gunvor, ex-*Général Mellinet* near Black Head, April 6 1912. Wrecked by bad landfall, but not by her Master. (*Forbin.*)

The French barque *Général de Négrier* loading grain at Oakland Long Wharf, early 20th century. (*Dickie Collection, San Francisco Maritime Museum.*)

Jacqueline at anchor in ballast. (*Marius Bar Photos, Toulon.*)

The French ship *Laënnec* is still afloat as the Finnish *Suomen Joutsen*, now a naval school-ship. (*Plummer Collection, San Francisco Maritime Museum.*)

Jeanne d'Arc awaiting breaking-up at Bayonne, December 1950. Perhaps the saddest end for a fine barque. (*Henri Picard Collection.*)

The *John*, formerly the French *Léon Bureau*, ashore in Valparaiso Bay, July 1919. (*Dr. Jürgen Meyer Collection.*)

French barque *Nantes* being intercepted by the German raider *Moëwe* on December 26 1916 before sinking. (*Dr. Jürgen Meyer Collection.*)

Under the French flag she was in the West Indies and French Guiana trade. 1902: Sold to G. Nossardi fu G., Genoa, and renamed *Era*. She was later owned by G. Drago, Genoa. She sailed without accident or oustanding incident until June 16 1916 when she was sunk by the German submarine *U-35* off Porto Maurizio in the Mediterranean. (This was the kind of handy vessel that Joseph Conrad could have sailed in.)

Iquique – Iron ship, 1,484 g., 1,436 n.
1868: Built by T. Royden & Son, Liverpool, for the British Shipowners' Co., Liverpool, as the *British Sceptre*.

Her name is remembered for the case of the New Zealand-bound emigrant ship *Cospatrick* which burned out south of the Cape of Good Hope on November 27 1874. The *British Sceptre* was bound from Calcutta to Dundee and picked up the very few survivors from the only two boats which got away from the fiery panic, crammed with people but without food, proper clothing or fresh water, for the *Cospatrick* had been crowded and burned furiously. Of 473 aboard her, 3 survived.

In 1891, the *British Sceptre* was sold to A. D. Bordes and renamed *Iquique,* but she was not to last long. On December 30 of the same year, on her first voyage under Bordes' ownership (from Newcastle-on-Tyne towards Valparaiso with coal) commanded by Captain Lanusse, she stranded in dense fog on Ooster Bank, near Brouwershaven (Holland). A gale prevented refloating and she became a total loss. Her crew were saved, being much more fortunate than the people of the *Cospatrick* 17 years earlier.

Jacobsen – Steel barque, 2,195 g., 1,950 n.
October 1 1901: Launched by Chantiers de la Loire, Nantes, for Sté. des Voiliers Dunkerquois, Dunkirk.

In her early days she was in the North Pacific grain trade and from 1909 until 1914 was chiefly on Chilean nitrate voyages.

On January 28 1915, while on passage from San Francisco towards Gloucester with barley, she was captured and sunk by the German raider *Prinz Eitel Friedrich* in 29°44′S., 26°57′W.

Jacobsen – Steel 4-masted barque, 2,150 g., 1,995 n.
1903: Built by Soc. Esercizio Baccini, Riva Trigoso, for E. Raffo fu E., Spezia, as *Erasmo*.

On her maiden voyage she left Genoa on June 12 1903 for New York, but was dismasted off the American coast and her first mate was injured by the fall of a yard. It was not until August 17 that she reached New York, under

J

jury rig, 66 days out. The *Erasmo*'s underwriters decided to effect her repairs in Italy and she was towed to Genoa by the Dutch tug *Titan*.

She continued under the Italian flag, always on Pacific voyages to Australia and Chile, until 1913, when she was sold to F. Laeisz, of Hamburg, and renamed *Pinguin*.

Two voyages to Chile were completed under the Laeisz house-flag, but she was laid up at Hamburg from 1914 until 1918. On September 15 1917 she was bought by C. J. Klingenberg & Co., Bremen, and renamed *Weser*. Some time later, in 1920, she was allocated to France as reparations, and sold by the French Government to the Sté. des Voiliers Dunkerquois for 161,434 francs and renamed *Jacobsen* in 1922. She made no voyage for her new owners, for she was sold for scrap in April 1923, and sailed from Dunkirk on December 25 1923, arriving at Bruges the following day to be broken up. It was a good ship wasted, but there was no work at the time.

Jacqueline – Steel 4-masted barque, 2,899 g., 2,613 n.
February 6 1897: Launched by Chantiers de la Méditerranée, La Seyne, for A. D. Bordes.
On her maiden voyage she left Marseilles with tiles for Australia and subsequently went to Chile, where she loaded nitrate. On February 9 1902, while on passage from Iquique to Dunkirk she went ashore near Calais, but was got off. In 1906 she made her best outward passage to Chile—Barry to Iquique, 72 days.

A curious accident happened to the *Jacqueline* on an August night in 1907. She and one of the two tugs which had her in tow from Dunkirk to Port Talbot were caught in thick summer fog as they crossed Mount's Bay from the Lizard, and ran straight into the headland at Carn-du. Her chief damage was a crumpled bowsprit, but both she and the tug slewed off the rocks as the tide rose and eventually reached Falmouth on August 21, where she was dry-docked and repaired. On her last voyage, she left Iquique for La Pallice on July 1 1917 with nitrate, under Captain Y. Nicolas. On September 25, spoken by British liner *Victoria* in lat. 46°25′N., long. 13°10′W. When the liner was going away a submarine was sighted coming near the barque, but both she and the U-boat were rapidly lost to sight from the *Victoria* because of a fog bank. The *Jacqueline* did not arrive and for some time her fate was a mystery.

Examining war records later, it was discovered that the U-boat was *U-101* (Kpt.-lt. Koopmann). Robbed of his target by the fog, he torpedoed her the following morning. She went down quickly, and there were no survivors.

Jacques – Steel barque, 1,877 g., 1,634 n.
November 5 1896: Launched by Chantiers de la Méditerranée, Havre, for G. Ehrenberg, Havre.

However, she capsized in port when fitting out afloat and was subsequently straightened. About 1910 she was bought by the Banque pour la Marine et l'Industrie of Paris, and in September 1912, sold (by the bank presumably) to Cie. Générale des Iles de Kerguelen, St. Paul et Amsterdam, of Havre, possibly for some sealing/whaling venture in the far south of the Indian Ocean. This did not happen it seems, as in 1914 she was sold to A/S Strix (Th. Jacobsen, Mgr.), of Sarpsborg, Norway, and renamed *Strix*, as a general trader throughout the war. In 1919 she came under the ownership of A/S Vigor (M. Hansen, Mgr.), Christiansand, and acquired yet another name, this time as the *Vicomte*. Slump soon followed: in 1924 she was broken up in Germany for her scrap value.

Jane Guillon – Steel barque, 2,303 g., 1,717 n.
August 1900: Completed by Chantiers de la Loire, St. Nazaire, for N. & C. Guillon, Nantes.

From January 1902 until February 1903 she made a voyage from the Tyne to San Francisco, returning to Leith. In 1905 her master and most of her crew were attacked by scurvy, and she put into St. Helena for a few days to refresh, eventually arriving at Nantes on December 10 1905.

At the end of December 1906 she left San Francisco for Europe with a cargo of barley, and reached Queenstown 111 days out. Ordered to Ipswich, she sailed on April 25 1907, but owing to head winds she was off Beachy Head only on May 2. Then her master, Captain Lech'vien, accepted the services of a tug, but it was blowing hard and matters grew worse hourly. On May 3 at 2 a.m. the weather cleared and the Cape Griz Nez light was sighted close by. The tug let go her tow rope and turned back. Captain Lech'vien tried to set sail but 20 minutes later the *Jane Guillon* went on the rocks near Audresselles. Continuous heavy seas submerged her almost entirely. The crew managed to hold on in the rigging until daybreak when they were rescued by the Audresselles lifeboat.

The barque became a total loss and the wreck was sold for £1,000. The case was tried and the tug was found at fault for abandoning her tow.

Jean – Steel barque, 2,207 g., 1,944 n.
February 16 1902: Launched by Chantiers de la Loire, St. Nazaire, for G. Ehrenberg, Havre.

Sold in May 1909 to Sté. des Armateurs Nantais, Nantes. On March 14 1910 left Port Victoria (South Australia) for the Channel (f.o.) and on August 10, not having been heard of for 149 days, she was posted overdue and reinsured for 8/10 gns. per cent. She subsequently turned up, reporting excessive delays by first very bad weather and then calms. She could sail well, as in 1910 she arrived at Adelaide 84 days from Prawle Point. She was an early war casualty, for on December 10 1914, while on passage from Port Talbot towards Antofagasta with coal, under Captain Le Dillinger, she was intercepted by the German raider *Prinz Eitel Friedrich* in lat. 44°50′S., long. 81°40′W. and a prize crew put on board to save the coal. The raider with the barque in tow made for Easter Island. Meanwhile, the British barque *Kildalton* was captured and sunk on December 12, 870 miles south-west of Valparaiso. The *Jean* arrived off Easter Island on December 23 and the raider the day after, when the *Prinz Eitel Friedrich*'s coaling from the barque began. Though the crews of the German ships had become used to coaling at sea and in open anchorages, this operation was long owing to the swell, and to avoid the barque capsizing and to reduce the range from which she could be seen her topgallant masts were sawn off. The work was over on December 31, and on January 5 1915 the *Jean* was towed off Easter Island, and after some target-practice was sunk in deep water. The crew were landed on the island, and later rescued by the British steamer *Skerries*.

Captain Le Dillinger refused to return home, preferring to espouse the daughter of a native Easter Island chief.

Jean Baptiste – Steel barque, 1,870 g., 1,668 n.
September 14 1897: Launched by Chantiers de la Loire, Nantes, for V. Vincent, Nantes.

Her maiden voyage was from Nantes to Saigon with patent fuel, thence to Mauritius and return to Dunkirk with rice. The second voyage was similar, but the third included a visit to Melbourne to load grain for Britain. On April 6 1904 she was bought by J. B. Etienne of Nantes and, seven years later, in 1911, was sold to Akties. Eidsvold (A. T. Simonsen) of Christiania, for £2,750, and renamed *Eidsvold*. (This was a low price.) She was under the Norwegian flag until her end under the names of *Hovda* and, later, *Storenes*. On March 1 1917 she was sunk by the German submarine *U-C-43*, about 20 miles south-east of Cape Clear.

The *U-C-43* was in turn torpedoed and sunk with all hands by the submarine H.M.S. *G-13* on March 10 1917, near Muckle Flugga (Shetlands).

Jean Bart – Steel barque, 2,224 g., 1,981 n.
June 3 1901: Launched by Chantiers de la Loire, St. Nazaire, for Sté. des Voiliers Dunkerquois, Dunkirk.

On March 6 1913, while bound from Antwerp to Wallaroo with 2,200 tons of coke and pig-iron, commanded by Captain Le Floch, she went ashore on the west coast of Wardang Island, South Australia. Owing to her critical position she was abandoned by all but her second mate, who remained on board. The *Jean Bart* was given up as a constructive total loss and was bought by J. Bell & Co. for £385, for conversion into a coal hulk. Refloated on May 26 1913, she was towed to Melbourne and drydocked. Found then to be in good condition the barque was sold to C. Krabbenhoft, Hamburg, who renamed her *Heinz* and sailed her for about a year. Now a German ship, she was captured in October 1914 off Port Nolloth by the *Kinfauns Castle,* then an armed merchant cruiser. She was approaching the anchorage under full sail but, seeing a mail steamer painted grey and flying the White Ensign, at once made a bold bid to escape. The *Kinfauns Castle* put her best foot forward before the *Heinz* was taken, for the wind was good. Condemned by the prize court, she arrived at Table Bay from Simon's Bay in tow on July 1 1915.

She was then sold to R. D. Brailli of London, for £11,150, and left Cape Town on July 30 as the *Tridonia* with a cargo of maize for Sydney. The following year she was lost by wreck in British waters, when on passage from Belfast for the River Plate, under Captain Stewart. Gales compelled her to put into Cork. When the first lull came she sailed but was soon battered by violent storms about 100 miles off the Irish coast, forcing her to make for the Bristol Channel for shelter. Anchored at Oxwich Point near the Mumbles, on October 30 1916, her cables parted and she was thrown on the rocks. This time she was a total loss, and Captain Stewart was drowned.

So ended the many-named old *Jean Bart.*

Jeanne Cordonnier – Steel barque, 2,194 g., 1,967 n.
December 20 1901: Launched by Chantiers de la Méditerranée, Havre, for Sté. des Voiliers Français, Havre.

On November 10 1904, sailing in the Channel in dense fog, she was involved in a collision with the Dutch full-rigged ship *Hainaut,* an oil sailer carrying petroleum in bulk for the American Petroleum Co., Rotterdam. The French barque put into Cherbourg for repairs. While on passage from Iquique to Havre with nitrate on May 31 1917, under Captain Arnaudtizon, she reached soundings when the unarmed barque was intercepted by the German submarine *U-88,* which ordered abandon ship and opened fire. Her starboard boat was damaged by a shell and the port boat took the crew, but one man was drowned. The sea was very rough and the boat reached the Scillies three days later.

Jeanne d'Arc – Steel barque, 1,303 g., 1,125 n.
1891: Built by Chantiers de la Loire, St. Nazaire, for H. Prentout-Leblond & Boniface, Rouen.
She began as another "slow-coach", being posted overdue on passage from Port Pirie for Antwerp with wheat in 1899-1900. Posted overdue in March, she was reinsured for 85 guineas per cent on the morning of April 7 1900, but in the afternoon she arrived in Flushing Roads, 168 days out—a long

passage, but there was surely no need for such pessimism. In 1901 she was sold to Paul Dor, Marseilles, retaining her name. The following year, in the Roaring Forties, Captain Bonhomme's son who was serving as a deck-boy was washed overboard and drowned. The ship was running heavily at the time and it was dark. The master was faced with a terrible decision, but he resolutely determined to risk no one by launching a boat which would certainly have been lost.

On August 11 1903 she left Marseilles bound for St. Denis (Reunion) with a full cargo of salt, but found 20 inches of water in the hold a fortnight later. The barque gradually took a heavy list. As she was 60 miles off Funchal, Madeira, next day the captain and crew decided by common consent to abandon her, and landed in two boats at Funchal on September 5. But their barque was not finished: on September 6, she was sighted by the British steamer *Obidense* (from Belem to St. Nazaire and Liverpool) which promptly towed the derelict to Funchal. Here she was temporarily repaired. After long litigation (on what grounds one does not know) the barque arrived on May 28 1904, back at Marseilles from Funchal, towed by the Marseilles tug *Phocéen*. In January 1905 she was sold for £2,730 to Flli. Pollio, Castellemare, and renamed *Doride*. She sailed profitably as an Italian vessel until September 19 1916, when she was sunk west of Sicily by the German submarine *U-35*.

Jeanne d'Arc ex-*Belen* – Steel barque, 2,202 g., 1,987 n.
April 18 1901: Launched by Chantiers de la Loire, St. Nazaire, for Cie. Celtique Maritime, Nantes, as the *Belen*.

On December 12 1904, arriving off Dunkirk in tow, she went ashore between the fairway and Malo-les-Bains, but was refloated on December 22. A few years later, in 1909, she was sold to Cie. Navale de l'Océanie (P. Tandonnet, Paris) and renamed *Jeanne d'Arc*, under which name A. D. Bordes bought her in 1912 and sailed her in the Chilean trade until 1921, when she was laid up.

She had a new lease of life when bought by M. Potet, of Havre, in 1923, for his West Indies and French Guiana trade, but this looked like ending when, in January 1930, she left Calais for the West Indies with 2,900 tons of cement, under Captain Joncour, and this turned into a poor voyage. Anchoring in the Downs, owing to head winds and bad weather, until January 16, she left the Channel after a week's delay only to be caught in a furious storm 110 miles off Ushant. The barque was disabled for three days, four men were injured, sails were lost, the cargo shifted, bulwarks and boats carried away. She managed to reach Belle Ile and put into St. Nazaire on February 1, but repairs took nearly two months before she could sail again. This sort of thing earns no money. When on April 27 1931 she arrived back at Havre from Jamaica, she was laid up.

Like the *Bonchamp* and the *Général de Sonis* under the same ownership, she was put up to auction on May 27 1932, at a cost of 20,000 francs. Sold as a hulk, she left Havre in tow for Cardiff on June 9 1932. Here a coal cargo was loaded and she was towed to Arcachon and converted into a coal hulk.

With her companion the *Duquesne,* the *Jeanne d'Arc* lay in Arcachon Bay for many years. Towards the end of 1949 she was towed to Bayonne and left idle until broken up in 1952. Monsieur Picard saved part of her mahogany bow scrolls (billet-heads) from the shipbreakers, and these are still well-preserved in his home at Royan.

Joinville – Steel barque, 2,212 g., 1,946 n.
March 1902: Completed by Chantiers Nantais de Constr. Maritimes, Nantes, for Sté. des Long-Courriers Français, Havre.

Her maiden voyage was unsuccessful, taking nearly two years. Just a few days after she had left St. Nazaire for Madagascar, commanded by Captain Allain, she experienced gale after gale in the Bay of Biscay; five of the crew were washed overboard and drowned. Three other men were gravely injured and her boats and spare spars carried away. She put into Lisbon for repairs and to complete crew, before continuing to Madagascar where her cargo of patent fuel was discharged; thence she headed for Tocopilla where a nitrate cargo was loaded for Hull. Again she was in trouble. Off Cape Horn in September, her hull suffered and began to leak. The steam pump coped with this, but later in the voyage, in November, in spite of the steam pump working continually, 19 inches of water were found in the hold. A day or two later as the boiler was damaged, part of cargo dissolved by water, rigging in very bad condition, and the barque taking a list, Captain Allain put into St. Nazaire and on November 21 1903 arrived St. Nazaire Roads, 125 days out.

Her cargo was discharged, the barque re-rigged after repairs, her cargo reloaded and the *Joinville* left St. Nazaire in tow for Hull on March 5 1904. This must have been a most unprofitable voyage, despite the Bounty.

In 1910 she showed that she could sail when she reached Adelaide from Dunkirk in 80 days. Just before World War I she was sold to Sté. Générale d'Armement. Her last voyage was in 1921, when on January 20 she sailed from Newcastle (N.S.W.) with coal for Chile, arrived Mejillones after a poor passage of 66 days, and sailed with nitrates to Falmouth in 121 days. After this, she was laid up in Canal de la Martinière, and left on October 1 1926 for breaking up.

Joliette – Steel barque (Jubilee rig), 2,698 g., 1,805 n.
October 16 1902: Launched by Chantiers de la Méditerranée, La Seyne, for Sté. Marseillaise de Voiliers, Marseilles.

She did not last long. On February 11 1909, when loading nickel ore at the wharf of Tchio (New Caledonia) for Havre, she was caught in a cyclone and foundered. Her crew were saved. The wharf where she was moored was partially destroyed at the same time.

Jules Gommès – Steel ship, 2,595 g., 2,234 n.
August 8 1901: Launched by Chantiers de St. Nazaire for Sté. Bayonnaise de Navigation, Bayonne.

In 1904 she had a great race home from San Francisco round the Horn with the British four-masted barque *Loch Carron*. The Scot hove up in 'Frisco Bay on the morning of Christmas Eve, the *Jules Gommès* leaving that afternoon. After six days in company the two ships lost sight of each other, to meet again on the equator in the Atlantic; the *Loch Carron* arrived at Queenstown 112 days out, the *Jules Gommès* arriving eight hours later at the same port.

In May 1911 she was sold to Sté. des Voiliers Normands (Prentout-Leblond-Leroux & Co., Mgrs.), Rouen (another bounty-expired ship). Between March 1915 and May 1916, she made a voyage from Cardiff to Montevideo, thence to Port Townsend and Seattle and afterwards to Queenstown where she arrived on April 14 1916. Ordered to Ipswich, she arrived there on May 3 1916. Freights were good at the time, but the German U-boats soon claimed her. On March 12 1917, while bound from Ipswich for Bahia Blanca, under Captain R. Nicole, she was captured by the *U-62* and sunk by explosive charges, in 49°10'N., 8°50'W. (106 miles west-south-west of Bishop Rock). Her crew were saved.

Jules Henry – Steel barque, 1,994 g., 1,673 n. (Carrying petroleum in bulk.)
March 19 1900: Launched by Chantiers de la Méditerranée, Havre, for A. Vimont & Co., Marseilles.

Like her sister-ship, the *France Marie*, she was in the petroleum trade between Philadelphia and Marseilles. In March 1901 she sailed to Marseilles from the American coast in the creditable time of 19 days and 12 hours. On April 1 1909 she was in Marseilles docks when an explosion in her tanks badly damaged the ship and nine lives were lost.

In 1913 the *Jules Henry* was converted into a full-powered motor-ship (possibly the first French motorship). The vessel was taken in hand by Wilton's Engineering & Slipway Co., of Rotterdam, lengthened, and reconstructed. The oil tank capacity was increased from 2,400 to 2,800 tons, of three different kinds of oil. The engines installed were two of 675 i.h.p., of the Werkspoor type. There was a gain in displacement by lengthening equivalent to 1,200 tons; the saving in weight owing to the lost masts and rigging was 80 tons.

Then, the *Jules Henry* was put in Black Sea voyages between Constantza and Marseilles until her end. She was broken up in 1934, when it had long been forgotten by most that she had ever been a sailing-ship.

Jules Verne – Steel barque, 1,394 g., 1,254 n.
1894: Built by A. Dubigeon, Nantes, for R. Guillon & R. Fleury, Nantes.

She was the first large sailing ship built with the benefit of the 1893 subsidy law. The *Jules Verne* was also the last large French sailer rigged with single topgallant sails, for all her later colleagues were rigged with double-top-gallants. In 1903, when nearly ten years of age, she was sold to Rederiaktie-selsk. Francis Hagerup (O. J. Olsen, of Tonsberg) and renamed *Francis Hagerup,* and in 1916 was bought by Aage Nielsen, Nykjöbing (Denmark), acquiring the name of *Consul N. Nielsen,* but was sunk by U-boat *U-69* off the Hebrides some 12 months later on May 29 1917. She was bound for Copenhagen from Buenos Aires with a cargo of linseed.

L'Hermite – Steel barque, 2,189 g., 1,946 n.
November 2 1901: Launched by Chantiers de la Loire, Nantes, for Sté. des Voiliers Dunkerquois, Dunkirk.

On May 16 1917 she was attacked north-west of Ushant by the German submarine *U-C-17.* The barque had been recently armed and made a very good fight, causing the U-boat to break off the action. *L'Hermite,* having been damaged by the submarine's shelling, was compelled to put into Brest for repairs. Captain and crew were commended. She survived the war and in April 1923 was sold for scrap to Italian shipbreakers. In 1921-22 she had made a passage to Falmouth from San Francisco with grain of 135 days.

La Banche – Steel barque, 2,348 g., 2,100 n.
January 22 1902: Launched by Chantiers de la Loire, Nantes, for J. B. Etienne, Nantes.

Between May 1913 and May 1914 she made a voyage from Antwerp to Rio de Janeiro, New Caledonia and Hamburg, details not given. Other voyages were from Hamburg to Caldera, Iquique, and Liverpool, and in the grain and nitrate trades. The voyage begun from Port Natal on June 16 1916 was her last, for fire broke out in her cargo of coal and matters grew worse rapidly, causing the barque to be abandoned. Fortunately, the French barque *Générale de Sonis* hove in sight and rescued the crew, and the *La Banche* sank in a few hours, north-east of the River Plate. Captain Lorant and his crew of 24 were landed at Bahia Blanca on September 6.

La Bruyère – Steel barque (Jubilee rig), 2,198 g., 1,944 n.
October 17 1899: Launched by Chantiers de la Loire, Nantes, for R.
Guillon & R. Fleury, Nantes.

In 1903, bound from Shields for Los Angeles under Captain Saint-Martin,
she left Cherbourg on May 21 and was posted missing in December, but
she arrived in California on December 22. She had taken 215 days via the
Cape of Good Hope, after losing her fore topgallant mast off Cape Horn
and turning eastwards round the world. In the circumstances this was a
creditable performance. In 1908, she was sold to Sté. Générale d'Armement,
and in 1909-10, while on passage from Cardiff for Iquique under Captain
Warneck, she was again battered off Cape Horn. Again, she faced about for
the Good Hope route, arriving at Iquique on January 15 1910 after a non-
stop passage of 180 days—again not bad for the distance, and probably
unique. On July 4 1921 she arrived at Falmouth from Caleta Coloso and
was laid up in the Canal de la Martinière, until she left on September 21
1927 for breaking up.

La Epoca – Steel 4-masted barque, 2,432 g., 2,268 n.
1893: Built by D. & W. Henderson & Co., Glasgow, for the Corunna Sailing
S. Co. (J. Hardie & Co.), Glasgow, as *Corunna*.

Hardie & Co. had a large fleet of first class ships and kept them in excellent
condition.

During her long career she made many good passages, among them Rio
de Janeiro from Glasgow in 40 days, 1893; Rio to Melbourne in 55 days,
and from the latter to London in 89 days the following year. She reached
Mauritius from Cardiff in 65 days and sailed from Mauritius to Newcastle
(N.S.W.) in 33 days, thence to San Francisco in 52 days. In 1895, she sailed
from 'Frisco and, despite partial dismasting north of the Equator, arrived at
Falmouth under jury rig only 124 days out. In 1896 she was 43 days from
Barry to Montevideo, thence to Philadelphia in 41 days, but was afterwards
136 days to Hiogo. She sailed from Hiogo to Port Townsend in 37 days, but
from Tacoma to Havre she was 149 days. In 1898, she made Nagasaki from
Barry in 136 days. Both this passage and that to Hiogo were made by the
long route round Australia—good for bounty payments but not for speed,
perhaps. The following year a passage of 27 days between Nagasaki and
Port Townsend was good. She was then said to have been only 17 days
between soundings, but the precise distance meant is far from clear. San
Francisco from the Tyne in 159 days at the turn of the century was not good,
but the same port to Antwerp the next year in 121 days (passed Kinsale 115
days out) made up for this. She was a good ship which moved nicely through
the water.

Her useful life came to an end on August 30 1904 when, 67 days out on passage Antwerp for Port Townsend with cement, under Captain Mason, she stranded about three miles west of Miramar, Argentina, during thick and squally weather, and immediately began to fill. Owing to her exposed position, and salt water having got into the fresh water tanks, Captain Mason abandoned the barque on September 2, the only casualty being a seaman drowned while trying to swim ashore. The *Corunna* was refloated on October 12 and taken to Montevideo where she was rigged down and used by Dodero Brothers as a hulk.

During the First World War she was re-rigged and sold by Dodero Brothers, Montevideo, to "buyers not stated" for £74,000 in 1917. These buyers were probably Société Boillard de Boisguilbert, Paris; at any rate she was under their ownership (Oriental Navigation Corp., Mgrs.) in September of that year. Later the same year, renamed *La Epoca* and under the Uruguayan flag, she left New York for Bordeaux, commanded by a Norwegian master, and her mixed crew of 26 were citizens of 13 nations. The barque was loaded with 4,000 tons of general cargo (steel, lubricant oil, nails, tobacco and paper), but she did not complete this passage. Instead, she was intercepted by the German submarine *U-93* on October 29 in 45°10′N., 1°45′W. The submarine sent a boarding party consisting of an officer and five armed ratings for the destruction and pillage of the barque (provisions, chronometers, clothes and so on were taken away). These placed explosive charges and *La Epoca* was abandoned and sank in three minutes at 10.30 a.m. All the crew were saved.

La Fontaine – Steel barque (Jubilee rig), 2,209 g., 1,966 n.
November 7 1899: Launched by Chantiers de la Loire, Nantes, for R. Guillon & R. Fleury, Nantes.

Sold in 1908 to the Sté. Générale d'Armement. She sailed safely right through the war and, on April 21 1920, left Port Lincoln for Nantes with a cargo of wheat. She never reached Nantes. Instead, on July 23 she was towed into Talcahuano with loss of fore and main topmasts, sails, and two boats. There was no apparent damage to the cargo, and this was transferred to the barque *Molière*, which left Talcahuano on February 1 1921, for the same owners. The cost of materials required to repair *La Fontaine*, together with labour, was estimated at about £18,000, so she was classed as a constructive total loss and hulked on the spot.

La Pérouse – Steel ship, 2,186 g., 1,913 n.
July 18 1901: Launched by Chantiers de la Loire, Nantes, for Cie. Maritime Française, Nantes.

She had a good turn of speed, shown by a run in 1910 to Queenstown from Seattle in 117 days. In 1913 she was sold to Sté. Générale d'Armement, and was wrecked in May 1917 when bound from Buenos Aires to Bordeaux with wheat. She was stranded near Hourtins about 22 miles south of the River Gironde, and was a total loss. Her crew were saved.

La Rochefoucauld – Steel barque (Jubilee rig), 2,200 g., 1,949 n.
September 16 1899: Launched by Chantiers de la Loire, Nantes, for R. Guillon & R. Fleury, Nantes.

She was the first bald-headed barque (no royals) to be built at Nantes, and local seamen did not like her looks because of the cut rig.

Her maiden voyage was to South Australia, and in 1902 she is said to have reached Europe from New York in 12 days, details not given: but the passage *could* have been made.

In 1903, on her return passage from New Caledonia, her master, Captain Le Hédé, died at sea, and the barque put into Dakar later with her rudder damaged. Then in 1908 she was sold to Sté. Générale d'Armement (which may have been a special company set up to manage non-bounty earners). On February 27 1917, while on passage from Iquique to Rochefort with nitrate, under Captain Malbert, she was captured in 5°N., 31°30′W. by the German raider *Seeadler,* and sunk by gunfire in order to satisfy her crew (it was said) that the *Seeadler*'s guns were not dummies.

La Rochejaquelein – Steel barque, 2,199 g., 1,954 n.
November 1901: Launched by Chantiers Nantais de Constr. Maritimes, Nantes, for Bureau Frères & Baillergeau, Nantes.

On her maiden voyage she reached Table Bay from Barry Docks in 41 days, and arrived at Cherbourg on March 5 1903 from Philadelphia, 11 days out, possibly a record for that run. She was chiefly in the California and Oregon grain trade until her end, and made some good passages; for example, on April 16 1910 she arrived at Falmouth from Astoria, 117 days out. On her last voyage the barque left London on September 26 1915 in ballast for Newcastle (N.S.W.) where coal was loaded for San Francisco. Returning from California to Ipswich with wheat she was sunk by the German submarine *U-C-17* when about 15 miles south of the Lizard, on November 14 1916.

La Tour d'Auvergne – Steel barque, 2,196 g., 1,948 n.
January 26 1901: Launched by Chantiers de la Loire, Nantes, for Cie. Maritime Française, Nantes.

During her tenth and last voyage she was sold to the Sté. Générale d'Armement. Details of this voyage follow:

May 20 1913   : Left Dunkirk for Tahiti and New Caledonia with

3,000 tons of patent fuel (2,000 tons for Papeete and 1,000 tons for Noumea).

October 16 : Left Papeete for Noumea.

October 23 : Wrecked near Palmerston Island. Her crew of 23 were saved by the Sydney barque *Antiope* and landed at Sydney about December 15. The wreck was sold for £90.

Laënnec – Steel ship, 2,299 g., 2,011 n.: later *Suomen Joutsen*.
October 1902: Completed by Chantiers de St. Nazaire for Sté. des Armateurs Nantais, Nantes.

Of her career under the French flag there seem two facts worth mentioning. On her maiden voyage, when sailing in ballast from St. Nazaire to Cardiff, she ran down and sank a British collier off the Bristol Channel, damaging her own bows in the process. At the subsequent enquiry, she was found to blame. It would appear that she had not sufficient stiffening at the time and was in consequence almost unmanageable. On December 12 1911 she was damaged in a storm while discharging a cargo of nitrate at Santander, and was repaired on the spot under the orders of Captain Louis Lacroix, then the ship's husband (Marine Superintendent).

She was laid up in St. Nazaire throughout 1921 and subsequently towed to the Canal de la Martinière to await better times. In November 1922 she was bought by Herr H. H. Schmidt of Hamburg, who converted her into a cargo-carrying training ship, with the name *Oldenburg*. In March 1925 she left Hamburg in ballast for Callao but while trying to round Cape Horn lost her main topgallant mast, main topmast, and mizzen topgallant mast. She put back to Montevideo under jury rig, arriving there on June 2, and lost five weeks for repairs. Her charter was cancelled and she was then ordered back to Hamburg, which she reached in 78 days.

In 1926 the *Oldenburg* made another voyage under the same shipowner, and in 1928 was bought by Seefahrt Segelschiffs Reed, G.m.b.H. of Bremen on behalf of North German Lloyd, with a view to use as a training ship. She seems to have been rather a sluggard, as her passages indicate. For example, in 1928, from Bremen to Valparaiso in 106 days and homewards, Iquique to Bremen, 97 days. The following year she took 170 days between Bremerhaven and Callao. After another accident at sea—she was thrown on her beam ends, her cargo shifted—she was sold in August 1930 to Finnish shipowners, for the Finnish Navy. She was then powered by twin oil engines, giving her a speed of about six knots, and renamed *Suomen Joutsen* (*Swan of Finland*). She made a six months' voyage each winter until 1939, giving excellent sail training to many Finnish cadets. She survived World War II and resumed her training duties in 1949, but was not seen outside the Baltic frequently. Her last cruise under sail was made in 1956, and the vessel then became a base ship for naval forces. In 1960 she was refitted and her accommodation modernized.

Since 1961, the *Suomen Joutsen* has been moored at Åbo (Turku) where she now serves as a stationary seamen's school for Merchant Service personnel.

Lafayette – Steel ship, 1,977 g., 1,766 n.
April 1902: Completed by Chantiers A. Dubigeon, Nantes, for Sté. des Armateurs Nantais, Nantes.

Captain Alexandre Boju took her in command on the stocks, and her maiden voyage was without incident. It was almost the only voyage she made, for on February 24 1905 she left New York bound for Saigon with case oil, and disappeared. No news of the *Lafayette* came to hand after she was spoken on February 25, about 150 miles west-south-west of Nantucket, and she was posted missing in November 1905. It was thought that she had struck an iceberg or had blown up, but this is speculation. Nothing was ever seen or found to throw light on her fate—a state of affairs necessarily accepted in the pre-radio sailing-ship era, and unfortunately far from uncommon.

Lamoricière – Steel barque, 1,931 g., 1,471 n.
1895: Built by Laporte & Co., Rouen, for Sté. des Voiliers Nantais, Nantes.

Another mystery—on November 3 1903 she left New Caledonia for Glasgow with nickel ore, under Captain Christian, and went missing. Her loss might have been caused by opening up and foundering, by collision with ice, or fatal damage from her own dismasting in some violent shift of winds, or hitting some rockbound coast or cliff and bouncing off to sink—the list is endless.

Le Pilier – Steel barque, 2,427 g., 2,036 n.
May 1902: Completed by Chantiers de la Loire, Nantes, for J. B. Etienne, Nantes.

On her maiden voyage she reached New Caledonia from Nantes in 92 days, which was good. So was her passage to Hobart from Brest in 84 days during 1910. The First World War killed her. On May 2 1916, while on passage from London to Buenos Aires, she was torpedoed and sunk by the German submarine *U-45* off Ushant.

Les Adelphes – Steel barque, 1,259 g., 1,144 n.
September 1891: Completed by A. Dubigeon, Nantes, for C. & F. Brunellière Frères, Nantes.

In 1901, when bound from Noumea to Rotterdam with nickel ore, she put into Falmouth having lost her main topmast. In 1902, she made a voyage to Madagascar and thence to Oregon, but after leaving Madagascar she was delayed by calms and put into Los Angeles later for medical assistance, several of the crew needing treatment for scurvy and fevers. In February 1903 she reached Falmouth from New York in 12 days, and in 1907 was sold for £4,400 to the Norwegian shipowner A. P. Ulriksen, of Mandal, and renamed *Eros*. She did well through the war and in January 1920, when at Havre, was bought by S. Saten, Gothenburg. She sailed from Pensacola the same year for Port Natal, and took 119 days which was slow, and so was her 35 days from Port Natal to Port Louis (Mauritius) in 1921. She was then acquired by the Indo-Mauritius Shipping Co. of Port Louis, and took 78 days to reach Port Natal, reporting some loss of sails. Then sold to Ismail A. Assmal, Durban, on July 22 1922, she sailed for Aden.

On September 28 1922 the *Eros* sailed from Aden to Rangoon taking 93 days. Here she was to have been named *Zubeda,* but was arrested for debt and sold at auction to one A. Ganny. Beached up the Pegu River in 1927, her masts came down when she touched the mud, and by 1929 she had sunk out of sight. Perhaps she was tired, though she was then only 38 years old. Many steel sailers lasted much longer.

Léon Blum – Steel ship, 2,733 g., 2,316 n.
Completed March 1902 by Chantiers de Normandie, Rouen, for Sté. des Voiliers de St. Nazaire.

She was named after Mr. Léon Blum who was a ship-chandler of San Francisco and an important shareholder of the Sté. des Voiliers de St. Nazaire. In 1903 she was transferred to the Sté. Générale d'Armement. In 1915, she made a slow passage between Antofagasta and Nantes, with loss of sails and other incidents. Two years later, in November 1917, while on passage from Adelaide to Dakar, commanded by Captain Grondin, she stranded by night near Dakar. Attempts to refloat her were unsuccessful and she was abandoned on November 27 and written off as a constructive total loss the following week—a pity, for the *Léon Blum* was a good, strong ship which had earned her "keep". (This was the ship in which Charlie Müller once sailed.)

Léon Bureau – Steel ship, 1,974 g., 1,767 n.
May 1902: Completed by A. Dubigeon, Nantes, for L. Bureau & Fils, Nantes.

She was an unlucky ship and experienced all sorts of misfortunes well described in Captain L. Lacroix's book "Les Derniers Grands Voiliers"—hurricane (1902), broken rudder twice (1904 and 1905), fire and scuttling

(1906), collision (1908), stranding twice (1909 and 1919). In 1909, she was
sold to Sté. des Armateurs Nantais, Nantes, and in 1913 was bought by
C. Krabbenhoft of Hamburg, and renamed *John*. The First World War
found her under the German flag at Valparaiso and there she remained until
1919. The *John* was one of 12 vessels, including three interned German
steamers, which broke their moorings and were driven on the rocks in
Valparaiso during a violent storm on the night of July 11-12 1919. She was
refloated and converted into a three-masted schooner-barge by S.A.C. Braun
& Blanchard, of Valparaiso, and registered at Punta Arenas. At first she
was renamed *Bruhimarie* and subsequently *Quellon*. In 1936 she was broken
up at Valparaiso.

Léon XIII – Steel ship, 2,089 g., 1,584 n.
June 22 1902: Launched by A. Dubigeon, Nantes, for Sté. des Armateurs
Nantais.

On April 20 1907 she left Portland (Oreg.) with wheat, under Captain
Lucas, and was 158 days to Queenstown, which was far from fast. The same
October she was caught in a storm, disabled, and driven ashore north of the
Shannon. The ship struck the rocks near Quilty and heavy seas almost
submerged her. She became a total loss but the crew of 22 were saved by
H.M.S. *Arrogant*. A small book entitled "The Wreck of the 'Leon XIII' ",
by an eye witness, was published in Dublin several months later and this was
her memorial. Some seamen said she should not have been named the 13th.

Loire – Steel 4-masted barque, 2,969 g., 2,685 n.
December 8 1896: Launched by Chantiers de la Loire, Nantes, for A. D.
Bordes.

Her best passage was in 1897, Portland to Iquique in 66 days. Another good
passage was Iquique to Prawle Point, 75 days, in 1898. Her name is remembered by the fine display of seamanship in October 1913, when she saved the
crew of the British full-rigged ship *Dalgonar*. On October 1 1913 the *Loire*
left Iquique for Dover for orders, commanded by Captain Michel Jaffré,
and on the 10th, in the night, saw rockets and blue lights. At daybreak the
capsized and part dismasted ship *Dalgonar* of Liverpool was in full sight.

  The case of the British ship *Dalgonar* was well known to all sailing-ship
seamen. She was a large full-rigged ship carrying almost 4,000 tons—a handful to manage. In October 1913 she was bound in ballast from Callao, Peru,
for Taltal in Chile to load. It *should* have been a simple passage in good
weather, though it meant first getting out of the north-setting Humboldt
Current on the South American coast and making south through the south-
east Trades. The weather was unusually atrocious, and the *Dalgonar* had
been badly ballasted at Callao. At the time, several large ships had gone

The *Jean Bart* stranded on Wardang Island, South Australia, March 6 1913.
(*A. D. Edwardes, South Australia.*)

The big French barque *Maréchal Davout* feels almost at home by Fisherman's Wharf, San Francisco, with the foreground of Mediterranean-type fishermen. The Limejuicer *Largo Law* is also in the picture. (*San Francisco Maritime Museum.*)

Trim decks of the big French barque *Marguerite Dollfus*, looking for'ard from the poop. (*San Francisco Maritime Museum.*)

Schooners, including the *Snow and Burgess,* and French ship *Madeleine,* loading lumber at Port Blakeley, Washington, early 20th century. (*Hester Collection, San Francisco Maritime Museum.*)

The *Quevilly* entering Dieppe under tow. (*Richard M. Cookson Collection.*)

The bowsprit of the French *Max* is knocked askew but the steamship *Walla Walla*, which did it, sank. (*Procter Collection, San Francisco Maritime Museum.*)

missing after leaving that port in ballast, and the reason would seem to be
that there was a "racket", a swindle, in the ballast business. Ships paid for
a sufficiency to keep them upright, but this was not put aboard. The ballast
sold was shingle dredged up from the harbour bed, wet and runny stuff at
best, hard to make secure, and the *Dalgonar* had one large hold in which
the shingle had plenty of room to move, though it was boxed in but not
thoroughly. In the Peruvian port at the time, masters were powerless to
fight the swindle which was said to have official backing. (The ships were
usually not going far: the weather was usually good: what difference did
some short delivery make, or inadequate safeguards against ballast movement? The ships shouldn't fall over. The matter of deliberate short delivery
was locally so well-known that a Notice in the British Consular office drew
masters' attention to the need to be on their guard against it.*)

The *Dalgonar* was out of luck. She met bad weather. Being insufficiently
ballasted she listed easily. This caused the treacherous shingle to move,
which listed her further over, causing the shingle to run until it was neither
the sides of its "box" nor the ship's side that held it but the actual under-
deck. It could not be shovelled back, for as fast as one shovel was pitched
to wind'ard six more rolled a-lee. It wouldn't bind. It could not be stabilised.

So the *Dalgonar* fell upon her side—her "beam-ends", as sailors say—and
stayed there, quite unmanageable. The weather remained unusually bad.
For days she lay there, wallowing, helpless, apparently doomed: but she did
not go right over. When efforts failed to get her anywhere near upright
again, an attempt was made to abandon her in her boats; but one skimmed
the breaking seas, the other was poised high atop the weather rail on the
skids. Trying to launch a boat, Captain Isbister—a fine old seaman—and
three of his men went in the sea heavily dressed and were not seen again.
The mate cut the masts away: she righted a little then, but far from sufficient. The gale increased.

Then the *Loire* came in sight: stood-by: and stayed, for the weather
remained atrocious, day after day—the hulk of the *Dalgonar* wallowing and
lurching in the sea as if any lurch would be her last, the *Loire* under easy
canvas making short boards, never out of sight, waiting for a moment's let
up, boats ready for her Breton seamen to make a dash to rescue the
Dalgonar's crew. Because the ship was on her side, they had to approach her
on the rolled down side. Pieces of iron-wire and broken steel masts writhed
in the water there, and their touch was death. Four days the men of the
Loire waited, the short international code hoist of flags meaning "I Will
Not Abandon You" flying from her gaff. The gale raged. Vicious squalls
raced over the ships, with stinging rain.

*This scandal is dealt with by the well-known and outspoken Captain James Learmont in his
autobiography "Master in Sail", published by Percival Marshall, London. He found the
deliberately contrived short delivery of ballast averaged between 14 and 15 per cent, and it was
customary to order only the essential minimum. No wonder many good ships went missing.

K

Then there was a slight easing—brief, but enough. While Captain Joffre handled his big four-masted barque like a yacht, Mate Yves Cadic brought the big life-boat across and rescued everybody: the *Loire* picked them up and sped on her way. This was on nearly 29°S., 87°W. Yves Cadic was an old man: he never recovered from the trials of that rescue and died quietly homeward-bound, off the Horn.

Oddly enough, the *Dalgonar* did not sink, for she was strong and well battened down, and the criminal shingle could move no more. She drifted slowly westwards over many months, finally stranding on the Pacific island called Maupihoa of the Society group. There her rusted steel shell remains.

The *Loire* arrived at Dunkirk, 96 days out. Ten years later, she was sold to Italy for breaking up. Old sailors still remember her and that rescue.

Louis Pasteur – Steel barque, 1,747 g., 1,612 n.
1895: Built by Laporte & Co., Rouen, for R. Guillon & R. Fleury, Nantes.

On her maiden voyage she reached Newcastle (N.S.W.) from Rouen in 74 days and, not long afterwards, in 1903, was sold for £4,400 to Eugen Cellier, Hamburg, retaining her name.

During the 1914-18 war she was laid up at Mejillones, Chile, and after sailing back to Delfzijl in 107 days, nitrate-laden, she was allocated to Great Britain as reparations. It seems that the Shipping Controller had little use for her, and she was broken up in 1923 after an abortive year or two as the *Hedwig* under the ownership of the Küstentransport und Bergungs A.G. of Hamburg, for whom she seems to have made no voyage.

Mac Mahon – Steel barque, 2,197 g., 1,952 n.
April 5 1898: Launched by Chantiers de la Loire, Nantes, for Sté. des Voiliers Nantais.

In 1906, the *Mac Mahon* made a long passage of 212 days from Swansea to San Francisco, and two years later was sold to the Sté. Générale d'Armement for £6,000. From December 1911 until September 1912 she made a voyage to Australia.
March 18 1921: Left Iquique for Europe.
May 22   : Put into Bahia with damaged rigging.
August 2   : Sailed Bahia, and arrived Queenstown in 69 days. She was ordered to Dunkirk, where she remained laid up until June 3 1922 when she arrived in the Canal de la Martinière. She left on August 30 1926, sold for breaking up.

Madeleine – Steel 4-masted barque, 2,893 g., 2,639 n.
July 23 1895: Launched by Chantiers de la Loire, Nantes, for A. D. Bordes.

Her best outward passage was made in 1898, from Shields to Valparaiso allegedly in 66 days, and her best return passage from Iquique to the Lizard was in 1896, 69 days. The 66 days is considered as improbable unless it was from departure (last sight of land) to landfall. On June 24 1911 she was anchored in Iquique Bay when an unexpected gale struck her. Drifting, she collided with her consort *Union,* went ashore and capsized at the bottom of the Bay, a total loss. The Italian full-rigger *Cavaliere Ciampa* was a total loss in the same storm, and the British ship *Grace Harwar* was damaged.

Madeleine – Steel ship, 2,709 g., 2,264 n.
September 20 1902: Launched by Chantiers de St. Nazaire, Rouen, for Sté. de Navigation du Sud-Ouest, Bordeaux.

In October 1904 she was sold to A. D. Bordes and was named *Madeleine II* as there was already a *Madeleine* in their fleet. Her best passage was probably made in 1913, 94 days from the Tyne to Iquique. On July 6 1917 she sailed from Le Verdon Roads for Sydney in ballast, under Captain A. Lévèque, in company with nine other sailing ships and three warships to convoy them. But after the convoy was dispersed, each vessel proceeding for her own destination, the *Madeleine* was shelled and sunk by the German submarine U-155 on July 31, in 33°45′N., 20°30′W., after a gallant action which lasted for two hours, despite the overwhelming superiority of the German guns. A third of the ship's crew were killed. The 20 survivors, among them several wounded, were picked up by an American steamer which handed them over to the French trawler *Marakchi,* arriving at Casablanca on August 7. Captain Lévèque and his crew were mentioned in dispatches for this action.

Maguy – Iron barque (Jubilee rig), 1,400 g., 1,294 n.
1890: Built by W. Pickersgill & Sons, Sunderland, for C. Neynaber of Elsfleth, as *Hanna Heye*.

She was sold to P. Razeto fu F., Genoa, in 1903, renamed *Vega,* later *Rio*. In 1912 she was sold to Buenos Aires interests and renamed again, this time *Tripolitalia*. She was later wrecked off the Argentine coast and salvaged a long time later. She was then hulked at Buenos Aires, but after refitting and re-rigging she was sold for £36,300 to Norwegian shipowners. A few months later she was resold to Italian interests and renamed *Garibaldi*. She arrived at Bordeaux in 1916 and was then bought by Gillet & Fils, dyers of Lyons, for the campeachy wood trade. Renamed *Maguy* she was registered at Bordeaux and later at Marseilles. The *Maguy* left Bordeaux at the end of 1916. Dismasted in the Bay of Biscay, she anchored at Belle Ile for shelter and was eventually towed to Nantes. Repairs took more than a year, after which she was in the West Indies trade. Arriving at Antwerp in October 1920, she was laid up there for a year. In 1922 she made a voyage to Santa Fe and the following year another to Jamaica. She continued to find Atlantic work, sailing in May 1923 from Cadiz with salt for Rosario, commanded by Captain Chéneau, thence from the River Plate to Antwerp with cuebracho wood. On January 7 1924, caught in a hurricane at sea and thrown on her beam ends, she was dismasted and four feet of water were in the hold, but four days later the Swedish steamer *Boren* hove in sight. The *Maguy* was abandoned, water-logged, in 43°50′N., 27°14′W. Her crew of 21 were rescued by the *Boren* and landed at Cherbourg.

Maréchal Davout – Steel barque, 2,192 g., 1,941 n.
August 30 1898: Launched by Chantiers de la Loire, Nantes, for R. Guillon & R. Fleury, Nantes.

In 1899 she arrived at Greenock from New Caledonia 84 days out, and was sold to Sté. Générale d'Armement in 1908 at the age of ten. While on passage from Melbourne to Dakar with wheat on December 15 1917, under Captain Bret, she was sunk by the German raider *Wolf* in the South Atlantic, south-south-east of Trinidad Island.

Maréchal de Castries – Steel ship, 1,973 g., 1,742 n.
October 10 1901: Launched by A. Dubigeon, Nantes, for Sté. des Armateurs Nantais.

On September 5 1910, bound from Dublin to Portland (Oreg.), she was thrown on her beam ends by a pampero off the River Plate when her cargo of railway material and bricks shifted. She was righted sufficiently to be under control, and ran for the Falklands where her cargo was re-stowed and partial repairs carried out. She then continued her passage to Portland via Hobart. On February 16 1918, when off the West African coast, she was chased by the German raider *Norefos* but managed to beat off the enemy with her two poop guns. (The Norwegian steamer *Norefos* was captured by the German submarine *U-157* and converted into an armed raider with a German crew.) The *Maréchal* was laid up at St. Nazaire for the whole of 1921, and in November 1922 was sold to H. H. Schmidt of Hamburg and renamed *Henriette*, later (in 1924) changed to *Hamburg*. During this period she is credited with a 68-day passage to Chile. Later fitted out as a cadet ship, she did not serve for long. Soon after leaving Melbourne with grain in 1925, her steering gear was damaged and she put into Sydney, and did not make Falmouth until October 19, 143 days out.

Ordered to discharge at Cork, on October 29 1925, she was driven to Dublin Bay by stress of weather and got ashore there in Sutton Bay during heavy weather, and remained for about a month. She was eventually refloated and towed into Dublin. She had not suffered as much damage as had been anticipated, but her owners decided that she was not worth repair, and the *Hamburg* was sold to Scottish shipbreakers for £2,000. On February 7 1926 she arrived in tow at Troon where she was scrapped.

Serving aboard at the time of her wreck was a young man named Gunther Prien, who was destined to command the German submarine *U-47* which sank the battleship *Royal Oak* at Scapa Flow, on October 14 1939 with the loss of 810 lives—a nasty blow to Britain, but a fine feat of seamanship and navigation.

Maréchal de Gontaut – Steel barque, 2,240 g., 2,025 n.
February 1902: Completed by Chantiers Nantais de Constr. Maritimes, Nantes, for Cie. de Navigation Française, Nantes.

On her maiden voyage she loaded a Chilean nitrate cargo for New York, where Captain Louis Lacroix took command. She left New York on August 31 1903 for Yokohama with case oil, crossed the Equator, 51 days out, and on February 20 1904 arrived at Yokohama after 173 days passage. March 25 1904, she sailed from Yokohama for Saigon, and left the latter port on May 27. Later in 1904 she was transferred to the Sté. Générale d'Armement. On November 26 1913 she left Callao for Sydney under Captain Huchon, ballasted with the same sort of shingle as the *Dalgonar,* and was never heard of again. It was assumed that she was lost through her ballast shifting.

Maréchal de Noailles – Steel barque, 2,707 g., 2,166 n.
June 22 1902: Launched by Cie. Française de Constr. Navales, Nantes, for Cie. de Navigation Française, Nantes.

In 1904 she was sold to Sté. des Voiliers Nantais. December 12 1912, left Glasgow for New Caledonia with general cargo (machines, coal, coke and lime), but she did not get far. Because of hard head winds and gales she had to put into Lamlash and later Belfast. She sailed from Belfast in tow on January 12 1913; the towage was stopped on January 13 off the Tuskar, but the barque was unable to clear before she was caught in another gale which wrecked her near Minehead lighthouse, on January 15 1913. Her crew of 24 were rescued.

Maréchal de Turenne – Steel barque, 2,204 g., 1,939 n.
April 22 1899: Launched by Chantiers de la Loire, Nantes, for R. Guillon & R. Fleury, Nantes.

On her maiden voyage she was severely battered off Cape Horn and arrived at San Francisco on December 30 1899, with her rigging damaged: but she kept the sea. In 1908 she was sold to the Sté. Générale d'Armement. On

October 27 1909, while bound from New York to Melbourne, she was involved by night in a collision with an unknown sailing vessel, but escaped with only slight damage. She was a lucky ship. Her last passage was from Melbourne with wheat to Queenstown in 1921, and the passage took 122 days, which was average for big carriers. She was then laid up in the Canal de la Martinière, and on January 27 1927 left the Canal for breaking up.

Maréchal de Villars – Steel barque, 2,198 g., 1,941 n.
May 24 1899: Launched by Chantiers de la Loire, Nantes, for R. Guillon & R. Fleury, Nantes.

On her maiden voyage she put into Montevideo on November 4 1899, partially dismasted. She could sail well. On July 13 1901 she left Hong Kong in ballast and reached San Francisco on August 19 in the creditable time of 37 days. It was the best run on this course since 1890 when the American wooden full-rigged ship *William H. Macy* made the passage in 34 days. She arrived at Queenstown from Wallaroo in May 1906 in 119 days. In the same year she sailed from Antwerp to Portland (Oreg.), but was forced back to Antwerp for repairs after colliding with a steamer. In 1908 she was sold to Société Générale d'Armement, and her end came on September 10 1916 when on passage from Seattle (Wash.) to Ipswich with wheat and barley. She was sunk by the German submarine *U-B-18*, about 60 miles north-west of Ushant.

Maréchal Lannes – Steel barque, 2,297 g., 1,955 n.
December 24 1898: Launched by Chantiers de la Loire, Nantes, for R. Guillon & R. Fleury, Nantes.

Captain C. Lepetit took her in command on the stocks, and the barque left Nantes on March 10 1899. She sailed from Swansea for San Francisco with coal on March 28, but on March 30 three of her boats were found empty at Broadhaven, Nolton, and Wertdale. Later part of her masts were sighted emerging near Grassholm Island, in the neighbourhood of the Smalls. It was supposed that the cause of her loss with her crew of 25 was a dense fog which set in not long after she sailed.

Maréchal Suchet – Steel ship, 2,270 g., 1,991 n.
November 1902: Completed by Chantiers de St. Nazaire for Cie. de Navigation Française, Nantes.

1904: Sold to the Sté. des Voiliers Nantais. On October 5 1909, while bound from Japan to Falmouth for orders, she put into Valparaiso with rudder damage and left again on the 28th. She was 106 days to Falmouth. There she was ordered to London and left Falmouth on February 16 1910 in tow, but on February 18 she stranded on Shingle Bank in a gale. The ship was refloated on February 22, badly damaged but was repaired to survive the coming war and get into more trouble afterwards. In 1921 she was sold to the Sté. des Voiliers Français, Havre. On her last voyage under the French flag the *Maréchal Suchet* arrived at Newcastle (N.S.W.) from Havre early in February 1921, 104 days out, and then took a coal cargo to Iquique in 82 days. She left Chile in August with nitrate and reached Bordeaux on Christmas Day, to lay up in the River Gironde. She next appeared in 1923, when she was sold to A./S. Freedom (E. Friis-Hansen, Mgr.) of Oslo, and renamed *Faith*. Despite the name, the only cargo she could get, apparently, was 1,900 tons of cattle bones from Ibicuy, Argentina. After this she was laid up in the Loire for months until she was bought for £3,100 by F. Laeisz of Hamburg for his Flying "P" Line. She was then renamed *Pellworm*. At the time there was a sudden increase in the nitrate freights from the West Coast of South America, and she was hastily commissioned under the German flag to share in this. She sailed in ballast from Nantes for Taltal in mid-July 1924 but could not get past Cape Horn, and her charter gave her no time to sail east-about. Her difficulties were bad ballast and crew trouble.

After a valiant effort, she was turned back and put into Montevideo, 119 days out, to find her charter had been cancelled. She was ordered to return and left Montevideo on December 20 1924. Arriving at Hamburg in 105 days having earned nothing, she was used as a hulk, while Mr. Laeisz commissioned some of his own ships and built another. The disgraced *Pellworm* ex-*Maréchal Suchet* was refurbished as a waterfront youth hostel at Hamburg, renamed *Hein Godenwind,* damaged during air-raids in the Second World War and finally used as target practice for Luftwaffe bomber pilots working-up in Baltic waters. Here she sank, perhaps not greatly mourned, at least in Hamburg. Mr. Laeisz was not accustomed to ships which could not (or did not) weather Cape Horn, no matter how handicapped.

It must be said in her favour that she was essentially a good ship. She was rushed off to sea to profit from that brief spurt in nitrate freights and her sand-ballast may not have been either adequate or properly stowed. At the time even German crews were somewhat bloody-minded. The *Pellworm* did not get a real chance to show her paces as a "P"-ship successor.

Marguerite Dollfus – Steel barque, 1,948 g., 1,724 n.
November 17 1898: Launched by Chantiers de la Loire, Nantes, for Sté. des Voiliers Français, Havre.

In 1901, she sailed to San Francisco from Melbourne in 50 days. On December 7 1916, while bound from Havre to Fort de France in ballast, under Captain J. Frostin, she was sunk by the German submarine *U-B-37,* in 49°45′N., 3°40′W., some 28 miles south of Start Point.

Marguerite Elise – Steel barque, 1,197 g., 1,085 n.
1891: Built by Chantiers de la Loire, Nantes, for V. Vincent, Nantes.

She made eight voyages under the French flag and was then sold in July 1903, for £6,400, to Seetzen Gebruder of Bremen. Renamed *Carl*, she retained the German flag until October 28 1914, when she was captured at sea by a British warship and taken into Falmouth with her cargo of guano —a useful fertiliser. Condemned as a prize in 1915, she was sold to the A./S. Transatlantic Motor Ship Co., of Christiania, and renamed *Lapwing*. Later bought by Gustav B. Bull, of Oslo, she was again renamed, this time as *Ivrig*. On May 1 1917, while on passage from Dublin to Newport News in ballast, she was shelled and sunk by the German submarine *U-C-65*, 12 miles west-north-west of the Mull of Galloway.

Marguerite Mirabaud – Steel barque, 2,293 g., 1,949 n.
October 13 1900: Launched by Chantiers de la Loire, Nantes, for Sté. des Voiliers Français, Havre.

The following year she put into Port Stanley leaking and repairs took three months before she left again for Havre. She did not last long, for on February 18 1907, while on passage from La Rochelle towards Tahiti with coal, via Hobart, she ran ashore in fog on the east coast of the South Island of New Zealand, about 30 miles south of Dunedin—rather an odd place to be at the time—and became a total loss. The crew were saved. Twenty years later part of her hull with bowsprit and fore lower-mast still marked the spot.

Marguerite Molinos – Steel barque, 1,928 g., 1,775 n.
July 17 1897: Launched by Chantiers de la Méditerranée, Havre, for Sté. des Voiliers Français, Havre. Called the "flyer" of the French bounty ships, she was renowned. A 2,500-deadweight tonner, she made a number of good passages in her early days, and was a notable hard-working bounty-earner. On her maiden voyage she left Penarth for San Francisco with 2,500 tons of coal on October 29 1897, and passed the Golden Gate on February 19 1898, 113 days out. On the homewards passage she was off the Lizard 90 days out, beating the British four-masted barques *Clan Galbraith* and *Pyrenees* by 11 and 14 days. Her excellent run compares with the record passages made on the route by the *Falls of Garry*, 88 days, in 1891-2, *Alcinous*, 93 days, in 1891-2, *Andelana*, 89 days in 1893 and *Susquehanna*, 94 days, in 1895. On December 11 1898 she sailed from Majunga for New Caledonia. In 1899, the *Marguerite Molinos* arrived at Noumea, 62 days out, and later arrived in San Francisco 113 days out from Swansea, full of coal. Her homewards passage, begun February 3 1900, was 108 days to the Lizard.

Again in 1901, she arrived at Falmouth from San Francisco in 103 days and in 112 days three years later.

The *Marguerite Molinos* survived the war but was laid up at Bordeaux for the whole of 1921. She sailed from there on April 12 1922 for La Martinière, but was soon bought by M. Potet, Havre, for his West Indian trade. She sailed without incident until February 17 1925 when she left Nantes for Brazil, was spoken 11 days later in 47°20′N., 7°W., and nothing more was heard of her until the following May, when she was quoted at 80 guineas on the reinsurance market on May 25 1925. Strangely, she turned up all well on that very day, arriving at Natal after a slow passage of 97 days. In January 1927 she was laid up at Havre and sold for scrap in April the following year.

Marguerite Thérèse – Iron barque, 1,215 g., 1,159 n.
1876: Built by Gourlay Bros., Dundee, for David Bruce & Co., Dundee, as *Stracathro*.
Twenty years later was sold to L. Le Provost de la Maissonnière, Dieppe, and renamed *Marguerite Thérèse*. She did not last long with her new name. On September 24 1897 she was abandoned at sea, dismasted, 125 miles southeast of Port Natal. She was towed to Durban by the French steamer *Entre-Rios,* condemned, and sold to Beira where she was used as a hulk. Her hull was still on the beach there in 1938.

Marie – Steel barque, 2,192 g., 1,958 n.
February 25 1899: Launched by Chantiers de la Loire, St. Nazaire, for Sté. des Voiliers de St. Nazaire.
On her maiden voyage she reached Table Bay from Barry in 60 days, and Newcastle (N.S.W.) from Table Bay in 32 days. Then in 1903 she was transferred to Sté. Générale d'Armement. On March 19 1913, when bound from California to Hull with wheat, she was caught in a snow-storm in the North Sea and stranded on Haisborough Sand. The barque bumped heavily and was abandoned by her crew of 24, who were rescued by the Grimsby trawler *Ameer*. However, the *Marie* managed to clear herself from the bank and was picked up by two Dutch trawlers and several tugs which towed her to Cuxhaven, arriving there on March 24. She had some seven feet of water in her hold but was in good order. On December 10 1913, off Easter Island, the *Marie* sighted the *Dalgonar*, drifting in the Pacific (see *Loire*).

On June 9 1916 she left Antofagasta, Chile, for Ellesmere Port with nitrate, but when 108 days at sea she was in collision with the British steamer *Wheatlands* and sank some 40 miles south-east of Waterford, Ireland. Crew saved.

Marie Alice – Steel barque, 1,114 g., 999 n.
1889: Built by Chantiers de la Loire, Nantes, for V. Vincent, Nantes.

Another mystery—she has been missing since February 12 1895, on passage from Sydney towards Antwerp with grain, commanded by Captain Ancelin —probably a victim of ice or Cape Horn.

Marie Madeleine – Steel barque, 1,462 g., 1,285 n.
September 1897: Completed by A. Dubigeon, Nantes, for Cie. Nationale d'Armement, Havre, as *Alice*.

In January 1904 she was sold to Cie. Havraise de Navigation (Ed. Corblet & Co., Mgrs.), Havre, and renamed *Marie Madeleine*. On June 9 1910, while bound from St. Nazaire to Santa Rosalia, Mexico, she was dismasted and lost four men 400 miles off the River Plate. Her master, Captain Langlois, managed to sail her to Montevideo under jury rig, reaching there on July 5 1910. The barque was surveyed, found not worth repair, sold on the spot and converted into a hulk. In the shipping shortage of World War I she was re-rigged, to sail at first under the Norwegian flag as *Mariota,* later as *Syvstjerne.* In 1919 she was sold to J. J. Larsen of Odense (Denmark) and renamed *Albert Höeg.* This was the last change, for while on passage from Savannah to Nyborg, in February 1920, she was wrecked near Gothenburg. Only four of her crew were saved.

Marie Molinos – Steel barque, 1,946 g., 1,715 n.
June 23 1899: Launched by Chantiers de la Loire, Nantes, for Sté. des Voiliers Français, Havre.

After a useful life she was shelled and sunk by the German submarine *U-20* in 46°40′N., 10°20′W. on passage from Nantes towards New York on May 3 1916.

Marthe – Iron and steel 4-masted barque, 2,946 g., 2,499 n.
1892: Built and owned by Alexander Stephen & Sons, Dundee, as *Melita*.

She was sold to A. D. Bordes in 1894 and renamed *Marthe* under the French flag. In 1896 she made a good passage of 75 days from Dunkirk to Iquique. May 12 1898, arriving from Pisagua with nitrate, under Captain Engrand, while being towed into Dunkirk Harbour in foggy weather, she touched on Ruytingen Bank. Several tugs were unable to refloat her, and the day after she sprang a serious leak, capsized and sank three miles south of the Ruytingen lightship. Her crew were saved. It was a pity—a good ship gone.

Marthe (another) – Steel 4-masted barque, 3,119 g., 2,754 n.
August 25 1900: Launched by Chantiers de Normandie, Rouen, for A. D. Bordes.

Her best outward passage to Chile was made in 1903-4, 70 days. In 1905 she was credited with the excellent run of 32 days between Newcastle (N.S.W.) and Valparaiso. Her last voyage began on July 6 1917, when she left Le Verdon Roads for Valparaiso in ballast, commanded by Captain Leff. On the following August 2, position 33°38'N., 23°30'W., the *Marthe* was shelled by the German submarine *U-155*. Captain Leff returned the fire but his small guns were hopelessly outmatched by the U-boat's two five-inch guns. The barque was abandoned with one man killed and five gravely wounded. The next day the *Marthe's* guns were transhipped to the submarine which then sank the barque by explosive charges, about 340 miles west of Madeira. The French crew were rescued in their boats three days later by a British submarine which handed them over to a British steamer to land them at Horta, Azores, on August 7. Captain Leff and his crew were mentioned in dispatches for their action.

Marthe Roux – Steel barque, 1,962 g., 1,726 n.
August 19 1899: Launched by Chantiers de la Loire, Nantes, for Sté. des Voiliers Français, Havre.

After a long and useful life, she was bought by Gillet & Fils, of Lyons, in 1916, for the log-wood trade, retaining her original name, but she did not last long before becoming yet another war casualty. The end came on passage from Black River (Jamaica) towards St. Louis du Rhône in 1917 with a cargo of 1,973 tons log-wood, under Captain A. Benoît. When 49 days out, on July 3 1917, she was captured and sunk by explosive charges by the German submarine *U-34*, about 25 miles north-north-east of Cape Ivi in the Mediterranean.

Marthe Solange – Steel 4-masted barque, 2,398 g., 2,269 n.
1890: Built by Russell & Co., Port Glasgow, for W. Price & Co., Liverpool, as *Holt Hill*, and still under that name in 1916.

Price had owned a predecessor of the same name, lost in 1889. On December 5 1916 she sailed from Nantes under the British flag for Gulfport, but was dismasted a few days later in a gale. Sighted by the Dutch steamer *Iberia*, her crew were taken aboard and the *Iberia* attempted to tow, but the hawser broke and the *Holt Hill* was abandoned. The *Iberia* proceeded, and the crew was landed at Plymouth on December 14. But the four-master was not finished. Found by a French steamer she was towed to Verdon Roads, arriving on December 30. On January 3 1917 she was taken to Bordeaux where she was used as a depot ship for port authorities and pilots.

Later sold to Sté. Maritime & Commercials (G. Kuranda, Mgr.), Bordeaux, and renamed *Marthe Solange*, she did not sail for her new owners.

Montmorency – Steel 4-masted barque, 2,892 g., 2,639 n.
March 16 1896: Launched by Chantiers de la Loire, Nantes, for A. D. Bordes.

Her best outward passage was on her maiden voyage, 65 days from St. Nazaire to Iquique. Her next best was Prawle Point to Valparaiso, 72 days, in 1899. In 1903-4, the *Montmorency* made a smart passage home. Leaving Iquique November 12 1903, she arrived Hamburg on January 24 1904, only 73 days out. She was still in the Chilean trade after World War I but no longer making such passages. On December 18 1923 she left Iquique for the English Channel (f.o.), and passed the Lizard 100 days out. On October 10 1924 she sailed from Caleta Coloso for Nantes and took 106 days for the passage. The *Montmorency* was laid up in Nantes and broken up in 1926.

Nantes – Steel barque, 2,679 g., 2,263 n.
November 16 1899: Launched by Chantiers de Normandie, Rouen, for Cie. Nantaise de Navigation à Vapeur, Nantes.

This big barque was the only sailing-ship to be built for the company. She was a good and solid vessel, always well maintained by competent ship-masters and well handled. In 1914 she was sold to Sté. Générale d'Armement and her last voyage came two years later. On October 9 1916 she left Iquique for London with 3,350 tons nitrate, commanded by Captain Carméné, and on December 26 was captured by the German raider *Moewe* in 12°37′N., 34°W., and sunk by explosive charges.

Neuilly – Steel barque, 2,186 g., 1,923 n.
October 27 1900: Launched by Chantiers Nantais de Constr. Maritimes, Nantes, for Sté. des Long-Courriers Français, Havre.

On her maiden return voyage in 1901 she arrived at Havre from New Caledonia in 148 days, with nearly half the crew attacked by scurvy. About 1914-15 the *Neuilly* was sold to Sté. Générale d'Armement. Yet another war casualty, on October 1 1917, while bound from Melbourne towards Bordeaux with 3,080 tons of grain, she was intercepted by the German submarine *U-90* and sunk by bombs in the Atlantic, 450 miles west-south-west of Penmarch Head.

Noëmi – Steel barque, 2,192 g., 1,958 n.
January 14 1899: Launched by Chantiers de la Loire, St. Nazaire, for Sté. des Voiliers de St. Nazaire.

On her maiden voyage she made Table Bay from Barry in 66 days, and Newcastle (N.S.W.) from Table Bay in 36 days, and in 1903 was transferred

Marthe sinking—another First World War casualty. Photograph taken from the *U-155* on August 3 1917. (*Dr. Jürgen Meyer Collection.*)

French bounty barque *Marie* with circular ventilators cut near the clews of several of the square sails—an idea to "spill dead wind". (It made no discernible difference in the ship's speed and was a fad of a few masters. (*Morrison Collection, San Francisco Maritime Museum.*)

Listing to a light fair wind, the barque *Maréchal de Villars* approaches San Francisco, her steel sides rust-scarred from her long voyage from France via Tasmania. (*Plummer Collection, San Francisco Maritime Museum.*)

Four-masted barque, *Seine*, ex-*Ernest Siegfried*, outward bound from San Francisco. (*Wm. Muir Collection, San Francisco Maritime Museum.*)

The short-lived school-ship *Richelieu*, ex-German *Pola*. (*By permission of the Trustees of the National Maritime Museum.*)

The barque *Suzanne* with her royals fast and no sail on the mizzen. (*A. D. Edwardes, South Australia.*)

to Sté. Générale d'Armement. On June 12 1913 she left Hamburg for San Francisco under Captain Le Gloahec, and very nearly never arrived for she had a narrow escape when she had just rounded the Horn. During the night of October 1-2 1913, the weather cold with heavy squalls of hail and snow, she was sailing with the wind on her port quarter when the second mate suddenly sighted a fixed green light a short distance away. Collision was avoided by throwing the *Noëmi* immediately aback—a dangerous manoeuvre in such weather. In fact the other ship being hove-to—stopped—could not have got out of the way. So close were the two vessels that it was easy to read the name of the other ship in the light of a flare. She was the Bordes' full-rigged ship *Cerro Alegre*. Such accidents may account for several missing ships. The *Noëmi* arrived at San Francisco in November, 152 days out, which was not at all speedy, but all hands thanked the Lord to be there.

After discharging her cargo the barque sailed in ballast for Portland (Oreg.), where she took a cargo of oats and barley, and arrived in the U.K. in July 1914, 145 days out. On her last voyage the *Noëmi* arrived at Ipswich from San Francisco on May 19 1921. After that, she was laid up in the Canal de la Martinière, and left on February 2 1927 to be broken up.

Nord – Steel 4-masted barque, 3,113 g., 2,905 n.
1889: Built by Barclay, Curle & Co., Glasgow, for A. D. Bordes.

She was a powerful vessel, a 5,000 deadweight tonner, with cellular double bottom and a deep-tank amidships in which she could take in 1,350 tons. The *Nord* was a fine ship. Her best passage was made in 1892 from Iquique to St. Catherine's, Isle of Wight, in 71 days. In 1915 she was partially dismasted off Cape Horn and put into Montevideo for repairs. On October 4 1917, in the Bay of Biscay, she was attacked by a German submarine but managed to beat the enemy off with her guns.

The *Nord* survived until April 1923, when she went to the shipbreakers.

Normandie – Steel barque, 2,056 g., 1,558 n.
July 1899: Completed by A. Dubigeon, Nantes, for Raoul Guillon, Nantes.

On her maiden voyage under Captain Le Provost de la Maissonnière—the only voyage she made—she arrived at San Francisco from Swansea on January 8 1900, after a slow passage. On February 25 1900 she left San Francisco for Falmouth for orders, but was wrecked on Ascension Island in May. Her crew were saved.

Notre Dame d'Arvor – Steel barque, 2,646 g., 2,232 n.
February 22 1902: Launched by Chantiers de la Loire, Nantes, for Cie. de Navigation Française, Nantes.

L

Between October 1903 and September 1905 she made the following voyage
which was then by no means an unusual round: Europe – San Francisco –
Australia – New Caledonia – Europe. Meanwhile, in 1904, she had been
transferred to the Sté. Générale d'Armement. On May 29 1906 she reached
Queenstown (Cobh, Ireland) from Port Pirie in 122 days—an average passage. On September 2 1909 she left Antwerp for Oregon with cement, but
was in collision with the British steamer *Raithwaite* a few days later in the
English Channel and put into Falmouth for repairs. On December 4, when
leaving dry dock, she struck the quay and was again badly damaged. Repairs
took six weeks before she could sail on January 21 1910. Calling at Hobart
on May 4, she arrived at Astoria (Oreg.), only on August 28, after a very
slow passage of 219 days from Falmouth and almost 12 months from
Antwerp. Again, leaving Tacoma November 19 1910 for Falmouth, she did
not arrive until April 21 1911, 153 days out. The round voyage took the
long time of 20 months, which was no way to earn a dividend. On March
22 1920, while on passage from Rochefort to Port Victoria in ballast, commanded by Captain Menguy, she went ashore by night on Wardang Island,
and attempts to get her off were unsuccessful. On May 20 1920 fire broke
out aboard and she was gutted.

Notre Dame de la Garde – Steel barque, 2,569 g., 1,954 n.
April 14 1900: Launched by Chantiers de la Loire, Nantes, for Sté. Marseillaise de Voiliers, Marseilles.

After a very short life, while bound from Havre to New Caledonia in
ballast, she stranded on Brany Reef, 18 miles south of Tchio on August 7
1901. The barque broke up but the crew were saved.

Olivier de Clisson – Steel barque, 2,202 g., 1,974 n.
May 22 1901: Launched by Chantiers Nantais de Constr. Maritimes, Nantes,
for Sté. Bretonne de Navigation (Prentout, Leblond & Leroux, Mgrs.),
Rouen.

She was another unlucky ship. On her maiden voyage from Penarth to San
Francisco, her master failed to weather Cape San Roque (Brazil) and put
into Cayenne (French Guiana), which he did not leave until September 9
1901. The crew was attacked by scurvy, perhaps understandably, and three
men died at sea. She arrived finally after a slow passage of 224 days. On her
next voyage which was from Plymouth to New York, her master died and
she stranded on Long Beach, near Fire Island, on February 9 1903. She was
refloated on March 13 and left New York for Japan with case oil, under
Captain Rault. The master's wife and baby died at sea during this voyage.
Her troubles were not over. On passage from New Caledonia for Havre in

1905, still commanded by Captain Rault, a serious leak was discovered on September 23. She developed a heavy list because of this and had to be abandoned. She capsized and sank the second day after when about 300 miles off the Cape Verde Islands. All the crew were saved.

Pacifique (the first) – Iron barque, 1,526 g., 1,472 n.
1867: Built by Barclay, Curle & Co., Glasgow, for G. Marshall & Sons, London, as *Berkshire*.

She was sold to A. D. Bordes in 1889 and renamed *Pacifique*. On October 14 1895, while on passage from Shields to Valparaiso with coal, she was run down off Dudgeon by the German steamer *Emma* (from Rotterdam for Bo'ness). The *Pacifique* sank almost immediately with her master, Captain Lebras, a coastal pilot and ten men. The remaining 11 were rescued by the *Emma* and landed at Hull.

Pacifique (the second) – Steel 4-masted barque, 2,241 g., 2,055 n.
1883: Built by W. B. Thompson, Glasgow, for R. L. Greenshields, Cowie & Co., Liverpool, as *Knight of St. Michael*.

She was a very good sailer under the British flag making passages like 90 days between Liverpool and Calcutta, and to Queenstown from San Francisco in 98 days. In March 1897 she was sold to A. D. Bordes and renamed *Pacifique*. In 1898 she left Astoria in company with the British four-masted barque *Province,* which arrived in Europe in 114 days, only 12 hours before the *Pacifique*. In 1899, another match was made, this time with the German four-masted barque *Athene* (ex-British *Conishead*) between Iquique and Europe. The *Pacifique* arrived at La Pallice on December 9 in 76 days, just as her rival passed Beachy Head. It was the *Pacifique's* best run in that trade. Two years later she was badly bashed up off the Horn on passage from the Tyne for Valparaiso with coal, under Captain Leyat, when she had to put into Montevideo with her decks swept, bulwarks gone, rigging damaged, three boats carried away, and her master and five men washed overboard. She was sold in 1916 to MM. Gaillard & Co. and registered at Bayonne, but she failed to arrive from her first voyage for these owners later the same year, when she left Penarth for Port Arthur on October 21 1916.

Pacifique (the third) – Iron 4-masted barque, 2,277 g., 2,108 n.
1886: Built by the Whitehaven Shipbuilding Co., Whitehaven, for North Western Shipping Co., Liverpool, as *Gilcruix*.

The famous English Poet Laureate, John Masefield, once served in this barque.

By 1895 she was sold to Knöhr & Burchard of Hamburg and renamed *Barmbek* until August 18 1914, when she was captured off the Lizard by the French auxiliary cruiser *Flandre* and taken to Brest. Her crew were in ignorance of the war, having left Portland (Oreg.), in April for Ipswich. The four-master was then managed by Ed. Corblet & Co., acquiring the name of *Pacifique,* port of registry, Brest, but about 1916 was transferred to the Cie. Navale de l'Océanie. In February 1921 she sailed from Fredrik-stad, Norway, for Melbourne with timber.

On the night of March 2 she was in collision with the American steamship *Naamhok,* eight miles south of St. Catherine's Point. The steamer proceeded but the barque was disabled. Eventually picked up by the Norwegian steamer *Tiro,* she was towed to Havre. She left Havre in January 1923 to be broken up at Caen.

The collision case went to court where the *Naamhok* was found at fault and her owners were required to pay £44,000 damages.

Paris – Steel barque, 2,333 g., 1,740 n.
April 14 1900: Launched by Chantiers Nantais de Constr. Maritimes, Nantes, for Sté. des Long-Courriers Français.

On May 10 1903 she left Hamburg bound for Honolulu and San Francisco with cement, her 27-man crew commanded by Captain Le Guével. She touched at Cherbourg and sailed from that port on May 16. She was spoken on June 26 in 19°S., 39°W., and never heard of again.

On March 4 1904 the *Paris* was posted missing at Lloyd's.

Pax – Steel barque, 1,437 g., 1,307 n.
1891: Built by Russell & Co., Port Glasgow, for J. H. Hustede, Elsfleth, Germany, as *Pax.*

Although she changed hands many times during her career all her owners retained her original name. She was also Dutch, British (from about 1902 until 1909-10) and Norwegian (owned by M. H. Gundersen, Tvedestrand) before she became French at Antwerp, where she was sold to the Cie. Navale de l'Océanie, of Noumea, in November 1920. After several successful voyages, she stranded near Noumea in January 1923. She was refloated and subsequently converted into a barge for carrying nickel ore from outports to the plant at Noumea for processing. She was used in this way until 1934 when she was beached in a bay near Noumea.

Persévérance – Iron 4-masted ship, 2,558 g., 2,511 n. (with water ballast).
1886: Built by W. B. Thompson, Glasgow, for A. D. Bordes.

She lasted only five years. On July 3 1891 she left Rio de Janeiro in ballast bound for Antofagasta, under Captain J. Lequerhic, and went missing. Bordes bought only good strong ships: no reason for her loss was ever found, but she would have been off the Horn before the end of winter there.

Persévérance – Steel 4-masted barque, 2,873 g., 2,588 n.
March 22 1896: Launched by Chantiers de la Méditerranée, La Seyne, for A. D. Bordes.

Her best homeward passage was 74 days in 1897 and her best outward passage 71 days, made in 1898. On March 1 1910 she grounded in the Schelde but was refloated and repaired at Antwerp. She was a World War I casualty. While bound from Iquique to St. Nazaire with 4,000 tons nitrate on September 24 1917, commanded by Captain F. Béquet, she was attacked by the German submarine *U-C-63* in 44°22'N., 9°10'W. After an action of an hour the barque was abandoned and sunk by explosive charges. Her crew were rescued the following day by the British liner *Victoria,* and landed at Ponta Delgada.

Pierre Antonine – Steel barque, 2,206 g., 2,030 n.
June 1902: Completed by Chantiers Nantais de Constr. Maritimes, Nantes, for P. Guillon, Nantes.

On August 30 1910 she arrived at Newcastle (N.S.W.) from London in 84 days. On February 21 1913, while on passage from Montevideo towards Newcastle (N.S.W.) in ballast, under Captain Nédelec, she was thrown on her beam ends through her ballast shifting in a mountainous sea. Her master ordered the masts to be cut away to prevent capsize. He managed to get her upright, and under jury rig the *Pierre Antonine* reached a position 45 miles off Sydney. Here she was picked up by a steamer which towed her to that port. Subsequently re-rigged, she was sold to Bureau Frères & Baillergeau, of Nantes. She survived the 1914-18 war, but in 1920 she made a slow passage from Europe to California and was posted overdue at Lloyd's. The same thing happened again on the homeward passage, begun from San Francisco on November 5 1920, when nothing was heard of her until the following May. She was then quoted at 40 guineas per cent on the re-insurance market. She turned up after a passage of 179 days, arriving at Ipswich on May 9 1921.
    The *Pierre Antonine* was afterwards laid up, and was broken up in 1926.

Pierre Corneille – Steel barque, 1,303 g., 1,125 n.
1891: Built by Chantiers de la Loire, St. Nazaire, for H. Prentout-Leblond & E. Boniface, Rouen.

She was commanded by Captain Leloquet from her completion until her end. In 1896 she made the best run of the year of 67 ships between Australia and the West Coast of North America—50 days. But she was doomed, too. On February 19 1898 she left San Francisco for Table Bay; was spoken by a passing vessel when three days out, and never heard of again.

Pierre Loti – Steel barque, 2,196 g., 1,926 n.
February 23 1901: Launched by Chantiers Nantais de Constr. Maritimes, Nantes, for N. & C. Guillon, Nantes.

She had an uneventful career, being sold in 1912 to the Sté. Générale d'Armement and lost in World War I. She met her end on January 27 1915, while on passage from San Francisco to Harwich with barley when she was captured and sunk by the German raider *Prinz Eitel Friedrich* in 29°53'S., 26°47'W.

Président Félix Faure – Steel 4-masted barque, 2,860 g., 2,410 n.
February 3 1896: Launched by Chantiers de la Méditerranée, Havre, for Cie. Havraise de Navigation à Voiles (C. Brown & E. Corblet, Mgrs.), Havre.

Mr. Brown had been master in American sail and rigged his four-master in the American fashion, with skysails. She was a smart vessel and a good sailer; her best outward passage was 79 days made in 1903 from Havre to New Caledonia. The *Président Félix Faure* was trading between Europe and New Caledonia until her end, which came 12 years later. Before that, she featured in one of the worst crew losses at sea known even in the Cape Horn trade. On February 2 1898 off Kerguelen Islands, in a violent storm, she was swept from stern to stem by tremendous seas and 15 men were washed overboard and not seen again. There were not enough men left even to launch a boat, had this been possible, but she sailed on to Port Adelaide, arriving there 131 days out. Ten years later she was lost when bound from New Caledonia for Havre with nickel ore, under Captain Noël. On March 13 1908 she was wrecked in dense fog on the Antipodes Islands. With only one boat and that badly damaged, the crew were fortunate enough to reach the shore in safety. The provision depot was on the other side of the island, but was not found by the French sailors who remained in a large shed close to the scene of the wreck. They found there 54 cases of biscuits and six blankets, but no rifles or cartridges.

In this desolate spot Captain Noël kept his crew alive with difficulty for two months until, on May 12 1908, H.M.S. *Pegasus* rescued all hands and took them to Lyttelton, N.Z.

Psyché – Iron barque, 1,015 g., 852 n.
1877: Built by A. Stephen & Sons, Glasgow, for A. C. Le Quellec, Bordeaux.

On January 30 1901, while bound from Caleta Buena towards the English

Channel for orders, commanded by Captain Tonnerre, she was abandoned in a sinking condition off the Horn. It was summer, fortunately, and all hands got away in the barque's two life-boats.

The mate's boat with five men aboard was found by the British full-rigged ship *Largiemore,* after 13 days, but the master's boat, with 13 aboard, was picked up by the British four-masted barque *Andromeda* after 38 days, when only nine men were left alive.

Quevilly – Steel 4-masted barque, 3,203 g., 2,418 n. (carrying petroleum in bulk).
March 20 1897: Launched by Laporte & Co., Rouen, for H. Prentout-Leblond & E. Boniface, Rouen.

She was among the first of the true sailing tankers, designed and built specifically for the carriage of petroleum in bulk. The *Quevilly* was no clipper for her ends were full, but she was a fine ship, beautifully sparred, and could sail well as a 17-day east-bound trans-atlantic run in 1898 showed. She was in the bulk-petroleum trade between Philadelphia and Rouen or Dieppe during her career under the French flag. On November 25 1903 the *Quevilly* rescued the crew of the sinking American schooner *Ira Bliss,* 80 miles off the mouth of the Delaware, and landed them at Dieppe where she completed that voyage.

Her best homeward passage under sail was 14 days in 1906, but in 1910 she was fitted with two M.A.N. six-cylinder oil engines driving twin screws to give her a speed of five knots. Whether these proved satisfactory or justified their cost is an open question—possibly not. She still carried her sails. On January 26 1917 the *Quevilly* was coming into New York Roads in fog when the American destroyer *Sampson* ran into her and she was badly damaged. The *Sampson* was found at fault, but $8,400 was paid by the American Government to the barque's owners only in 1934. On November 23 1917 the *Quevilly* had a narrow escape from torpedoes off La Pallice.

On January 31 1918 she left La Pallice, under Captain F. Rault, with a cargo of petroleum for the Azores where she was used as a depot tanker for the bunkering of ships until 1919. She left La Pallice escorted by the French submarine *Diane.* On the night of February 11 a violent explosion was heard. Believing it was a German submarine attacking, the *Quevilly* managed to escape by carrying a press of sails, but the *Diane,* commanded by Captain H. J. Le Masne, was not seen again. In March 1919 the barque resumed her voyages but by 1921 she was laid up at Rouen until sold to A/S. Sörlandske Lloyd (K. A. Thorbjörnsen, Mgr.), Oslo, and converted to a full-powered whale-oil tanker, with two new engines, and superstructure aft. The only sign of her sailing ship origin left was the clipper bow, shorn of its bowsprit. Renamed *Deodata* in due course, and unrecognisable, she left Rouen on March 13 1924 for Port Arthur (Tex.), and continued to give useful service chiefly in the Black Sea oil trade under the Norwegian flag until 1939, for various owners, carrying not only whale-oil.

On October 21 1939, while bound from Constantza for Grangemouth in ballast, she struck a mine 1½ miles off the Inner Dowsing light-vessel and began to sink rapidly. Her men took to a raft and lifeboat. Within ten minutes they were picked up by a British vessel. Three of them were badly injured, and all were landed at an East coast port that same night.

Quillota – Iron ship, 1,335 g., 1,112 n.
1876: Built by R. Steele & Co., Greenock, for J. & W. Stewart, Greenock, as *Brahmin*.

She was sold to A. D. Bordes in 1893 and renamed *Quillota*. On October 27 1901 she left Nantes for North Shields in ballast but off the Tyne she was caught in a strong gale. Compelled to anchor off Sunderland, she parted from her anchors and drove on Hendon Rock where she sank, with the loss of 19 lives on November 12 1901.

Quillota – Steel barque, 2,559 g., 2,073 n.
June 21 1902: Launched by Chantiers de St. Nazaire, Rouen, for the Sté. des Voiliers de St. Nazaire, as *Jehan d'Ust*.

She was bought by A. D. Bordes before completion and renamed *Quillota*. She had a useful if undistinguished career until September 29 1917, when she sailed from St. Nazaire Roads for Fremantle, under Captain A. Mal, in company with the French four-masted ship *A. D. Bordes* and the barquen-tine *Saint Suliac*. The convoy was escorted as far as Belle Ile by the armed trawler *Chevrette,* which returned to St. Nazaire the day after. A week later, on October 6 about 9 a.m., a steamer hove in sight astern coming up rapidly and opened fire. Captain Mal, convinced he had fallen in with a German raider returned the fire. The action lasted 40 minutes, but having been hit below the waterline twice, with her forecastle on fire and rigging badly damaged, the barque became unmanageable and was abandoned sinking. One man was drowned. Her crew were picked up by the steamer which was then discovered to be British.

The *Quillota* was victim to one of those mishaps which can always occur in war time. H.M. merchant cruiser *Mantua*, formerly a P. & O. liner, was patrolling the Atlantic when she sighted a sailing vessel carrying no flag, which was taken to be the German raider *Seeadler*. Fire was opened. The *Mantua* had six seamen wounded, one of them badly injured.

Apologies were subsequently made by the Foreign Office to the French Government. But this was an error of recognition as well, perhaps, as of challenging procedure: the French barque did not at all resemble the German raider, which had begun life as, and still looked like, a British full-rigged ship. It could be that the *Mantua's* gunnery officer did not know one from the other.

Rancagua – Iron ship, 1,704 g., 1,443 n.
1877: Built by Harland & Wolff, Belfast, for W. P. Sinclair & Co., Liverpool, as *Slieve Bawn*.

Sold to A. D. Bordes and renamed *Rancagua* in April 1894. In December 1901 she was bought by J. D. Thompson, Glasgow, and given back her original name. Three years later she was lost on the Chilean coast while on passage from Independencia Bay to the United Kingdom. It was a pity, for she was a fine and fast ship. Basil Lubbock speaks of her as an "out-and-out jute clipper".*

Rancagua – Steel ship, 2,729 g., 2,315 n.
May 1902: Launched by Chantiers de St. Nazaire, Rouen, for Sté. des Voiliers de St. Nazaire, as *Pilote Hervé Rielle*.

She was bought by A. D. Bordes when she was fitting out, and named *Rancagua*. After a useful career she went missing on a passage homewards from Chile. She was bound from Mejillones towards Bordeaux, commanded by Captain Grégoire, was spoken on January 20 1917 by a passing vessel, and subsequently posted missing when there was no further news and she did not arrive. Several months later it was learned that she had been sunk on February 10 1917, by the German submarine *U-B-39* in the Bay of Biscay. Her crew were lost without trace.

Reine Blanche – Steel barque, 1,854 g., 1,653 n.
June 1896: Completed by Laporte & Co., Rouen, for R. Guillon & R. Fleury, Nantes.

In 1897-98 she made a round voyage from Swansea to San Francisco, Capetown, New Caledonia and back to Havre. Amount of freight was 237,642 francs to which the navigation bounty must be added, being another 133,481 francs (for the whole voyage). In 1899-1900 she made another long voyage of the same sort, being Havre – Cardiff – Capetown – Melbourne – Iquique – Rouen. In 1903 she was bought by A. D. Bordes and retained her original name. She was a good ship which had an uneventful career, and was broken up in Spain in 1923.

---

* In his *Last of the Windjammers*, Vol. I, Brown, Son and Ferguson, Glasgow.

René – Steel barque, 2,463 g., 1,976 n.
November 1902: Completed by Chantiers de la Loire, St. Nazaire, for
L. Guillon, Nantes.

She made an excellent passage in 1910 when, on August 12, she arrived at
Newcastle (N.S.W.) in 80 days from London. Again on September 30 1911,
she reached Newcastle from Cherbourg in 87 days despite loss of boats and
several sails in a gale. The same year she left Newcastle for Portland (Oreg.)
with coal and arrived at Astoria, 60 days out, but with more damage. On
April 18 1919 she left New Orleans for Nantes with general cargo and soon
had some sort of mutiny aboard, which was unusual. She had a mixed crew
that voyage. The second mate suffered a knife wound but authority was
restored and the voyage continued. The *René* arrived off the Loire 63 days
out on June 20 1919. She remained under the French flag with several brief
changes of ownership until the autumn of 1921 when she changed both
name and flag to become the *Lisbeth* of Hamburg, owned by H. H. Schmidt.
In 1925 he disposed of her to Seefahrt Segelschiffs Reederei G.m.b.H., of
Bremen (the Bremen Shipowners' Association).

Her new owners renamed her *Bremen* and sent her to sea as a cargo-
carrying cadet ship. She proved satisfactory in this role, although in 1930
she created some interest on the re-insurance market by taking the excessive
time of 152 days from Iquique to the Channel. She was largely employed
in the nitrate trade; typical of many of her passages was the following. Fixed
to carry 3,310 tons of nitrate at 16 shillings per ton with full options, she
left Iquique on November 8 1930 and arrived at Ghent 98 days later on
February 14 1931. On February 12, when off Dover, she was in collision
with the French steamer *Député Abel Ferry,* and damaged above the waterline.

In August 1932 the *Bremen* was sold to the scrappers. She was a good ship,
and had at least ten years of earning life left at the time. But the freight
markets were very poor.

René Kerviler – Steel ship, 2,677 g., 2,291 n.
March 1902: Completed by Chantiers de St. Nazaire for Sté. des Voiliers
de St. Nazaire.

On October 25 1902 she left Zanzibar for Hobart for orders, and was spoken
by the British steamer *Ettrickdale* (London for Albany) in 40°S., 43°E. on
January 14 1903.

She arrived at Hobart only in March 1903, over 130 days out, a very slow
passage, said to be due to continual calm. It may be that she tried to cross
the Indian Ocean rather far to the north. In 1903 she was transferred to Sté.
Générale d'Armement and sailed usefully throughout the First World War.
On January 30 1920 she left Geelong with wheat and arrived at Nantes on

May 24, 115 days out—a reasonable, average passage. After a voyage to California the following year, she was laid up in the Canal de la Martinière until July 16 1927, when she was towed away for breaking up. She was a big full-rigged ship and could have been rather difficult to move in light winds.

Rhône – Steel 4-masted barque, 2,896 g., 2,610 n.
July 21 1896: Launched by Chantiers de la Méditerranée, La Seyne, for A. D. Bordes.

Her best outward passage was 73 days from Beachy Head to Iquique in 1902; her best homeward, Iquique to the Lizard, 78 days in 1902. These were very good. She went ashore east of Dungeness on October 7 1904, but was refloated the day after by the Belgian tug *John Bull,* which took her to Dunkirk. In 1907 the *Rhône* was in collision with another Bordes' four-poster, the *Pacifique,* in fine weather and broad daylight, off the Falklands. The latter managed to reach her destination, but the *Rhône* put into Valparaiso for repairs. The owners found their masters at fault and both captains were dismissed.

Her last voyage was in 1924, from Cardiff to Taltal, 111 days. She was laid up in 1925 and went to the breakers in July 1926.

Richelieu – Steel 4-masted barque, 3,116 g., 2,808 n.
1916: Launched by Blohm & Voss, Hamburg, for F. Laeisz, Hamburg, as *Pola,* and completed just after the armistice.

In 1919 she was taken over by the Allies and handed to the French Government in 1920 in accordance with the Treaty of Versailles. The *Pola* arrived in October 1920 at Dunkirk where she remained idle until 1923. Meanwhile, the Government sold her to the Sté. des Armateurs Français for 511,050 francs, as a cargo-carrying training ship. In September 1923 she arrived in St. Nazaire Roads in tow from Dunkirk, and she was then laid up in the Canal de la Martinière for a year because of the poor freight market and the high operating costs of school-ships. In 1924 she passed to the ownership of the Sté. de Navigation "Les Navires Ecoles Français"—a subsidiary of the Sté. des Armateurs Français—which had been founded by the leading shipowners. She was towed to Nantes and fitted out as a cargo-cadet ship under the name of *Richelieu,* of Nantes.

On November 20 1924 she left the River Loire for Port Lincoln, Australia, under Captain Ch. Populaire. Her crew numbered 50, including only 14 apprentices. These boys went aloft only at their own request, in very fine weather and not higher than the lower topgallant sails, which was unusual in any sailing vessel but particularly in an alleged school-ship. On February 17 1925, she reached Port Lincoln, 89 days out. Her return passage with grain was one of the best that season—102 days to 120 miles west of Land's End. The Swedish four-masted barque *Beatrice* (ex-British *Routenburn*) arrived only 12 hours before the *Richelieu,* and the *Routenburn* was an old Scots wool-clipper. The *Richelieu* discharged at Liverpool where she was much admired. She sailed back to Brest but was then laid up for a year. Her next voyage the following year was to Baltimore in ballast, under Captain Cornec, with only 11 cadets. (France was never very keen on the cargo-carrying school-ship idea.) On December 16 1926 she reached Baltimore 39 days out from Brest via Madeira, but in January 1927, while loading 3,200 tons of pitch for Lorient, fire following an explosion caused her end, written off as a constructive total loss. She was sunk to put the fire out, salved afterwards, and sold for $3,000 to be used as a towed barge. She was scrapped at Baltimore about 1933.

The *Richelieu* had a brief career. She was the only large sailing vessel ever used as a French school-ship, but she was not replaced, for sail-training of this organised, costly type was always much criticised by many French shipping people. For one thing, the idea of learning such a profession in this way was quite foreign to the old school of thought, not merely among the practical Bretons. Not only many French seamen held the view that, in any event, the *Richelieu* experiment was oddly conducted.

Rochambeau – Steel barque, 2,725 g., 2,311 n.
November 1902: Completed by Cie. Française de Constr. Navales, Nantes, for Cie. de Navigation Française, of the same port.

She was the last of the big sailers launched at Nantes. In 1904 she was sold to the Sté. des Voiliers Nantais.

Leaving Europe for San Francisco in March 1907, she was delayed nearly two months off Cape Horn by violent and continual gales.

In March 1911 she ran down and sank the British schooner *Flora Emily* whose crew were landed at Queenstown, and later the same year when bound from Glasgow towards Tchio, New Caledonia, under Captain Créquer, she stranded and remained on the Main Reef some 25 miles from Tchio on August 30 1911 and eventually broke up. All the crew were saved.

Saint Donatien – Steel barque, 1,648 g., 1,259 n.
November 20 1900: Launched by A. Dubigeon, Nantes, for L. Bureau & Fils, of that port.

On her maiden voyage she left Cardiff on March 9 1901 for Nagasaki with coal, commanded by Captain Dejoie, and arrived in Japan 125 days out. She sailed for Oregon on August 7, and from the Columbia River on October 17 that year with wheat for Queenstown, and arrived there in 122 days.

These were good average passages, perhaps a little better. On her fourth voyage the *Saint Donatien* left Bordeaux for Adelaide in ballast, under Captain R. Bertrand, on May 25 1905. She sailed from Verdon Roads on June 8, was spoken on July 6 in 5°N., 27°W., and then disappeared with her crew of 22. She was posted missing in February 1906—yet another of the great ships gone with their crews in silence to add to the mysteries of the sea.

Saint Louis – Steel barque, 1,997 g., 1,779 n.
November 1902: Completed by A. Dubigeon, Nantes, for L. Bureau & Fils, Nantes.

1906: Sold to the Sté. Générale d'Armement. On October 3 1916 Captain Tiercelin took over in Ipswich and sailed for Chile with cement. A nitrate cargo was then loaded for Australia, and the *Saint Louis* traded in the Pacific regularly between Australia and San Francisco. Here she arrived for the last time, from Sydney, on January 20 1919, and sailed later for Nantes with flour. The following year she left Port Pirie bound for Nantes with wheat but had to put into Port Natal for medical assistance, leaving again on May 1. She was obviously making this passage round the Cape of Good Hope instead of by Cape Horn. The *Saint Louis* sailed from Spencer Gulf in company with the Nantes barque *Molière* (Captain Delanoë), which headed for Cape Horn. Curiously enough, the two barques arrived in the River Loire on the same day. The *Saint Louis* followed this with another South Australian voyage, first to Port Germein in ballast in 106 days, and back from Port Germein to Bordeaux with 33,500 bags of wheat, via the Cape of Good Hope again. Sailing January 25 1921, she passed St. Helena Island 73 days out and arrived in Verdon Roads under sail, 133 days from Australia, on June 7 of that year. There was not another such charter and so, on July 4 1921, she left Bordeaux in tow for the Canal de la Martinière. Here she became the 13th big sailing ship laid up, on July 7 1921. Soon there were many more. Captain Tiercelin became responsible for the maintenance of seven sailing-vessels left idle in the sailers' cemetery, until 1926. One crew was in charge of each seven ships for several years, in the hope of sailing again. Very few did so, and on September 10 1926, Captain Tiercelin, to his great regret, had to take his old ship to Lorient for breaking up.

Saint Rogatien – Steel barque, 1,581 g., 1,389 n.
September 1901: Completed by A. Dubigeon, Nantes, for L. Bureau & Fils, Nantes.

Captain Illiaquer took her in 1905 and commanded this fine barque until her end which came after a long and useful career on November 17 1916, while on passage from Dieppe towards Buenos Aires. She was torpedoed by the German submarine *U-B-40* off Falmouth. With great courage, and although his ship was gravely damaged, Captain Illiaquer and his devoted bos'n, named Huguen, remained on board until the very last moment in hope of saving the vessel, but she sank suddenly and they disappeared with her. The rest of the crew were rescued.

In 1921 and 1922 two French steamers were named *Capitaine Illiaquer* and *Matelot Huguen* after these brave men.

Sainte Anne – Steel barque, 1,629 g., 1,282 n.
April 1899: Completed by A. Dubigeon, Nantes, for L. Bureau & Fils, Nantes.

On her maiden voyage she was chartered from Swansea with coal to San Francisco and return to the United Kingdom with grain. In 1903 she was partially dismasted off the Cape of Good Hope and put into Fremantle for repairs. The following year, in March, dismasted in the North Atlantic again with the loss of three men, she was spoken by the White Star liner *Oceanic,* which signalled news of her accident to a German steamer. The latter picked up the barque in 46°19′N., 34°33′W., and towed her to the Azores. The *Sainte Anne* was later taken to St. Nazaire for repairs. In 1910 she was sold to Pedersen & Mosvold of Farsund, Norway, and renamed *Knygen.*

From 1917 until 1921 she appears in the Register as the *Skarv,* owned by Akties. Excelsior (S.O. Stray & Co., Mgrs.) of Christiansand, and was broken up in Germany about 1924.

Sainte Catherine – Steel 4-masted barque, 3,104 g., 2,754 n. (See *Seine.*)

Sainte Marguerite – Steel 4-masted barque, 3,104 g., 2,754 n. (See *Blanche.*)

Sandvigen – Steel ship, 1,907 g., 1,768 n.
1892: Built by A. Rodger & Co., Port Glasgow, for H. Hogarth & Sons, Ardrossan, as the *Ballachulish.*

She was sold in 1910 to S. O. Stray & Co. of Christiansand and renamed *Sandvigen.* She remained under this ownership until 1924, when she was bought by the Sté. des Hauts Fourneaux de Noumea (New Caledonia) and converted into a barge. She did not sail under the French flag. Several old sailing-ship hulks were used in New Caledonia, including the *Bonneveine, Bougainville* and *Pax.* The *Scimitar* later *Rangitiki,* a record-maker, was hulked and renamed *Paul Bouquet* at Noumea in 1909. She was reported as being in use in Australian waters during 1914-18 and, after the war, returned to Noumea. The *Chillicothe* and *Tonawanda*, both ex-German full-riggers, were converted into barges in 1927.

The barges were towed by the steamer *Tayo* between New Caledonian small ports and Noumea. This system of transporting nickel ore began in 1900 and lasted until 1934, when the towed hulks were replaced by three powered cargo vessels. Abandoned in a bay near Noumea, partially submerged under sand, three or four rusted hulls were still recognizable as former sailing vessels in the early 1970s, among them the *Sandvigen*.

Seine – Steel barque, 2,185 g., 1,587 n.
July 25 1899: Launched by Chantiers de Normandie, Rouen, for A. D. Bordes, she made only one voyage.

On December 28 1900, when returning from her maiden voyage 81 days out from Iquique to Falmouth for orders with nitrate, the *Seine* was thrown ashore in Perran Bay near Newquay, Cornwall. Her crew of 24 were rescued with difficulty. By dawn the *Seine* was dismasted, on her beam ends, and open to the breakers. The wreck was eventually sold to a Newquay sea captain for £42, for whatever he could get out of her. In May 1954 what remained of the *Seine* was blasted apart to allow a cable to be run ashore at the spot.

Seine – Steel 4-masted barque, 3,104 g., 2,754 n.
April 20 1898: Launched by Chantiers de la Méditerranée, Havre, for E. Corblet & Co., Havre, as *Ernest Siegfried*.

Her first owners put her in the New Caledonia nickel ore trade. She made several good runs on this route: 91 days in 1899, 94 and 97 days in 1904 were her best. In April 1909 she was purchased by Cie. Navale de l'Océanie, Havre, and renamed *Sainte Catherine,* but in 1912 came under the ownership of A. D. Bordes who gave her the name of *Seine*. She sailed successfully through the 1914-18 war, but in October 1919 had serious fire in her cotton cargo while lying in Havre harbour and was scuttled, but later was raised and repaired.

Laid up at Bordeaux in the "slump", the *Seine* left that port in February 1923 for Bilbao where she was scrapped.

Socoa – Steel ship, 2,613 g., 2,251 n. (See *Thiers*.)

Strasbourg – Iron ship, 1,770 g., 1,653 n.
1884: Built by Flensburger Schiffsb. Ges., Flensburg, for J. C. Pflugk, of Hamburg, as *Libussa*.

She was sold to A. D. Bordes in 1893 and renamed *Strasbourg*. Five years later, on January 31 1898, she was in collision in fog near Folkestone with the British steamer *Ardoe,* and severely damaged. On January 21 1910 she left Port Talbot for Valparaiso with 2,300 tons of coal, under Captain Le Depessier, but less than a week later lost her main mast and her mizzen-topmast in a long gale, and the day after her foremast also went overboard. Nonetheless, she managed to stagger into Palais Roads (Belle Ile) for shelter, unaided, under jury rig, with only her lower mizzen mast left standing and a jib set on a spar above her forecastle. Towed to St. Nazaire, she was con-demned and sold for scrap. This was in August 1910: she was 26 years old, too old to warrant further heavy capital outlay.

Sully – Steel barque, 2,649 g., 1,995 n.
June 22 1902: Launched by Chantiers de la Loire, Nantes, for Cie. Mari-time Française, Nantes.

In 1913 she was sold to Sté. Générale d'Armement. After a useful and accident-free career, on a passage from Bahia Blanca to Brest in March 1917, she was sunk by the German submarine *U-C-47*, 15 miles west of Ushant. Captain Populaire was then in command.

Surcouf – Steel barque, 2,212 g., 1,947 n.
December 23 1901: Launched by Chantiers Nantais de Constr. Maritimes, Nantes, for Sté. des Voiliers Nantais.

She lasted only seven years. On February 25 1909, while bound from New Caledonia to Glasgow with nickel, she stranded in fog at Black Nob near Tara, County Down, and was a total loss. Her crew of 24 were saved.

Suzanne – Steel barque, 2,691 g., 2,270 n.
March 23 1901: Launched by Chantiers de Normandie, Rouen, for E. Corblet & Co., Havre.
She reached Noumea from Havre on her maiden voyage in 89 days. She had a long, useful and uneventful career, sailing through the war. On Sep-tember 15 1921, she arrived at Falmouth from Port Victoria 143 days out—not very good, but this was a year of poor Atlantic winds and long passages. Others did much worse. She was subsequently laid up in France and broken up in Spain in 1925.

Tarapaca – Iron 4-masted ship, 2,506 g., 2,338 n. (with water ballast).
1886: Built by W. B. Thompson, Glasgow, for A. D. Bordes.
She was in an odd accident on September 9 1902. Arriving at La Pallice from

The four-masted *Seine,* ex-*Ernest Siegfried,* seen from her lee beam. The fore lower topgallantsail is being loosed to the beam wind. (*Wm. Muir Collection, San Francisco Maritime Museum.*)

Flush-decker *Sully* off Wallaroo, South Australia. The crew have been chipping off rust and paint amidships. (*A. D. Edwardes, South Australia.*)

French barque *Turgot* on slip on the West Coast of North America.
(*H. D. Huycke Collection, Lincoln-Port Blakeley.*)

Yet another war casualty—the *Union* sinking, seen from the *Kronprinz Wilhelm*
on November 22 1914. (*Dr. Jürgen Meyer Collection.*)

Ville de Mulhouse, still in full commission, at Cardiff in December 1927.
(*Dr. Jürgen Meyer Collection.*)

Hulk *Andalucia,* ex-four-masted barque *Ville de Mulhouse.* View taken at Punta
Arenas in December 1969. (*Norman J. Brouwer.*)

Vercingétorix, sailing to sea, probably in South Tasmania.
(Dr. R. Grimard Collection.)

Wrecked on a Sydney beach—the barque *Vincennes.* She came off.
(Ship Shop, Sydney, 1920.)

Tocopilla with 4,000 tons of nitrate, under Captain E. Robert, she struck the pier and sank in the lock with a heavy list, blocking the harbour for five days. She met her end on September 1 1917, while on passage from Iquique to Bordeaux, commanded by Captain Hunault. When 100 days out she was captured by the German submarine *U-52* about 64 miles west-south-west of Oléron. After pillage she was sunk in two minutes, by explosive charges. Her crew managed to reach the French coast the same day.

Thiers – Steel ship, 2,613 g., 2,251 n.
October 25 1901: Launched by Chantiers de St. Nazaire, for Sté. Bayonnaise de Navigation, Bayonne, as *Socoa*.

She was a rather slow ship but profitable with her 3,450 tons cargo capacity, despite the occasional accident. On August 2 1906, when bound from Stettin towards San Francisco with cement, she stranded in thick weather and sank near the Lizard, off Cadgwith. She was abandoned, but a salvage agreement was agreed with the Western Marine Salvage Co. on a "no cure no pay" basis, for £2,120. Several attempts to refloat her failed, and 50,000 barrels of cement had to be jettisoned, when three tugs succeeded in refloating the *Socoa*. She was towed from the Kildown Rocks to Cadgwith Bay where she was beached and temporarily repaired, and later taken to Falmouth for final repairs. The *Socoa* was perhaps the only modern sailing-ship ever salved from the dangerous rocks round the Lizard.

While in Falmouth she was sold to the Cie. Maritime Française and renamed *Thiers*. Later sold again to the Sté. Générale d'Armement, she sailed successfully through the First World War. Afterwards she crossed the North Atlantic westwards to Newport News in 55 days, and returned in 29. Her last voyage began on May 8 1921 when she left Port Germein, South Australia, for the English Channel for orders. She arrived at Queenstown, 155 days out, and sailed for London. After discharge she was towed to St. Nazaire and, on December 10 1921, laid up in the Canal de la Martinière, which she left for breaking up early in 1927.

Tijuca – Steel 4-masted barque, 2,394 g., 2,257 n.
1892: Built by C. Connell & Co., Glasgow, for J. C. Rogers & Co., Glasgow, as *Marion Josiah*.

She was sold to A. D. Bordes and renamed *Tijuca* in 1910. Seven years later, when on passage in November 1917 from La Pallice for Taltal in ballast, under Captain J. M. Ollivier, she was shelled by the German submarine *U-151* some 220 miles north-north-west of Madeira. Captain Ollivier returned the fire but his small guns were outmatched, and at last the *Tijuca* was sent to the bottom by torpedo.

M

Touraine – Steel barque, 1,989 g., 1,778 n.
December 26 1898: Launched by A. Dubigeon, Nantes, for R. Guillon, Nantes.

She was a successful barque with an uneventful career. On her maiden voyage she was chartered for coal from Swansea to San Francisco. About 900 miles west of the Golden Gate, she spoke the big British full-rigger *Claverdon* which was bound for the same port. The *Touraine* arrived in less than a week but the *Claverdon* took 44 more days—an extraordinary difference on the face of it. Early in 1909 she was sold for £4,900 to the Sté. Générale d'Armement, for whom she sailed successfully throughout the First World War. On November 29 1918 she was spoken by the French tug *Pluvier* which told her that war was over, and gave her orders for Nantes. She was then 85 days out on passage from Australia. Delayed by calms until December 5, she arrived in St. Nazaire Roads on December 30 1918, 116 days from Fremantle. She sailed until 1921 when she was laid up in the Canal de la Martinière, which she left on September 11 1926 for Lorient, to be scrapped.

Tourny – Iron ship, 1,117 g., 906 n.
1864: Built by Pile, Hay & Co., Sunderland, for G. D. Tyser & Co., London, as *Howrah*.

Sold in 1890 to A. & L. Verdeau Frères & Co., Bordeaux, who renamed her *Tourny*. Her rig was later altered to barque, and in 1901 she came under the ownership of P. Dor of Marseilles. On October 26 of that year, she was found by the French liner *Italie* disabled and nearly capsizing in the Valencia Gulf. The barque was abandoned and 15 of her crew rescued by the liner, with the exception of an A.B. named Denis who refused to abandon the *Tourny* in spite of the orders of Captain Jagoret. On October 31 the barque was spoken by the *Isère,* of the French Navy, 140 miles north-east of Oran, but Denis—a headstrong Breton—refused again to abandon the vessel. On November 1 the *Tourny* was finally picked up and towed to Algiers by the British steamer *Syrian Prince.* The British master claimed salvage. The case went to Algiers Court in December 1901, and the *Tourny's* owner was required to pay £480 to the *Syrian Prince's* owners for the towage only, because legally the "headstrong Breton" had remained aboard as his lawful representative. Whether Seaman Denis was rewarded is not recorded, but one rather hopes he was.

In September 1903, the *Tourny* was bought by Luigi Mortola, Genoa, and renamed *Agostino M.* On May 1 1909 she left Haiti for Marseilles with logwood, under Captain L. Mari. On May 25 the crew were attacked by a tropical disease, and Captain Mari died at sea. Command fell to the chief officer, Filippo Razeto; and although he was ill himself. he succeeded in reaching Cadiz on July 9, 69 days out. By then he was at the point of death.

The *Agostino M.* was broken up at Genoa in 1911.

Tourville – Steel barque, 2,314 g., 1,741 n.
June 1902: Completed by Chantiers Nantais de Constr. Maritimes, Nantes, for Bureau Frères & Baillergeau, Nantes.

Another one-voyage-only, ill-fated ship. On her maiden (and last) voyage she left St. Nazaire on June 18 1902 commanded by Captain Yvon, for New York, to load 80,000 cases of kerosene for Melbourne and Adelaide. She sailed from Australia to Taltal and Caleta Coloso, where she loaded nitrates for New York. Laden with case oil again, she left New York for Hobart and Hakodate, delivered this second cargo safely, and then sailed from Japan in ballast for New Caledonia. On the night of June 1 1904 she was lost on a coral reef near Mare Island in the Loyalty Islands. Her crew were saved. Inquiry showed that both the position and extent of the reef on her charts were incorrect. (Although she had sailed to eight ports and was lost on her way to the ninth, these were all *passages*: she had not completed the round voyage, back to Europe.)

Trielen – Steel barque, 1,072 g., 996 n. (See *Corumoc*.)

Turgot – Steel barque, 2,611 g., 1,959 n.
1902: Completed by Chantiers de la Loire, Nantes, for Cie. Maritime Française, Nantes.

On June 11 1909 while on passage from Antwerp (via Hobart) towards Seattle, with coke, bricks and tarred oakum, under Captain Roze, she caught fire. At the time she was in sight of San Antonio, Cape Verde Islands. The fire grew worse so rapidly that the crew had to abandon the ship, which stranded still afire and was lost on the rocks of the island.

Union – Iron 4-masted ship, 2,183 g., 2,023 n.
September 1882: Launched by Russell & Co., Greenock, for A. D. Bordes.

She was given two small steam engines, driving two screws, to help her when becalmed or entering and leaving harbour. The propellers could be raised when under sail. This auxiliary machinery proved unhelpful and was soon discarded. On June 24 1911 when at anchor in Iquique Bay she was collided with by her consort *Madeleine*. The *Union* lost her mizzen mast, and her rig was afterwards altered to four-masted barque. She was lost early in the First World War while bound from Port Talbot to the River Plate and Valparaiso with coal, commanded by Captain V. Gregoire. She was captured in 34°S., 52°W., by the German raider *Kronprinz Wilhelm* on

October 28, 1914. The German was pleased to fill her bunkers, but the transfer proved long and difficult. The *Union* finally capsized and sank on November 22, alongside the captor, with 800 tons of coal still in her hold. Her crew were landed at Montevideo two days later.

Valentine – Iron barque, 1,213 g., 1,167 n.
1885: Built by A. M'Millan, Dumbarton, for M. Little, London, as *Ariadne*.

Sold in May 1893 to A. D. Bordes and renamed *Valentine*. On January 28 1898, when arriving at Totoralillo (Chile) in 72 days from Cardiff with coal, under Captain L. F. Bourgain, she struck a badly charted rock. Although she was soon beached, the *Valentine* became a total loss.

Valentine – Steel 4-masted barque, 3,120 g., 2,756 n.
November 8 1900: Launched by Chantiers de Normandie, Rouen, for A. D. Bordes.

She made the finest outward passage round the Horn ever recorded by a ship of the Bordes fleet. She left Shields on November 24 1903 and arrived at Iquique on January 29 1904, 66 days from port to port and only 61 from the Isle of Wight. Captain L. Gardanne took her from the stocks, and in 1902 he had also made the best passage home of the year of the Bordes fleet, 73 days from Iquique to Falmouth. In 1904 the *Valentine* reached Dunkirk from Iquique in 70 days.

Her end came in the war. In August 1914, she left Port Talbot for Iquique with coal, commanded by Captain F. Guillou. On the night of November 2 1914, when off the Chilean coast 90 days out from Port Talbot, the *Valentine* was captured by the German cruiser *Leipzig*. A prize crew was put on board and the raider *Prinz Eitel Friedrich*, which was accompanying the *Leipzig*, took her in tow for the anchorage of Mas-a-Fuera where they arrived on November 4 1914. The obvious plan was to use her cargo for bunkering German ships, as long as it lasted.

Captain Guillou refused to rig down his vessel to facilitate the coaling and was transferred with his crew to the *Prinz Eitel Friedrich*. The French crew were replaced by a prize crew, who lost no time unbending the sails and dismantling the rigging. After taking nearly 1,200 tons of coal from the French barque, she was anchored some distance away with a prize crew on board. One night her saloon took fire but the fire was put out. Several days later the *Valentine* was towed outside territorial waters and sunk in deep water. Her crew was taken to Valparaiso by the steamer *Sacramento*, and landed there on November 21.

Valparaiso – Iron ship, 1,266 g., 1,076 n.
June 1874: Completed by Macfadyen & Co., Port Glasgow, for Hargrove, Fergusson & Jackson, Liverpool, as *Workington*.

By 1874-75 she had been sold to French interests and renamed *Suffren,* her port of registry Bordeaux. A year later she was the *Port de Montevideo,* still registered at Bordeaux. In 1877 she was sold to A. D. Bordes and renamed *Valparaiso*. In 1883 she was in collision with the British steamer *Labarrouere* in the River Charente: but this was the last incident in a long career during which her best passage was from Pisagua to the Lizard in 81 days, in 1894. In July 1900 she was sold for £5,200 to T. Gazzolo fu A., Genoa, acquiring the name of *Sacro Cuor di Gesu,* and in 1909, renamed *Graciosa,* she was converted into a coal hulk at Bahia, doing good service there for many years as she was a strong old ship.

Valparaiso – Steel 4-masted barque, 3,081 g., 2,664 n.
October 30 1902: Launched by Chantiers de France, Dunkirk, for A. D. Bordes.

She was another fine ship, combining a good earning capacity with a good turn of speed and reasonable docility of handling. Although she was no record-breaker, she made successful and uneventful voyages and once was in the Channel from Iquique in 80 days.

Her last voyages to Chile were made between 1923 and 1925. The *Valparaiso* was laid up at Nantes about February 1925 until September 1927, when she was towed to Dunkirk for breaking up. A well-remembered ship, she left a good name.

Van Stabel – Steel barque, 2,349 g., 1,741 n.
December 7 1901: Launched by Chantiers de la Loire, Nantes, for Sté. des Voiliers Dunkerquois, Dunkirk.

She sailed for less than a year. On January 17 1903 she left Glasgow bound for San Francisco with coal, under Captain Quemper, but within a fortnight had lost her main and mizzen masts in a wild gale. Then hopelessly handicapped she was thrown on Durbury Reef, west coast of North Uist*, and lost with her crew of 27. This was on February 1 1903.

---

*The coast of North Uist on which the *Van Stabel* was lost, received special mention in the Admiralty Sailing Directions a century ago. "Many causes combine to make this portion of the coast the most dangerous perhaps on the west side of Great Britain; the prevalent south-westerly and westerly gales, the long dark nights, the projecting position of the islands and their little elevation above the sea as well as the numerous rocks and reefs which surround them . . ." made the low islands an absolute death trap then.

Vauban – Steel ship, 2,391 g., 1,735 n.
April 7 1902: Launched by Chantiers de St. Nazaire for Cie. Maritime
Française, Nantes.

Lasted four years until, on June 30 1906, while on passage from Cherbourg
towards San Francisco commanded by Captain Le Dantec, she was driven
ashore by calm and currents on Varandina Rocks, south-west of Boavista
(Cape Verde Islands) and became a total loss. Her crew were saved.

Vendée – Steel barque, 1,964 g., 1,765 n.
June 1900: Completed by A. Dubigeon, Nantes, for R. Guillon, Nantes.

Sold in 1904 to Ch. Vallée, of the same port. Later in 1908, she was bought
by the Sté. Générale d'Armement. On June 24 1908 she left Astoria for the
United Kingdom with wheat, under Captain Rigault, and was very nearly
a total loss.

On the night of September 1, in thick and snowy weather, she became
embayed in Kendall Cove, south-west coast of Wollaston Island about 14
miles north of Cape Horn. Luckily she stranded on a sandbank, and her
crew of 25—after several days in the boats—were rescued by a small wooden
steamer, the *Oreste* of Punta Arenas. A salvage agreement was subsequently
established on a "no cure no pay basis" and the *Vendée* was refloated several
weeks later and towed to Montevideo for repairs. She sailed successfully until
and through the 1914-18 war. On her last voyage she left Newcastle (N.S.W.)
for the River Plate on January 19 1921 with coal, and on July 21 of that
year arrived in the Canal de la Martinière from Montevideo and laid up,
in the absence of paying freights. There she stayed until April 27 1926, when
she left the Canal for Lorient to be broken up.

Vercingétorix – Steel ship, 2,273 g., 1,988 n.
September 1902: Completed by Chantiers de St. Nazaire for Cie. de Navigation Française, Nantes.

In 1904 she was sold to the Sté. des Voiliers Nantais, for whom she sailed on
world voyages until August 1914, when she was captured in Antwerp's docks
on the arrival of the German troops. She was sold, rigged down, for 448,000
marks to C. J. Klingenberg, of Bremen, who refitted and re-rigged her under
the new name of *Bremen*. In 1919 she was restored to her French owners,
the Sté. des Voiliers Nantais-Chargeurs de l'Ouest, arriving at Cherbourg
from Dunkirk on November 4 1919, and was later towed to Lorient for
repairs under her original name.

Her last voyage was to Wellington from Nantes in 1921, thence to the
United Kingdom with wool. On December 27 1921 she reached London 108
days out, and was subsequently laid up. She was reported as sold for scrap

in September 1923. This vessel was later confused with the *Vindicatrix* which was at one time a stationary school-ship for the Gravesend Sea School. As such, the *Vindicatrix* was still afloat in 1921.

Versailles – Steel barque, 2,201 g., 1,939 n.
August 25 1900: Launched by Chantiers Nantais de Constr. Maritimes, Nantes, for Sté. des Long-Courriers Français, Havre.

She kept out of the casualty lists and news columns. About 1914-15 she was sold to Sté. Générale d'Armement, survived the war, and made her last voyage in 1921. On January 26 that year she arrived off Cape Borda, South Australia, for orders, from Swansea, at Adelaide two days later, and at Port Germein to load on February 10. Thence she sailed for Queenstown for orders in 157 days, which was not at all fast. But why hurry in from sea only to be laid up in the Canal de la Martinière? Here she inevitably arrived early in October 1921, and remained until she left for breaking up on September 3 1926.

Victorine – Iron barque, 1,241 g., 1,126 n.
1879: Built by A. Stephen & Sons, Dundee, for A. D. Bordes.

Her best outward passage was made in 72 days from Dartmouth to Valparaiso in 1893. She had a long and very useful life until destroyed in the First World War on October 6 1917, when bound from Bordeaux for Fort de France under the command of Captain A. Mathieu. She maintained an unequal fight against the German submarine *U-89*, about 96 miles north-west of Cape Ortegal. Overwhelmed by the superiority of the German guns, the *Victorine* was sunk on the morning of October 7. She was 38 years old but could have been good for at least 50, for the old iron sailers were hard ships to wear out.

Ville d'Orléans – Steel barque, 2,553 g., 1,738 n.
March 2 1901: Launched by Chantiers de la Loire, Nantes, for Cie. des Voiliers Havrais (H. Genestal & Fils, Mgrs.), Havre.

She reached Greenock from New Caledonia on her maiden voyage in 102 days, but she had a very brief life. On July 11 1902, while on passage from the Clyde to Brisbane with rails, coke and cast-iron, she was abandoned sinking in 46°41'S., 137°17'E. Her crew were taken off by the Nantes barque *Gaël* which landed them at Hobart.

Ville de Belfort – Steel barque, 1,930 g., 1,695 n. (See *Germaine*.)

Ville de Dieppe – Steel and iron barque, 1,254 g., 1,228 n. (carrying petroleum in bulk).
1888: Built by Oswald, Mordaunt & Co., Southampton, for L. Robbe Fils, of Dieppe.

She was the first French sailing-ship built as a tanker, and made a number of voyages on the North Atlantic route, mainly to Philadelphia. In 1900 she was badly damaged by fire in port, and was sold to Prentout & Leblond of Rouen. In July 1903 she changed hands again, being bought by Acties Union (Jens Pay, Mgr.), of Christiania, retaining her original name though flying the Norwegian flag. She was lost in the war while bound from La Pallice to New York in ballast, in April 1917. Under the Norwegian flag, she fell to the guns of the German submarine *U-C-21* when about 20 miles west of Oléron Island.

Ville de Dijon – Steel barque, 1,946 g., 1,702 n.
October 8 1899: Launched by Chantiers de la Méditerranée, Havre, for Cie. des Voiliers Havrais (H. Genestal & Fils, Mgrs.), Havre.

On her maiden return voyage she left New Caledonia on July 6 1900 for Swansea, with 2,700 tons of nickel ore, under Captain Bony, and was dismasted about a month later in a storm not far from Cape Horn. A jury rig was contrived and the Horn rounded, luckily in moderate weather. This was towards the end of August 1900. On September 14, after making a 1,800-mile run with only her lower masts standing, she was found about 300 miles off the River Plate by the German steamer *Amasis* and towed to Montevideo, where the pair arrived two days later. The *Ville de Dijon* was then towed to Swansea by the British tug *Blazer*. Some years later, on the night of July 26 1907, the barque was in collision with a German liner in the English Channel and had to put into Havre for repairs. In July 1909, she was sold to the Sté. Générale d'Armement, at the age of ten years. On July 15 1913, she arrived at Papudo (Chile) from Newcastle (N.S.W.) with coal, but a week later was driven ashore in a storm and became a total loss. Of the crew of 22, only three were saved.

Ville de Mulhouse – Steel 4-masted barque, 3,110 g., 2,798 n.
April 28 1899: Launched by Chantiers de la Méditerranée, Havre, for Cie. des Voiliers Havrais (H. Genestal & Fils, Mgrs.), Havre.

This big four-master was still afloat in Chilean waters early in 1972. Her design is said to have been based on that of the *Président Félix Faure*, built in the same yard in 1896, but with double topgallants and royals—no skysails, which were not French. The Cie. des Voiliers Havrais were engaged primarily in the nickel-ore trade from New Caledonia to the Clyde or Havre.

On her maiden voyage under Captain Girard, she sailed from Havre on July 7 1899 with a cargo of patent fuel in blocks for New Caledonia, arriving on October 1, having made the run in 86 days which was good. The following voyage, the *Ville de Mulhouse* was sent to California to take advantage of wheat rates of 35 shillings a ton, arriving at San Francisco from Swansea in October 1900, 126 days out. She later returned to the ore trade and in 1902 reached Greenock from New Caledonia in 97 days—again an excellent passage.

Her voyages were indeed generally good except for a slow passage of 185 days from Antwerp to Los Angeles in 1906, under Captain Bony. She was delayed by calms off California.

In April 1909 she was sold to Sté. Générale d'Armement—again at the end of ten years, strengthening one's view that this was a financial arrangement of some sort when the bounty-earning years were ended. The *Ville de Mulhouse* survived the war and in 1919 was trading between Dakar and Brazil. She was home in December and then went to the River Plate. Next she turned up at San Francisco where she loaded wheat for the last time, and passed Dover on March 7 1921, arriving at Ipswich on March 9, 140 days out. She then returned to Nantes and was laid up in the Canal de la Martinière on May 22 1921, as freight rates were very low and useful charters non-existent. But on June 28 1927 she left the Canal having been bought by Soc. Anon. Ganadera y Comercial Menendez Behety, of Punta Arenas, Chile. On December 24 1927 she sailed from Cardiff under the Chilean flag for Punta Arenas with coal, under Captain H. Kahler, a German master, and part German, part Norwegian crew. The Norwegians came from the Argentine full-rigged ship *Fortuna* which had burnt out and sank on October 28. She arrived at Punta Arenas in 63 days, on February 25 1928, and was converted to a coal hulk in that port with the new name of *Andalucia*.

With the outbreak of the Second World War her owners, the Cia. Chilena de Navegacion Interoceanica, fitted her out for further service at sea. Together with the *Alejandrina* (ex-British four-masted barque *Andrina*), she was used more-or-less as a deep-sea barge. They carried cargoes of local coal to Buenos Aires, being towed by the owners' steamers, and on the return voyage a certain amount of general cargo from the River Plate to Punta Arenas. They also used their lower sails in fair winds. The *Andalucia* ex-*Ville de Mulhouse* was built with pole lower-and-topmasts—in one steel tube—and never had been rigged down entirely. She kept her course and topsail yards aloft so that it was a simple matter for square-rigger seamen to give her back some sail, and she was in good order aloft and below. (And still was when I was aboard off Punta Arenas, in 1969, writes Alan Villiers.)

This sea service finished with the war, the *Andalucia* and her companion again became hulks. The former Frenchman was used as a store-ship for the Chilean Navy for many years. In May 1972 she was still afloat, anchored off

Punta Arenas, but was not in active use by the Chilean Navy, and her final
fate was uncertain.

Ville de Redon – Iron barque, 1,142 g., 1.061 n.
1864: Built by M. Samuelson & Co., Hull, as *Marian*.

In 1879 she was owned by A. B. Geddes, Liverpool. In 1889 she appears as
Brillant under the ownership of C. M. D. Jorgensen, Hamburg. In 1895
she was bought by C. Mabon, Nantes, and renamed *Ville de Redon*. She
made a slow passage of 208 days from Shanghai to Europe a year or two
later, and in 1898 was in serious trouble when she stranded. However, she
was refloated not too badly damaged, and towed to Bremerhaven. Sold to
C. A. H. Witte, Bremen, she acquired the name of *Charlotte*. From 1905
until 1930 she was owned by P. Molins, Montevideo, as the *San Pedro*. Laid
up in 1929, she was broken up in 1930 when 66 years old. She appears to
have sailed when under the Uruguayan flag mainly on local and coastal
Atlantic voyages.

Ville de Rouen – Steel barque, 1,303 g., 1.125 n.
1891: Built by Chantiers de la Loire, St. Nazaire, for H. Prentout, Leblond
& Boniface, Rouen.

She lasted ten years. On October 30 1901, while bound from Cardiff towards
Fremantle, she stranded and sank in the River Moore, near Fremantle, and
became a total loss. Her wreck was sold for £101 and she disappeared from
the register.

Ville de Saint Nazaire – Steel ship, 2,790 g., 1,818 n.
1902: Built by Chantiers de St. Nazaire for Sté. des Voiliers de St. Nazaire.

She was transferred to Sté. Générale d'Armement in 1903, before sailing.
On her maiden voyage that year she was in collision with the French full-
rigger *Desaix* in Astoria Roads, damage not stated. On May 27 1904 she left
Kanala (New Caledonia) for Havre with nickel ore, commanded by Captain
David, and two days later was wrecked on Kuakue Rocks. Her crew were
saved, but she had had little time to show her paces. Perhaps large square-
rigged ships were not ideal for trading to or among reef-bound Pacific
islands: but they were wonderful carriers and inexpensive to build and
operate.

Ville du Havre – Steel 4-masted barque, 3,109 g., 2,806 n.
July 24 1899: Launched by Chantiers de la Méditerranée, Havre, for Cie.
des Voiliers Havrais (H. Genestal & Fils, Mgrs.), Havre.

On her maiden voyage she made a slow passage of 146 days between Havre and Saigon. Loading in New Caledonia a year later, she was thrown ashore in a cyclone but was refloated and repaired at Sydney. In 1902 she reached Batavia from Rotterdam in 90 days, which showed what she could do, but three years later, in 1905, she stranded again in New Caledonia and was again refloated, this time by the s.s. *St. Antoine*. Sold to the Sté. Générale d'Armement in 1909, she was another war casualty. The *Ville du Havre* left Ipswich on March 1 1916 for Buenos Aires in ballast, under Captain E. Ybert, with a crew of 28, but was captured on March 7 and sunk by the German submarine *U-32* off Ushant, in 48°48′N., 6°36′W. Her crew was rescued by two steamers but one life was lost.

Vincennes – Steel barque, 2,210 g., 1,964 n.
June 27 1900: Launched by Chantiers Nantais de Constr. Maritimes, Nantes, for Sté. des Long-Courriers Français, Havre.

While on passage on May 25 1906 from Yokohama for Sydney in ballast, commanded by Captain Le Vaillant, she got ashore on Manly Beach close to Sydney Heads, but was refloated and towed a few miles into port for repairs. About 1914-15 she was sold to Sté. Générale d'Armement and sailed safely throughout the war, despite raiders, submarines, and a cyclone. On her last voyage she left Sydney on January 11 1921 for Falmouth for orders with wheat, and arrived in the River Loire on May 31, 140 days out—again, the year of long passages. Perhaps some of those surviving sailing-ships just did not want to come back to a Europe (which did not want them then) too quickly. On June 17 1921 she was laid up in the Canal de la Martinière, and left on September 13 1926 to be broken up though only 26 years old and still a fine barque.

Wulfran Puget – Steel 4-masted barque, 2,872 g., 2,588 n.
December 16 1895: Launched by Chantiers de la Méditerranée, La Seyne, for A. D. Bordes.

Her best voyage was in 1903 when she sailed to Iquique in 73 days from Dungeness, and on her return passed the Isle of Wight 74 days out from Chile—excellent work. She also survived the war, and her last voyage was again the familiar run to Chile. On May 11 1924 she left Dunkirk for Iquique: arrived September 7 1924, 119 days out: sailed again September 27, with nitrate, and on January 20 1925 arrived at Dunkirk after a passage of 115 days. She was laid up the day after.

The *Wulfran Puget* was sold to the shipbreakers in June the following year—yet another fine ship gone for a song. But no one then wanted her.

Yvonne et Marie – Iron barque, 1,059 g., 1,024 n.
1876: Built by Jollet & Babin, Nantes, for L. Lozach & R. Sageran, Nantes.

She was sold in 1883 to V. Vincent, Nantes, retaining her original name. Bought in July 1900 by Vincenzo Sabia of Naples, and renamed *Geni,* she stranded near Great Inagua (West Indies) in June 1912, and became a total loss. At the time she was on a passage from Port de Paix to Marseilles with a cargo of campeachy wood. Her crew were saved and landed at Port au Prince.

She was an excellent old iron barque of handy size for the West Indies trade but too small for 20th century long voyaging of the world-girdling kind, at which the big square-riggers were so good—as long as anyone wanted them to be, and still had the courage and skill to sail them.

NOTE by Henri Picard:

It is obvious from my List that in the great Sailing-ships days the ships of Nantes were most prominent. They formed some half of all the last Bounty Fleet, from 1902 to 1921. The Société Générale d'Armement of Nantes bought new ships from year to year. In 1914, for example, the Société owned 52 big square-rigged ships of 119,704 gross tons, compared then with 45 of 112,531 tons owned by the Maison A. D. Bordes of Dunkirk. But all these ships (save for a few remnants) soon disappeared after the First World War.

Though the ships have gone they still live on in the hearts of many of us who knew their worth and quiet sea beauty, and the worth, too, of those who sailed them and sailed in them. My work I offer therefore as my modest attempt to preserve something of the memory of the last days of Deepwater Sail in France, before the sun may sink finally below the horizon and the memory be lost for ever.

Ships' Final Fate

The fates of the French sailers are summarised in the following table.

Wrecked		68
Missing		21
Foundered		10
Lost by fire		7
Lost by collision		4
War losses	Submarine	60
	Sunk by raiders	13
	Mined	2
	Sunk in error (by "friends")	1
Broken up		91
Hulked and abandoned		10
Still afloat in 1970-71		5
Still in service in 1972 as an auxiliary full-rigged ship		1
	Total	293

The ship still in service is now the Finnish school-ship *Suomen Joutsen,* ex-*Laënnec,* moored at Åbo.

Acknowledgements by M. Picard

Many private individuals, public authorities and shipping organisations have given me assistance in my research. I append a list of these, trusting that those to whom I owe so much will accept this as an acknowledgement of my thanks.

Adam, Amiral M.	Brest
Affaires Maritimes	Nantes, Le Havre, Rouen, Dunkirk, Bordeaux
Anderson, A. O.	Washington, D.C.
Barbé, Captain P.	Nantes
Bourgneuf, Captain L.	Dinan
Brouwer, Norman J.	Washington, D.C.
Buchet, Colonel G.	Royan
Bureau Veritas	Paris
Cookson, Richard M.	Ndola, Zambia
Det Norske Veritas	Oslo
Durrieux, Captain J.	Bordeaux
Edwardes, A. D. The late	Glenunga, South Australia
Glass, Captain W.	Belvedere
Godeau, M.	St. Malo
Guiader, Captain J-L.	Levallois-Perret
Hacquebord, H.	Epe, Holland
Huycke, Captain Harold D., Jr.	Mill Valley, California
Karl Kortum	San Francisco
Keys, Richard E.	Newcastle-upon-Tyne
Klebingat, Captain Fred K.	Coos Bay, Oregon, U.S.A.
Lamiotte, Capton P.	Bordeaux
Lloyd's Register of Shipping	London
Lyman, Dr. John	Chapel Hill, N.C.
MacDonald, Dan	Glasgow
Meirat, Jean	Menton
Mellert, Captain Friedr.	Bremen
Meyer, Dr. Jürgen	Hamburg
Paillé, Captain Marc	Nantes
Public Record Office	London
Service Historique de la Marine	Paris
Shepherd, R. H.	Ruislip
Townsend, K. A.	Great Yarmouth

Thanks are also due to the following for permission to reproduce photographs:

Adamson	Rothesay
Alexandersson, Gustav	Klinten, Sweden
Barnard, M.	Hull
Beattie	Hobart
Chapeau, F.	Nantes
Cookson, Richard M.	
Forbin, Ph.	
Grimard, Dr. R.	Marseilles
Huycke, H. D.	Lincoln – Port Blakeley
Marius Bar Photos	Toulon
Mitchell Library,	Sydney
National Maritime Museum	Greenwich
Neurdein Frères	Paris-Corbeil
Randall, James	
San Francisco Maritime Museum	

Bibliography by Henri Picard

Cornish Shipwrecks	Richard Larn and Clive Carter (David and Charles
Deep-Water Sail	Harold A. Underhill (Brown Son & Ferguson)
Il Romanzo della Vela	Tomaso Gropallo (Maralunga, Genoa)
Journal de la Marine Marchande	Paris
La Guerre Sous-Marine 1914-1918	Admiral Arno Spindler (Payot, Paris)
Last of the Windjammers	Basil Lubbock (Brown Son & Ferguson)
Les Derniers Cap-Horniers Français	Captain Louis Lacroix (Luçon: S. Pacteau)
Les Derniers Grands Voiliers	Captain Louis Lacroix (Paris: Peyronnet)
Nitrate Clippers, The	Basil Lubbock (Brown Son & Ferguson)
Sail Training and Cadet Ships	Harold A. Underhill (Brown Son & Ferguson)
Sea Breezes Magazine	Liverpool
Sea-Dogs of Today	Alan Villiers (Harrap)
The Way of a Ship	Alan Villiers (Hodder & Stoughton)
The War with Cape Horn	Alan Villiers (Hodder & Stoughton)
Nous Les Cap-Horniers	Captain Georges Aubin (Flammarion, Paris)
Us et Coutumes à bord des Long-Courriers	Captain Armand Hayet (Denoël)
Hamburgs Segelschiffe 1795-1945	Dr. Jürgen Meyer (Heinemann, Norderstedt)
Ultima Vela—The Last Sail	Tomaso Gropallo (Maralunga, Genoa)